Cricket and community in England

MANCHESTER
1824

Manchester University Press

Cricket and community in England

1800 to the present day

Peter Davies
with Robert Light

Manchester University Press
Manchester and New York
distributed exclusively in the USA by Palgrave

Published by Manchester University Press
Oxford Road, Manchester M13 9NR, UK
and Room 400, 175 Fifth Avenue, New York, NY 10010, USA
www.manchesteruniversitypress.co.uk

Distributed exclusively in the USA by
Palgrave, 175 Fifth Avenue, New York,
NY 10010, USA

Distributed exclusively in Canada by
UBC Press, University of British Columbia, 2029 West Mall,
Vancouver, BC, Canada V6T 1Z2

British Library Cataloguing-in-Publication Data
A catalogue record for this book is available from the British Library

Library of Congress Cataloging-in-Publication Data applied for

ISBN 978 0 7190 8279 5 hardback

15 14 13 12 11 10 09 08 07 06   10 9 8 7 6 5 4 3 2 1

Typeset
by Helen Skelton, Brighton, UK
Printed in Great Britain
by CPI Antony Rowe Ltd, Chippenham, Wiltshire

This book is dedicated to all those people who have devoted their lives to local cricket and local cricket clubs.

Contents

List of tables

Acknowledgements

We would like to thank Brian Heywood for reading, and offering his thoughts, on the manuscript. Thanks you also to the University of Huddersfield Library – its Yorkshire Cricket Collection was an invaluable resource – and to all the postgraduate students at the University of Huddersfield Cricket Research Centre.

Introduction

We are hoping that this book will fill a gap in the market. The literature on cricket, and in particular cricket history, is vast, but there are few broad-ranging histories of the sport. Obviously, cricket has some very fine academic historians but it could be argued that it is slightly lacking in all-embracing social histories. This volume is a social history of grassroots cricket in England. It will touch on county and Test cricket, just like it will refer in passing to cricket in Wales, Scotland and Ireland, but its focus will remain cricket in England.[1]

It would be fair to say that sport history has been taken more seriously in recent decades. Richard Holt set the pace with his book, *Sport and the British: A Modern History* (1990). It traces the development of sport since 1800 and is particularly interested in the contribution of the Victorians to the growth of sport. That said, Holt can still say, 'A remarkable range of popular games and contests was played and enjoyed in Britain before the advent of modern sports. Each town or village had its ball games, running races, and varieties of fighting and animal sports.'[2] After chapters on early sport and amateurism, Holt goes on to consider sport in an urban context and sport and empire. His final chapter brings the story of sport up to date, looking at issues such as television and hooliganism.

Similar issues interested Jeff Hill in his book, *Sport, Leisure and Culture in Twentieth-Century Britain* (2002). His main concern is recreation and 'free time'. He says, 'Over the past couple of decades in Britain there has been an immense outpouring of work on sport alone, so much so that there is now a strong case for regarding the study of sport as a distinct sub-branch of the discipline of history'.[3] Hill is interested in many key themes including economics, the media, cinema and tourism. His chapter on clubs is also interesting. He notes a particular British tendency towards 'voluntary organisation'.[4]

Martin Polley has written about the Olympics and also the history of sport in *Moving the Goalposts: A History of Sport and Society in Britain Since 1945* (1998), *The History of Sport in Britain, 1880–1914* (ed. 2003) and *Sports History: A Practical Guide* (2006). With regard to the Olympics, he argues, 'It's misguided to think that the Olympic

Games went from their classical Greek dissolution straight to de Coubertin's revival without anything in between, and a lot of those in between events took place in Britain. A couple of important ones are still going on: Robert Dover's Olympick Games at Chipping Campden in the Cotswolds; and the Much Wenlock Olympian Games in Shropshire. I've been to both this year: nothing beats visiting a living event with deep historical roots to get a sense of the event's history and identity.'[5]

We should note the work by H.A. Harris, *Sport in Britain: Its Origins and Development* (1975). This book looks at the nature of early sport – looking at Roman Britain, for example – and then goes on to assess the evolution of a variety of sports including cricket. Harris is particularly interested in the amateur/professional divide and focuses on the landmark year of 1963, when the distinction was abolished.[6] He also assesses the significance of the two world wars for cricket. He says that in 1919 every effort was made to put sport back on its feet; in 1945, after six years of war, he argues that very little had changed. His social history also considers the nature of women's cricket and the way in which the sport originated in girls' boarding schools as an alternative to tennis.[7]

J.A. Mangan's edited collection, *Pleasure, Profit and Proselytism* (1988), focuses on sport as a 'cultural phenomenon'. He emphasises the fact that over time leisure and sport became more important. Mangan's book comprises fourteen chapters, with contributors focusing on such themes as industrialisation, social stratification, popular culture, imperialism, Social Darwinism and colonialism.[8] Mangan argues that people made their own culture and that sport, in a sense, was a replacement for religion. More controversially, he asserts that through sport the bourgeoisie was able to take up class positions against the masses.[9]

In *Sport in Britain: A Social History* (1989), Tony Mason talks about the importance of sport to the study of social history. He says: 'Its place in the popular culture has been recognised by sportsmen and non-sportsmen, men and women, radicals and conservatives, intellectuals and hearties.'[10] He goes on to devote chapters to all the main sports, with Jack Williams writing the section on cricket. He looks at the role of the MCC, issues of finance, levels of participation, the nature of recreational cricket, the nature of league cricket and women's involvement. His contention is that, 'Throughout the twentieth century cricket has been inseparably intertwined with the class system and its history does much to make clear the changing nuances of social relationships within Britain'.[11]

Derek Birley also takes a long-term perspective in *Sport and the Making of Modern Britain* (1993). His first chapters on the very early history of sport are subtitled 'AD43–1199', '1200–1485' and '1485–1603', and he finishes his historical survey in 1888. Like other authors, he seeks to justify the study of sport. He quotes Joseph Strutt: 'In order to form a just estimate of the character of any particular people it is absolutely necessary to investigate the sports and pastimes most prevalent amongst them.'[12] He goes on to argue: 'As for sport it is not only older than the British Isles but older than man.'[13]

In his book, *The Evolution of English Sport* (1996), Neil Wigglesworth says he wishes to consider the way in which people 'enjoy themselves' away from work. He traces the evolution of sport in the nineteenth century and bemoans the fact that, up until recently, little effort has been made to place this in a cultural context.[14] Interestingly, he also focuses on geography. His argument is that the 'rich' south was at odds with the 'depressed' north, and that the southern counties could never match the 'northern sporting fervour'.[15] He traces the history of professionalism and concludes that cricket, possibly more than other sports, was able to assimilate amateurs and professionals with relative ease.

Eric Dunning, in *Sport Matters: Sociological Studies of Sport, Violence and Civilisation* (1999), looks at the role of sport in the 'Western civilising process' and also examines the relationship between sport and race and gender. He argues: 'In my judgement the sociology of sport has recently emerged as one of the liveliest areas in the subject. A central part of its liveliness consists in the fact that the subdiscipline has become a terrain contested by protagonists of all the main sociological paradigms.'[16]

In their book, *Sport in Britain 1945–2000* (2000), Richard Holt and Tony Mason focus on seven major themes: playing and watching, reconstruction, amateurism, the professionals, media, identity and government. They are particularly interested in the amateur ethos and its decline over the decades.[17] They equate amateurism to a gentlemanly spirit and voluntary organisation and talk about the 'strenuous effort' that helped shape the cultural identity of Britain. As with many other authors, they are fascinated by the relationship between amateurs and professionals and argue that it was hardly ever questioned that the two brands of sportsmen could play together, side by side.[18]

Wray Vamplew has written about horse racing, football, physical education, sport in general and rural sport. He has also co-authored books on sport and alcohol, sport and the weather, and sport in Australia. For us, his most relevant work is *Pay Up and Play the Game: Professional Sport in Britain, 1875–1914* (2004). Here, Vamplew looks at different aspects of professional sport including gate money, touring teams, Muscular Christianity, the birth of clubs and leagues, and the distinction between amateurs and professionals. He sees the birth of league cricket in the late nineteenth century, in the north and the Midlands, as a crucial development.[19] His general argument is that economic historians in particular have marginalised sport.[20]

In *Sport and Society: A Student Introduction* (2008), Barrie Houlihan looks at a range of modern and contemporary issues in sport, from human rights and doping to tourism and the environment. His main contention is that sport is now fundamental to society rather than being 'an oasis in an increasingly complex and compromised society'. He goes on: 'Sport, sports organisations and sports practice are at the heart of a number of major social issues either in their own right as sites of tension over social values ... or as policy instruments of government.'[21] It is this contention that has motivated Houlihan to take a multi-disciplinary approach to the study of sport and society.

On football, we should note the work of Dave Russell and Stephen Wagg. Russell has taken part in some general projects about the history of the game – the *Encyclopedia of British Football* (2002), for example, with Richard Cox and Wray Vamplew – and has also specialised in local and regional studies. His main works are *Preston North End: 100 Years in the Football League* (1988), *Looking North: Northern England and the National Imagination* (2004), *Sport in Manchester* (2009), and *Sporting Heroes of the North* with Stephen Wagg (2010). Given that the cricket leagues of Lancashire and Yorkshire were fundamental to the growth of the game in England – an issue that is covered in Chapter 3 of this book – Russell's work is very relevant for us.

Likewise, Wagg has written on sport in general, football and cricket. His book, *Amateurism in British Sport: It Matters Not Who Won or Lost?* (2007) has relevance for our early discussions of amateurism and professionalism. In a more general sense, we should note the following works: *Key Concepts in Sports Studies* (2009), *Sport, Leisure and Culture in the Postmodern City* (2009), *Sporting Heroes of the North* with Dave Russell (2010), and *Myths and Milestones in the History of Sport* (2011). On football, he has authored *British Football and Social Exclusion* (2009), and on cricket, *Cricket and National Identity in the Postcolonial Age* (2007) and *Cricket and Globalization* (2010 with Chris Rumford). At first glance, the issue of globalisation would appear not to have too much relevance for a book on grassroots cricket in England but as the final chapter of this volume makes plain, even small village clubs have been affected by this important trend.[23]

On rugby, Tony Collins is the major historian and his research has much relevance for those of us interested in cricket and sport in general: *Rugby's Great Split: Class, Culture and the Origins of Rugby League Football* (2006), *Rugby League in Twentieth Century Britain* (2007), *1895 And All That ...: Inside Rugby League's Hidden History* (2009) and *A Social History of English Rugby Union* (2009). Of his latest book, he has said:

> I wanted to see what motivated people when it came to the idea of rugby as a moral force which gave people confidence. I went back to *Tom Brown's Schooldays* – which is not an easy book to read, it's really dated – it's clear that much of its [sic] comes from that. Rugby School had immense self-confidence – at one point, a character in the book says it's the only part of the empire that's properly ruled – so if you come from that background, then it explains how the English Rugby Union became, and remains, so self-confident. Those involved in the RFU, players and officials, have tremendous self-confidence to this day, even if England aren't playing well. They convey a sense of being superior to everyone else. When I revisited Tom Brown's Schoolboys, I saw that the reviews when the book was first published commented on this self-confidence; one reviewer said it was as if these people were in a secret society.[24]

As regards cricket specifically, we should note that in recent times Sir Derek Birley and Sir John Major have authored significant works on cricket history. Birley's *A Social History of English Cricket* (1999) is a broad-ranging study that traces the history of the sport from medieval times right up to the current day. It interweaves the social history of cricket with the social and political history of Britain – England, in particular – in recent centuries. His chapters on the two world wars are particularly instructive. He uses the phrase, 'Turn the Dark Clouds Inside Out', as the title for Chapter 14 on the Great War, while 'Shaken, not Stirred' is utilised for Chapter 17 on the Second World War. He talks about the disruption caused by the two world wars but also notes the optimism that was synonymous with the two post-war periods.[25]

Major's work, More Than a Game (2007), focuses on cricket's early development. He is particularly interested in changes in technique, the birth of competition, and the role of cricket's early patrons. His argument is that rich aristocratic patrons helped to popularise the game. They, alongside pubs and breweries, were, in his view, the 'midwives' of the sport. He names three in particular: Edward Stead in Kent and the Duke of Richmond and Sir William Gage in Sussex. He also identifies a 'second wave' of patrons, which involved the third Duke of Dorset, Sir Horace Mann and the Earl of Tankerville. As with the first, the geographical focal-point was the Home Counties.[26]

The significance of Hambledon is also spotlighted by E.V. Lucas in The Hambledon Men (1907). John Arlott called this 'one of the great landmarks in cricket literature'. The book is a compilation of articles: two by the cricketer-writer John Nyren – including 'The Cricketers of My Time' (1832) – and also contributions from Rev. John Mitford, Arthur Haygarth and others. Lucas provides the commentary and he is clear on the significance of Nyren's book: '[It] stands alone in English literature. It had no predecessor; it has had no successor.'[27]

Christopher Brookes has written a helpful overview of cricket's development in England, assessing the early period in English Cricket: The Game and its Players through the Ages (1978). He assesses cricket as a 'folk game', looks at the impact of gambling, and also focuses on the significance of professional touring elevens. In his tenth chapter, he looks at 'Amateurs and Professionals', and argues that, 'At first sight it may seem slightly odd that the distinction between "amateurs" and "professionals" should have assumed such importance at exactly the time that cricket was supposed to be taking on the mantle of the "national" game'.[28] This is an issue we will return to.

For his part, Ric Sissons has focused on the rise of the professional cricketer. John Arlott called The Players: A Social History of the Professional Cricketer (1988), 'a landmark book in cricket literature … That is to say, it is concerned with cricket not simply in the round, but linked to the related aspects of the social scene in which it is played … This is, indeed, the history of cricket played for money – a game played for pleasure yet paid for …'[29] In the book, Sissons traces the history of professionalism through the era of the All-England XI, the 'Not-So-Golden Age', the inter-war era and the modern period.

In his book, Cricket and the Victorians (1994), Keith Sandiford traces the growth of cricket in the Victorian era. He talks about the 'direct link' between Victorian politics and Victorian cricket, and argues that the Victorians put a major emphasis on games and recreations as opposed to, or in addition to, work.[30] He also looks at the role of professional cricketers and their 'serious' attitude to the game. He argues that the notion of sportsmanship was jeopardised by the emergence of paid professional players.[31]

The formative years of the sport are examined by David Underdown in *Start of Play: Cricket and Culture in Eighteenth-Century England* (2000). He depicts a sport that was strong in rural areas, and then spread to the main urban centres, London in particular. Significantly, he devotes two chapters to the story of Hambledon, and argues that, 'By the 1770s cricket was ... a familiar part of the social scene throughout southeastern England, and it was spreading among people of all sorts and conditions. There may even have been women's cricket at Broadhalfpenny.'[32]

Jack Williams has emerged as the historian of the inter-war years. His book, *Cricket and England: A Cultural and Social History of the Inter-War Years* (2000) argues that cricket was far more than a game in the inter-war period. It stood for a 'vision of England' and was a barometer of social harmony. In essence, it was a metaphor for England and a reflection of English qualities. In general, he argues that studying cricket helps to deepen our understanding of the inter-war period. By necessity too, he assesses the legacy of the Great War and argues that this conflict, 'strengthened associations of cricket with Englishness'.[33]

The same author has also authored *Cricket and Race* (2001). This book looks at the relationship between cricket and empire, and the relationship between cricket and racism between the wars. Williams also goes on to consider key case studies, including Apartheid and the D'Oliveira Affair. Towards the end of the book he devotes chapters to anti-West Indian and anti-Pakistani racism. His main conclusion is the first line of the book's introduction: 'Race was at the heart of cricket throughout the twentieth century'.[34]

Jeff Hill has written about various aspects of cricket history. His *Sport and Identity in the North of England* (1996) – with Jack Williams – explores the significance of the Lancashire cricket leagues. In more recent times, he has edited *The Cambridge Companion to Cricket* (2011) with Anthony Bateman. This book covers an array of themes and issues, and as one reviewer put it, 'this is a noble addition to the literature of a game which has attracted more fine writing than any other. It is the product of 20 international contributors, each an authority. Chapters range from the early development of the game to its growing popularity in former British colonies, its celebration in literature, the wealth, in recent times, that accrues to individuals – and some controversies.'[35]

As regards the history of local clubs, we should note the work of Brian, Freda and Malcolm Heywood, whose two-volume history of Todmorden CC, of the Lancashire League, is both comprehensive and illuminating. The first volume, *Cloth Caps and Cricket Crazy* (2004) deals with the nineteenth-century history of the club, while the second, *In a League of Their Own: Cricket and Leisure in 20th Century Todmorden* (2011), assesses the last hundred years.[36] Throughout, they situate the history of the club against the backdrop of the town's history and changing leisure patterns.

Other writers have written useful histories of clubs and competitions, including Martin Abbot (Filleigh, Devon), Martin Bishop (Reading Biscuit Factory), Mike Butler (the Heavy Woollen Cup), R. Cavanagh (cricket in Lancashire), S. Eccles (Clifton, Manchester), C. Farnworth and S. Hall (Bacup), David Goodall (Wavertree, Liverpool), Andrew Hardcastle (Calderdale), J.H. Kell (Menston, Leeds), Tony Lister (Burnley), Pat Neal (Mirfield, West Yorkshire), Dennis O'Keefe (Illingworth St Mary's, Halifax), Roy Pearce (Wirksworth, Derbyshire), J. Rushton (Ramsbottom), C. Ruston (Leeds), B. Shaw (Evesham), Andrew Smith (Illingworth St Mary's, Halifax), Jeffrey Stanyer (Exeter), P.N. Walker (Liverpool), A. West (Ribblesdale, Lancashire) and many others.

We should also note the work of Andrew Hignell, who has explored the growth of the game in Wales in several books and through a special heritage project, 'Tailenders', which is based at Glamorgan CCC in Cardiff. Hignell is particularly interested in the growth of cricket in Cardiff and South Wales and his book, *A Favourit' Game: Cricket in South Wales Before 1914* (1992) is a very helpful overview of the game's development in the Principality.[37] Another historian, Sean Reid, is currently working on the social history of cricket in Ireland, and again his work will be a useful contribution to the growing literature on the social history of the game.[38] And on cricket overseas – which is beyond the scope of this book – we must recognise the contribution of Dean Allen (South Africa), Hilary Beckles (West Indies), Mihir Bose and Boria Majumdar (India), Michael Manley (West Indies), Greg Ryan (New Zealand) and Wray Vamplew/Brian Stoddart/Gideon Haigh (Australia).

Finally, we should acknowledge the contribution of key journalists. Writers such as Neville Cardus, J.M. Kilburn and Raymond Robertson-Glasgow have shone a fascinating light on the history of the game.

At this juncture we should introduce two linked themes in the social history of sport: community and the voluntary tradition. They are particularly important issues so far as this study is concerned.

According to Hill: 'Marx considered British working men to be great "joiners": their support for clubs of all kinds outstripped even that of their mutualist-inclined French counterparts. It was a habit that prompted the French literary brothers Goncourt to remark that the first thing two Englishmen would do if cast away on a desert island would be to form a club.' He goes on: 'Voluntary association was, indeed, a classic British cultural form, stretching back at least to the eighteenth century ... Of all the sectors in which British sports and leisure pursuits are to be found it is the voluntary – the one created by people themselves as part of everyday life – that is the most extensive and deeply embedded, reaching into the very fabric of social life.'[39] We see this impulse strongly in local cricket – people coming together, either formally or informally, to form clubs.

Holt argues along similar lines: 'The unifying thread which runs through the vast and diverse world of popular sports is the idea that workers make their own culture rather than having their play organized for them or sold to them. For popular sports have often been seen as the product of initiatives from above that were imposed upon, or passively adopted by, those below. This "diffusionist" view of popular culture needs close and critical scrutiny.'[40] In Chapter 2, we will use a selection of examples to emphasise the fact that cricket clubs were voluntary bodies, formed by groups of enthusiasts and like-minded people in a particular village, town or locale.

The influence of churches, public houses and places of work was particularly strong. In the late nineteenth century, there were many church cricket teams. Historians argue about whether they were formed on the say-so of the vicar or whether it was the congregation that was crucial in pushing for the opportunity to play cricket. Dennis O'Keefe, who is researching his PhD on cricket in Halifax and district, says: 'I think the most compelling evidence is indirect – the surge in church clubs which followed the arrival of the leagues, which brought a boom in all types of cricket. In other words they were demand-driven, with players seeking a home in order to join the league and the church/chapel was an obvious solution at the time. The men trying to get the Halifax and District Church (Sunday School) League off the ground actually complained about the apathy of the clergy at the churches involved.'[41] Either way, churches became crucial to the early development of the sport. We will cite many examples of church-based cricket clubs. And of course they had many natural advantages: a pool of would-be cricketers (the congregation), the backing of an established organisation (the chapel or church), and resources (many church clubs would play on local church land). There was also established leadership in the form of the minister or vicar – a not-to-be-underestimated factor. Spen Victoria CC, near Dewsbury, was linked to Cleckheaton Wesleyan Sunday School in its early days. In this period, team members had to attend chapel, but this regulation gradually lost its force.[42]

Villages would also have their public house or houses. Locals would congregate there to drink, eat and socialise. There was a natural sense of community. And once the landlord of the pub realised that a cricket club bearing the name of his establishment would be a good thing – not least for trade and the reputation of his business – there were all kinds of possibilities. The players would meet in the pub before the match and also celebrate or commiserate in the same establishment after the game. At Leymoor CC in Huddersfield, the Walker's Arms public house is located on the boundary edge. The club has a good relationship with the pub: it holds meetings there, puts on social events, and patronises it on matchdays as well as during the week.[43]

Industry played its role too. Many cricket clubs emerged as 'works teams', established or at least encouraged (or certainly not discouraged) by enlightened entrepreneurs. Workers 'worked' as a team; many also wished to 'play' as a team.

And works teams had many advantages: the players worked together so were already very familiar with each other; businesses would often own land, which could be used for sport; and through working together, workers' teams would often have a well-developed sense of team spirit. At Bridgeholme CC, near Todmorden, the cricket club was established in 1950 by the owners of two local businesses, Nanholme Mills and Moss Brothers. At first, players had to be employees of either company, but in time this regulation was relaxed.[44]

In these ways, and others, we see an emerging relationship between sport and community.

The current book, *Cricket and Community in England: 1800 to the Present Day*, is about cricket in England. It is different to others in that it puts the emphasis on grassroots cricket rather than the first-class game. We should also explain that since 2004 we have been working on a major Heritage Lottery Fund-sponsored project about the history of cricket in Calderdale (centring on Halifax) and Kirklees (Huddersfield). Many of our case studies come from this area but we have also made a conscious effort to diversify our geographical examples as much as possible. That said, we make no apology for using many exemplars from Yorkshire, and the north more generally, because this is where many of the key developments took place and, even today, it is estimated that around two-thirds of all league cricket takes place in the north. So we will make a virtue out of a necessity and give the northern counties plenty of coverage. We can justify this geographical balance – because it was in the north where important things were taking place as regards the evolution of the game.

We have four main goals: to provide readers with an accessible introduction to the history of grassroots cricket in England; to supply a clear overview of the different phases of this history; to mix basic narrative with helpful and incisive analysis; we will also refer to material collated by specialist historians in other areas of England (e.g. Martin Abbot in Devon, Martin Bishop in Reading, Dennis O'Keefe and Andrew Smith in West Yorkshire, Roy Pearce in Derbyshire, Duncan Stone in Surrey and Willie Sugg in Cambridgeshire) whose work will be referenced throughout the book.

The structure of book is chronological but also thematic. Our analysis begins in Chapter 1, in the eighteenth and nineteenth centuries, with an inquiry into the nature of early sport and early cricket. The key events will be placed within the context of the social, economic and cultural development of the country. We will focus on pre-modern cricket, its formative development in the south-east of England and the role played by competition, commercialism and professionalism, and also the initial growth of cricket in the north and the influence of pre-modern sport on its structure and character. In this period, sport and recreation were shaped by the new social, economic and cultural pressures of capitalist industrialisation, and cricket became an emerging expression of local and civic identity.

The following chapter, Chapter 2, investigates the way in which the early cricket clubs were formed. It will relate the development of cricket clubs to the social, economic and cultural changes that took place during the last four decades of the nineteenth century. We will evaluate the key social, economic and spatial resources necessary to form cricket clubs and the pattern of social exclusivity that marked early organisations. Here, three important themes are: broadening access to leisure opportunities during the 1860s and the impact of this upon cricket; new socially inclusive cricket clubs and the role of other secular and non-secular institutions in their formation; and community identity, cricket clubs and social and economic change at the end of the nineteenth century. In the same period, cup and league competitions were being instituted for the first time.

We then move on, in Chapter 3, to the issue of competition. What was the nature of early competition? We will assess the concept of the challenge match and also evaluate how such events contributed to the early development of the sport. We will take examples from across the country and from different phases of the nineteenth century. We will then move on to a consideration of leagues and cups. In their time, they were revolutionary developments. Today we accept them as the norm, but then, they were new and novel. How and why did leagues and cups emerge? And what kind of reaction did they elicit?

Moving into the twentieth century, in Chapter 4 we investigate the significance of the two world wars as regards the development of cricket. In what sense were they a rupture? How was grassroots cricket affected by the conflicts? This section will deal with a variety of issues including: the moral dilemmas faced by clubs and cricketers; the logistical impact of the wars on local league cricket; the 'pulling together' that went on in the face of war; and why some clubs went into hibernation and others went on playing. We will also assess the significance of the inter-war period and the immediate post-Second World War era as key formative years.

As regards the post-war era, Chapter 5 examines a range of issues, including multiculturalism in the grassroots game, the role of women, equipment and junior cricket. Grassroots cricket faced a number of challenges in the latter years of the twentieth century. It was affected adversely by the economic downturn and had to adapt to survive. This chapter will trace the downturn but also focus on the ways in which the sport at a local level renewed itself.

The final chapter, Chapter 6, brings the story of cricket up to date and investigates such issues as competition, globalisation, commercialisation, and the role of the English Cricket Board (ECB). Local cricket has changed and modernised itself. There are still problems and challenges, but the sport, at grassroots level, has modernised itself. It has embraced new forms of competition and been unafraid to exploit the effects of globalisation. In a sense, local cricket clubs are small business units and in this modern era we see them evolving into more commercial entities and interacting with the government and ECB.

Throughout we have used a variety of sources. We have revisited some of the classic secondary texts, but we have also made a conscious effort to base our arguments on primary sources, whether nineteenth-century newspaper reports or twenty-first century extracts from the Internet.

This book takes us on a journey from the eighteenth to the twenty-first century. But it should be noted that, in one sense, the story of cricket has turned full circle. The advent of the Indian Premier League and the Indian Cricket League reminds us that two centuries on from the epoch of challenge and stake matches, cricket is still at the mercy of speculators.

Notes

1   See www.independent.co.uk/sport/cricket-how-the-game-fares-below-county-level-1109196.html for a helpful overview (last accessed 13 March 2012).
2   R. Holt, Sport and the British: A Modern History (Oxford, OUP, 1990), p. 13.
3   J. Hill, Sport, Leisure and Culture in Twentieth-Century Britain (Basingstoke, Palgrave, 2002), p. 1.
4   Ibid., p. 130.
5   http://palgrave.typepad.com/polley (last accessed 13 March 2012).
6   H.A. Harris, Sport in Britain: Its Origins and Development (London, Stanley Paul, 1975), pp. 52–3.
7   Ibid., p. 75.
8   J.A. Mangan (ed.), Pleasure, Profit and Proselytism (London, Frank Cass, 1988).
9   Ibid., p. 2.
10 T. Mason, Sport in Britain: A Social History (Cambridge, Cambridge University Press, 1989), p. 1.
11 J. Williams, 'Cricket', in Mason (ed.), Sport in Britain, p. 116.
12 D. Birley, Sport and the Making of Britain (Manchester, Manchester University Press, 2001), p. 1.
13 Ibid., p. 1.
14 N. Wigglesworth, The Evolution of English Sport (London, Routledge, 2009).
15 Ibid.
16 E. Dunning, Sport Matters: Sociological Studies of Sport, Violence and Civilisation (London, Routledge, 1999).
17 R. Holt and T. Mason, Sport in Britain 1945–2000 (Oxford, Blackwell, 2000), Chapter 3.
18 Ibid., Chapters 3 and 4.
19 W. Vamplew, Pay Up and Play the Game (Cambridge, Cambridge University Press, 2004), p. 58.
20 Ibid., p. 283.
21 B. Houlihan, Sport and Society: A Student Introduction (London, Sage, 2008), p. 8.
22 See, in particular, S. Wagg and D. Russell, Sporting Heroes of the North (Newcastle, Northumbria Press, 2010).
23 Ibid.
24 www.irishexaminer.com/sport/the-problem-with-english-rugby-111054.html (last accessed 13 March 2012).
25 D. Birley, A Social History of English Cricket (London, Aurum Press, 2003).
26 J. Major, More Than a Game: The Story of Cricket's Early Years (London, HarperPress, 2007).
27 E.V. Lucas, The Hambledon Men (London, Henry Frowde, 1907), p. 120.
28 C. Brookes, English Cricket: The Game and its Players through the Ages (Newton Abbot, Readers Union, 1978), p. 138.
29 R. Sissons, The Players: A Social History of the Professional Cricketer (London, Kingswood, 1988), pp. xiii/xiv.

30 K. Sandiford, *Cricket and the Victorians* (London, Ashgate, 1994), p. 81.

31 Ibid.

32 D. Underdown, *Start of Play: Cricket and Culture in Eighteenth-Century England* (London, Penguin, 2001), p. 111.

33 J. Williams, *Cricket and England: A Cultural and Social History of the Inter-War Years* (London, Frank Cass, 2000), p. 6.

34 J. Williams, *Cricket and Race* (London, Berg, 2001), p. 1.

35 *The Independent*, 6 May 2011.

36 M.F. and B. Heywood, *Cloth Caps and Cricket Crazy: Todmorden and Cricket 1835–1896* (Todmorden, Upper Calder Valley Publications, 2004) and *In a League of Their Own: Cricket and Leisure in 20th Century Todmorden* (Todmorden, Upper Calder Valley Publications, 2011).

37 A. Hignell, *A Favourit' Game: Cricket in South Wales Before 1914* (Cardiff, University of Wales Press, 1992).

38 Reid is a PhD student at the University of Huddersfield.

39 Hill, *Sport, Leisure and Culture*, p. 130.

40 Holt, *Sport and the British*, p. 135.

41 Note to authors, 15 Sep 2011.

42 See www.ckcricketheritage.org.uk/northkirklees/spen/clubhome.htm (last accessed 13 March 2012).

43 See www.ckcricketheritage.org.uk/southkirklees/leymoor/clubhome.htm (last accessed 13 March 2012).

44 See www.ckcricketheritage.org.uk/calderdale/bridgeholme/clubhome.htm (last accessed 13 March 2012).

1 Early sport and cricket

One of the key components in studying sport history is to recognise that sport reflects society. So, by looking at how changes in society influenced the development of modern sport the structure of pre-modern sport can be more clearly explained.

Sport in England underwent massive changes during the nineteenth century. The modern conception of sport was formed during the middle-1800s, and refined over the next fifty years, so that virtually all today's major sports and types of sporting competition had been formed by the beginning of the twentieth century. These changes in sport were linked to parallel developments in English society, economy and culture.

Three major influences in this process were:

- The reform of the public schools, which were refashioned to provide an education that groomed students for social and imperial leadership. Sport became a major part of this process and was codified to instil a sense of discipline and moral purpose.
- Urban industrialisation: The industrial capitalist economy totally refashioned the way many people lived their lives. In particular, the new work discipline regulated working practices and hours. Also, for many, payment was now made for the value of their labour and not for the goods they produced.
- Rational recreation and Muscular Christianity: To these new movements, many pre-modern or traditional leisure activities contradicted the new values of respectability which were developed during the nineteenth century. So, these and other social and religious groups felt the need to reform the working classes by replacing traditional activities with new ones.

So to examine the shape of pre-modern sport it is important to look at how the social, economic and cultural make-up of British society before the nineteenth century was reflected in contemporary sport and leisure.

Time for leisure: economic influence on sport and leisure

The most fundamental difference between pre-modern and modern sport was related to the availability of free time which could be used for leisure activities. Like the later allocation of free time, such as the Saturday half-day holiday, this was dictated by the contemporary economic structure.

The modern working week was not established until after the 1850s. Before this time the pattern of work, and therefore leisure, was based on the agrarian economy, which in certain areas included cottage industries such as textiles. Consequently, time for leisure was dictated by the agricultural and religious calendar.

This meant that regular spare time was in short supply and, with the exception of the Sabbath, was only available at times of religious holidays or local feasts and festivals. Along with the general religious holidays, such as Christmas, Shrove Tuesday, Lent, Easter and Whitsun, individual Saints days were often days when local feasts and festivals were held. Other holidays marked the beginning or end of the agricultural phases, such as ploughing, sowing, harvesting, sheep shearing and the slaughter of livestock.

Perhaps the most famous example of games being played at these times of year are the folk football matches which were regularly played on public holidays, and in some cases are still played today. Shrove Tuesday was a popular time for folk football, along with other sports such as cockfighting. Wakes weeks were more localised holidays during which blood sports and combat sports were often staged. Most towns and villages also had their own feast at which sports were an integral part of the celebrations, with horse-racing a popular occurrence.

Although sports were banned on the Sabbath, many still used this time for leisure. Consequently, prosecutions for Sabbath-breaking have provided important source material for the study of early sport. Cricket, in particular, has benefited from this source. One of the first known references to the game was at Boxgrove in Sussex in 1622, when several men were prosecuted for playing on Sunday.

Regular time available for playing sport was clearly restricted by local variations and seasonal demands. But another source of leisure time was provided by irregular time away from work. Spontaneous holidays could be relatively common, especially among those employed in the trades and other craft-specific industries where employees were paid on piece rates. Perhaps the most common of these spontaneous holidays was St Monday, whereby production was increased towards the end of the week, on Saturday, and Monday was taken as an unofficial holiday. The cutlery trades in Sheffield were famous for their observance of St Monday. In the mid-nineteenth century a Mr Hutton, who had moved from Sheffield to work in Birmingham, described the practice in his former home town:

In Summer the men ... often sacrifice a Monday afternoon to the exercise of sports, which, at all events, is better than drinking away the Monday, as thousands do in Birmingham.[1]

The relative autonomy of some trades also meant that time off could occasionally be taken for specific events. These were mostly spectator contests, such as prize fights or cockfights, at which the main attraction was the opportunity to gamble.

Clearly, contemporary economic and social practices obstructed the development of a regulated and rationalised programme of sport before the middle of the nineteenth century. Allied to the difficulties in travel and communications, this meant that in many cases sports remained highly localised and practised as little more than folk customs. However, as the eighteenth and early nineteenth centuries unfolded, continued economic and population growth, especially in London and the emerging urban centres, meant that within these constraints a relatively sophisticated framework of sport was also developed.

One of the most striking characteristics of pre-modern sport was its diversity. One way to understand the structure of sport during this period is to split sporting contests into two distinct categories. First, participation sports, i.e. those events which were primarily staged for the enjoyment of the people who played in them; and second, spectator sports, i.e. those sports which were primarily staged as a form of entertainment.

Participation sports were mainly in the form of folk games. A huge array of events were popular, from folk football and cricket to knur and spell and bull-running. Because the predominantly parochial nature of sport prevented any widespread standardisation, many variants of similar traditional games existed. Cricket provides a good example of this, and while the sport had barely spread outside the south-east of England before the end of the eighteenth century, many similar folk games already existed elsewhere in the country. They included cat and dog, club ball, creag, stool ball, bad and trap ball.

There were two main categories of participation games. First of all, 'organised' events. These pre-arranged 'traditional' contests usually took place on religious and local holidays. Folk football matches fall into this category and Boxing Day and Shrove Tuesday were the most popular days for annual games. These contests often included large numbers of players with around 1,000 men taking part in the annual game in Derby; a much smaller community such as Sedgefield still staged a game in which 400 men on each side took part.

Blood sports such as 'throwing at cocks' were also common at holiday times. In this event stones were thrown at the bird and whoever knocked it over and caught it before it got up, took the animal home to eat. In some places a variety of sports were played at holiday times. Each Easter thousands met at Sancton near Market Weighton 'for the purpose of horse-racing, football, cudgel playing and other events'.[2]

The other type of organised sporting events were matches which resulted from a specific challenge. In many cases these contests were primarily spectator events, but in cricket they were also staged for the benefit of participants. In these more social matches the challenge was a means of arranging the fixture to coincide with the availability of the players. While, to some extent, the need to make specific arrangements reflected the irregular nature of working patterns, these matches mainly involved members of the gentry whose main concern was fitting the fixtures into a busy social calendar. The challenge matches were particularly prominent among the eighteenth-century aristocracy and a wager was almost always involved.

One of the earliest examples of such matches being arranged is provided by a letter from Sir William Gage to the Duke of Richmond in 1725. He wrote:

My Lord Duke

I received this moment your Grace's letter and am extremely happy your Grace intends us ye honour of making one a Tuesday, and will without fail bring a gentleman to play against you …[3]

This form of pre-arranged fixture also provides the first examples of cricket matches being played in Yorkshire. Around about the middle years of the eighteenth century, references begin to appear to matches such as this one which appeared in the *Leeds Times* on 14 May 1776:

Yesterday a cricket match was played on Chapeltown Moor by the gentlemen of the Town for 5 Guineas and a dinner – married men against bachelors, which was won by the latter, as there were six to come in when the game was out.[4]

The second form of participation sport was played between groups of local working people when free time became available. Although they are less well documented than 'organised' participation events, these spontaneous matches were probably more common. Little evidence survives about this form of sport partly because of its spontaneity. Any organised event requires some form of communication, such as the correspondence which was used to arrange the early challenge matches.

The availability of source material relating to these forms of sport also reveals much about the contemporary social structure and its influence upon early sport. Leisure time was more available to those of a higher social standing and this meant that they were able to pre-arrange fixtures in advance. They were also literate and communicated with their opponents through correspondence, which in some cases has survived to provide valuable source material.

Leisure time for the working classes was less freely available and had to be taken when it became possible to do so. Therefore, by necessity, participation in sport was more spontaneous and could not be planned ahead. It is also likely that few working-class people were literate and would not be able to record the events that took place even if they were of note.

This point is supported by the nature of many references to spontaneous cricket matches which have survived. These often come from the reminiscences of professional cricketers, who were by definition working class and learned the game by playing in spontaneous matches.

Allen Hill, the Yorkshire and England player who made his name playing for Lascelles Hall in Huddersfield, provides one such example. His early memories show how work and leisure were closely linked:

> We were all weavers, and spent half our time in playing Cricket. The time we spent in practising in the daytime we made up for by sticking to the loom at night.[5]

Tom Emmett, who captained Yorkshire in the 1880s, learned his cricket in a lane near Illingworth, Halifax, where:

> At the entrance to the drive were two stone posts, and it was one of these that we used for our wickets. That was where I was initiated into cricket, and where I first found I could hit the post with a round arm delivery.

Spectator sports or entertainment events

The second main type of pre-modern sporting contests were spectator events. These were often sports in which general participation was not possible, like blood sports (such as cockfighting), or was not desirable, like combat sports (such as prize-fighting). Consequently, the participants were generally accomplished, well-known performers, which added to the attraction of the event, as did the ubiquitous prevalence of gambling. It was through this type of spectacle that sport became a form of popular entertainment. This raised commercial possibilities that attracted the attention of entrepreneurs.

By the middle of the eighteenth century, most towns had at least one cockpit and these could often be found in public houses. Likewise, outdoor arenas for prize-fighting could also be found in many major towns and especially in London. Promoters staged regular events at these venues, which mostly featured professional sportsmen. Men like Jack Broughton, Tom Cribb and Tom Molyneux became well known popular figures through their performances in the ring. Of the less barbarous large-scale spectator events, horse-racing was perhaps the most popular and demand had seen grandstands built at York, Doncaster and Richmond racecourses before the 1780s.

Cricket was perhaps the one sport that crossed the divide between participation and spectator sport. By the middle of the eighteenth century, the rapid growth of stake matches, which were played between teams representing members of the aristocracy, had led to major matches which featured the best players of the day.

These fixtures were called 'Great Matches' and led to the employment of professional players, as wealthy backers strove to assemble the best teams possible. They initially took place in London and the south-east of England and also attracted the attention of entrepreneurs. Proprietor-owned grounds were built at which the Great Matches were staged. The events were promoted in the press, and admission charges made for spectators, who could also buy refreshments and lay bets on the result.

One of the earliest of these venues was the Artillery Ground in London, which in 1732 was managed by Christopher Jones who was landlord of the nearby Pyed Horse public house. In 1738, an estimated crowd of 10,000 watched a match between Kent and England at the venue. Around fifty years later Thomas Lord, the most famous cricket proprietor of all, opened his first ground, near what is now Dorset Square.

As well as these elaborately staged events, cricket was also being played as a form of popular entertainment at traditional times of leisure. Early references to cricket being played in Yorkshire provide good examples of this type of sporting event being staged on public holidays. In 1751, 'The Sheffield authorities engaged professional cricketers to amuse the populace, and so draw them from cock fighting exhibitions', and in 1757 Leeds Church Burgesses' accounts record that they had 'paid cricket players on Shrove Tuesday, to entertain the populace and to prevent the infamous practice of throwing at cocks', the sum expended being 14s6d.[6]

As the sport spread rapidly during the first half of the nineteenth century, major cricket events also began to be held in Yorkshire. This development was made possible when George Steer built the first major cricket venue in the county, at Darnall in Sheffield in 1821. Major cricket matches were regularly staged at Darnall during the early 1820s. They proved extremely popular and in August 1824 a match between Sheffield and Bingham attracted an estimated crowd of between 15,000 and 20,000, while a month later Sheffield v Leicester was watched by between 20,000 and 25,000. These matches were promoted in the same way as the earlier 'great matches' in London had been and adverts were placed in the press. By this time a second major venue for cricket had been opened in Sheffield, at Hyde Park, and it was soon to overtake Darnall as the city's main venue.

Despite the relative sophistication of these large spectator events, one definitive theme in all pre-modern sport was its informality or lack of standardisation. Rationalised rules and regulations in sport were developed during the Victorian era. They reflected a more general movement towards regulation in most aspects of society. As the population and economy grew, they required greater administration which led to, among other things, an expansion in local and national government. Elsewhere, voluntary societies became popular. They were run by a uniform structure of elected officials and committees, which provided the blueprint for the administrative bodies which were created to run many sports. The public schools also played a role in this process, by first codifying many sports, such as football, and making way for a generally accepted set of rules.

Before this, specific agreements were made for each contest. This was usually done through the challenge and mostly involved peripheral issues which lay outside the general principles of the sport. The need to agree set rules in what were originally folk games probably arose through the prevalence of gambling and was therefore necessary in almost all types of contest.

By their definition, organised matches provide the best references to the way agreements were made through the challenge. Usually they were closely linked to gambling and often simply stated who could take part on each side. However, specific agreements were often made to even out the contest, making it more lucrative both for a weaker opponent to accept the challenge and for spectators to bet on the result. Consequently, a variety of what now seem bizarre contests took place.

This is perhaps most effectively demonstrated in the ambiguous sport of pedestrianism. All types of walking or running challenges were grouped under this heading. Some were straightforward contests, as when 'Joseph Wright of Birkenshaw', was ready to race 'William Hargreaves of Bowling Lane, near Bradford, 110 yards, from £5 to £10 a-side'.[7] On other occasions, however, far more imaginative challenges were often undertaken. These commonly involved individual contestants who attempted to complete some form of task usually in a given time. Townshend, 'the champion pedestrian', accepted one such challenge in 1827 when the *Sheffield Independent* reported, 'We understand on Monday morning at 7 o'clock he starts from Hyde Park to walk forty miles backwards for six days following – for a wager of £20'.[8]

Early cricket matches could also be played with informal variations to the normal rules. Odds matches were a relatively common occurrence. These fixtures involved a particularly strong eleven, which often included a collection of professionals, playing a team which was recognised as being weaker and therefore was allowed to field extra players. Odds matches were favoured by the teams of touring professional elevens that travelled around England, playing local eighteens and twenty-twos in exhibition matches during the middle of the nineteenth century.

The allocation of given men was another way to even out the sides. This could happen on the most prestigious occasions, and to make the early Gentleman v Players matches more equally contested, professional 'players' were sometimes 'given' to the Gentlemen and in 1829 Lillywhite and Broadridge took nineteen of the twenty Players' wickets to fall in the Gentlemen's victory.

Changes to the more generally accepted laws were also occasionally made to even out the contest. The 1837 Gentleman v Players encounter became known as the 'Barn Door' match, after the Players were required to defend a wicket which was twice the normal size.

Single- and double-wicket matches were another example of such variations. These matches could resemble prize-fights, with leading players attracting groups of backers who sought challengers for big-money contests. The games were held as popular spectacles and challenges were advertised in the press to attract interest. But leading players also accepted challenges from lesser opponents and John Thewlis, the Yorkshire player from Lascelles Hall, described how he once agreed to play against eleven landlords residing within a mile of Chickenley, near Dewsbury, and then had

> a long disputation as to the method of scoring, but finally I carried my point that all runs were to be made in front of the wicket.[9]

The need for informal variations in sport was perhaps more understandable in the spontaneous participation matches that took place. Conditions and the available resources would rarely be consistent. Variations were likely in the number of players available at any given time, the dimensions of whatever ad hoc playing area could be found and the resources which were at hand with which to play the game.

Like the spread of the capitalist industrial economy, modern sporting concepts were not formed immediately. They took time to develop and spread. This meant that old and new ideas often coexisted and at times interacted. Many aspects of pre-modern sport still disappeared. Sport became rationalised and formalised, with organised clubs and rules. It was also played more often and at regular times of the week and year, and it was more civilised, with the end of barbaric human and animal sports.

But perhaps the most lasting influence of this pre-modern period can be seen in the cultural values which remained in some sports. As we have seen, the challenge and stake matches, with their integral link to gambling, dominated many aspects of sport in the pre-modern period. Crucially, they provided sport with a strong and vibrant sense of competition which remains today.

Alongside other features of pre-modern sport such as commercialism, professionalism and viewing sport as entertainment, competition conflicted with the values which emerged in cricket during the second half of the nineteenth century. However, these cultural values remained strong, particularly in the urban industrial regions of Britain, like the West Riding of Yorkshire, and they played a major role in the development of the modern spectator sports which now dominate the sporting landscape.

Early cricket

At the start of his chapter on the game's history in the 1888 *Badminton Book of Cricket*, Andrew Lang could already recount how, 'Hundreds of pages have been written on the origin and early history of Cricket'.[10] Lang's observation reflects a deep fascination which continues today. It has encompassed a number of inventive theories which are drawn from a diverse range of sources, but all have failed to reach any firm conclusion.[11] For, as David Underdown has pointed out, 'the almost total absence of written sources regarding cricket before about 1600 ensures that there is nothing that the historian can usefully say about it [sic] we can speculate, but what do we know?'[12]

Yet the emergence of this enduring desire to reconstruct the game's origins and early history has a deep significance that far outweighs the value of any results which were subsequently produced. It offers an important insight into how cricket came to play a key role in common perceptions of English culture and national character during the nineteenth century in a way that placed growing importance on the manner in which the past was viewed. During the middle decades of the nineteenth century, sport and leisure became a key issue as British society was transformed by the growth of capitalist urban industrialisation. Over the previous half-century, social, economic and cultural relations had been transformed as the ideals of an expanding middle class became increasingly predominant. These changes conflicted fundamentally with many of the values that had previously underscored the fabric of society in England and placed new demands on those at both ends of the social scale.

Few aspects of life represented the rift between pre-modern society and the demands of urban industrial capitalism more than leisure and recreation. The previously informal, often excessive and profligate culture of leisure, which crossed class divisions, was incompatible with the new work discipline, evangelical morality and social respectability that characterised the way in which English society was being reshaped. Consequently, leisure became a key issue for those involved in new social and cultural movements such as public school reform, 'Muscular Christianity' and the ideal of the 'Gentleman Amateur', which looked to create a social elite fit to lead the nation and its rapidly expanding empire. Games, especially, came to be seen as an ideal means through which values that it was felt should represent the character of the English gentleman could be promoted. As a pastime of increasingly national dimensions, cricket was at the forefront of these developments and in his book *The Cricket Field*, which was published in 1851, Rev. James Pycroft decreed,

> The game of cricket, philosophically considered, is a standing panegyric on the English character: none but an orderly and sensible people would so amuse themselves.[13]

In this changing context the game's relatively long history also provided a means through which the new approach to leisure could be promoted in a way that offered a reassuring link with the past. Consequently, Pycroft was able to ascribe the new values to cricket by associating them with an idealised vision of the social relations which predominated in rural England over previous centuries. In it he proclaimed that,

> It is no small praise of cricket that it occupies the place of less innocent sports. Drinking, gambling, cudgel-playing insensibly disappear before a manly recreation, which draws the labourer from the dark haunts of vice and misery to the open common ... where 'the squire or parson o' th' parish Or the attorney' may raise him without lowering themselves, by taking an interest if not a part in his sport.[14]

But in order to fully cement its status as a definitively English pastime, cricket's English roots had to be confirmed. So speculation over the game's origins increased and, for example, in the introduction to his book *The English Game of Cricket*, Charles Box explained that, 'In the compilation hereof one great object has been kept steadily in view – viz. that of proving cricket to be purely of English origin'.[15] Box concluded that 'cricket is pre-eminently an English game – English in its origin, English in its character'. But how far did the picture of cricket's history which was painted by writers such as Box and Pycroft provide a representative view of the game's past?

For all the speculation about its origins, there is little doubt that the game which first came to be known as cricket was a variant of the numerous generic bat and ball folk games. As Mike Marqusee has pointed out, initially these games were 'pre-national', and part of common pan-European folk culture. In England, variants such as stool ball, cat and dog, club ball, trap ball and tip cat all encompassed the basic tenets of cricket. They were played and spread informally, causing a degree of adaptation and reinterpretation between place and time and in the south-east of England during the sixteenth century cricket emerged as the popular derivative form of these generic games.

It is from this point onwards that the written references to cricket that Underdown referred to begin to appear and many are closely linked to the game's status as a popular recreation. Until restrictions were relaxed following the Restoration of the monarchy in 1688, sabbatarianism and fear of civil and economic disorder resulted in the suppression of such pastimes. Consequently, prohibitive legislation and prosecutions provide sporadic early written references to the game in the south-eastern counties of England.[16] Indeed, even as late as 1733 the *St James' Evening Post* reported that,

> The [sic] Grand Jury presented (as very great grievances) the assemblies at Moorfields of loose, idle and disorderly persons playing at cricket and using many other new-invented ways of gaming to the depravatoir and corruption of youth and good manners.[17]

By the time this report was published, however, the social and cultural dynamics of cricket had been transformed by the rapid growth of interest in the game among the English gentry. Cricket became one of many pastimes on which members of the English aristocracy used to spend their wealth and leisure time and which grew significantly during the long period of political and economic stability that followed the Restoration. Notices of matches in which members of aristocracy took part became common and they reflected how general perceptions of the game had begun to alter. For example, in 1730 the *British Journal* explained that,

> His Grace the Duke of Richmond, and several other young Noblemen and Gentlemen, have begun to divert themselves each Morning, at the Play of Cricket in [sic] Hyde Park and design to pursue that wholesome Exercise every fair Morning during Spring.[18]

Cricket provided a convivial environment which was perfectly suited to the distinctive recreational habits which emerged among the English social elite during the long eighteenth century. As Peter Clarke has shown, this period was marked by the growth of a diverse associational leisure culture which began to permeate throughout British society. It spurred the formation of numerous clubs and societies and by the 1770s cricket had become a prominent focal point for such organisations.[19] The first known reference to a cricket club appeared in 1722 when 'the Gentlemen known by the name of the London Club, who are composed of several parishes in London, Southwark &c' attended 'a meeting at the Three Tons and Rummer in Grace Church Street' in 1722.[20] Early clubs such as the one established at the Star and Garter Inn in Pall Mall were formed among members of the aristocracy. But alongside these more august organisations it is likely that those which became active in the market towns that surrounded London at Dartford, Bromley and Coxheath in Kent, and Croydon in Surrey, were established by members of the expanding urban gentry.

The activities of these early cricket clubs also mirrored those of other contemporary clubs and societies. Playing cricket was often combined with more sociable activities and pick-up matches between members were common with dining and drinking usually providing a cordial end to proceedings. At Coxheath in Kent play was also concluded with a dinner which cost 2s for members and 3s for non-members, while at Hambledon three dozen bottles of wine were ordered for the club's annual general meeting in 1784. But Clarke has also shown how the eighteenth-century associational culture provided an important locus of social formation for the expanding middle classes.[21] Indeed, at the Hambledon club the members included professional men, such as Edward Hale, the son of a local surgeon, and recent arrivals in Hampshire society whose status was built upon new wealth, like Richard Barwell. Through their involvement with the cricket club they were consequently able to mix both with each other and members of the traditional landed elite.[22]

But the increase in aristocratic involvement in cricket also served a wider purpose. The game provided an ideal opportunity to hold the type of large-scale inclusive events which reinforced the distinctive social relations of pre-modern Britain. Patronage of popular recreation provided an important means through which the aristocracy could display their wealth and power while also promoting a common English culture which crossed class divisions. Major matches in which members of the aristocracy took part were staged in front of large, socially mixed crowds and for example, when the Duke of Richmond played a match against a Mr Chambers, '11 on each side for 200 guineas [sic] on Richmond Green' in 1731, as well as a 'great number of persons of distinction of both sexes', thousands of spectators from the lower orders were also present.[23]

The increasing focus of aristocratic patronage upon cricket in south-east England reflected the game's origins as a popular recreation in rural communities across the region. Because of its setting and the relatively humble status of the participants, written references to cricket in this context are scarce and it is likely that matches retained an informal structure that could fit around the demands of the agrarian economy throughout the eighteenth century. It is certainly unlikely that those who took part in the popular rural game had sufficient access to either the necessary resources or regular leisure time required to establish formally organised cricket clubs. But the games which took place in these towns clearly developed a compelling competitive culture which built upon the vibrant sense of communal identity that existed among the lower orders and in 1708 saw a Kentish farmer declare in his diary that, 'Wee beat Ash Street at Cricketts'.[24]

One common dynamic, however, underscored both aristocratic involvement in cricket and the popular rural game and that was gambling, which was arguably the most popular form of leisure in the eighteenth century. Playing cricket for money underscored the inherent competitive dynamics of the sport and gave expressions of communal and individual aristocratic rivalry a heightened significance. But for members of the aristocracy, especially, cricket also provided a compelling means through which gambling could be combined with other social and recreational activities. So it became common for matches to carry a wager between the participants, whoever they were. For example, at the lower end of the social scale, Thomas Turner, a shopkeeper from East Hoathly in Sussex, took part in a seemingly inconsequential match, on the local common in 1756. He played for the 'Street' quarter of the Parish against the 'Nursery [sic] each time paying his due as a "gamester" [sic] in this case a shilling a match'.[25]

But much larger sums of money were at stake when teams assembled by members of the aristocracy met in the Great Matches. As early as 1735 one such contest took place between teams representing 'his Royal Highness the Prince of Wales and the Earl of Middlesex'.[26] By the middle decades of the eighteenth century a regular circuit of matches between the aristocratic patrons of cricket had emerged. Often contests took place between two sides that represented individual patrons such as the one mentioned above, while individuals or groups of backers also put together teams that played in the guise of counties, such as Kent and Sussex, or as All-England. Sometimes, however, teams represented the leading aristocratic clubs and, for example, in 1776, Hambledon, arguably the most famous of all such organisations, played matches against England in June for £525 and Surrey in August for £1,050.[27]

The importance of gambling on cricket consequently had a profound influence upon the distinctive culture and structure which shaped the game in its pre-modern context and beyond. Its impact is perhaps most clearly evident in the innate informality which characterised the game during this period. Playing for stake money meant there was little reason for teams to take on opponents of superior strength and a variety of means were used to make matches more even. So as well as the straightforward contests between teams of equal numbers, many matches took on a different form and sometimes stronger teams allowed their opponents to field one or more 'given men'. This was the case when 'the Gentlemen of London, and the Gentlemen of Dartford' met in 1756 and as the latter side had previously 'beat the Gentlemen of Hampshire the matches successively for Fifty Pounds a side' they were 'allowing London to have Bryant, Smith, Durling and Job Harris'.[28] On other occasions, however, odds matches were played: for example, eleven of Hambledon played against twenty-two of 'Other Counties' in June 1772.[29]

But the inherent flexibility of these contests masked a high degree of organisation which had important consequences for the game's development. Matches were arranged on an individual basis through a system of challenges which reflected the exigencies of pre-modern economic and social demands. Before the second half of the nineteenth century, when the capitalist economic structure had been adopted in the majority of industries and a uniform weekly pattern of work was established, leisure time was sporadic and a systematic programme of sporting fixtures could not be arranged. So matches had to be arranged to fit around the availability of those involved. As in other sports, this was done in the form of a specific challenge which was issued and accepted through an exchange of correspondence.

It was through this system of challenges for stake money that the first written laws for cricket emerged. In the early decades of the eighteenth century cricket remained an informal game with variant local rules. So it was necessary to clarify which of these would be used in any single contest. As significant amounts of money could be wagered, disputes frequently occurred and it became common for matches to be governed by some form of written contractual agreement. The earliest known example of these 'Articles of Agreement' was drawn up for two matches between the Duke of Richmond and Mr Alan Broderick in 1727. Such documents almost certainly provided a model which was adhered to in other contests before the first attempt to set out a uniform code of regulations was made at a meeting of representatives from various leading London clubs at the Star and Garter Inn, Pall Mall in 1744.

But the inception of written rules in cricket bore little relation to the concept of fair play that is widely associated with the widespread development of codified rules in sport around 150 years later. Their main purpose was to specify the terms of the wager which included setting out the size and composition of the teams, the number of matches which were to take place, the venues and, most importantly, the size of the stake. The distinction between these dual functions was illustrated in a set of 'Articles' which were agreed for the match between Sheffield and Leicester in 1828 and published in *Bell's Life*. It was agreed,

> to play two matches at cricket, home and home, for Fifty Pounds each, eleven players, residents of Sheffield, against ten players of the county of Leicester, with a given player of All England, to be played according to the Maryl-la-bonne Rules.[30]

The last condition of the agreement suggests that the MCC laws may have been relatively unfamiliar to the parties involved in this contest and were still yet to gain full acceptance as late as the 1820s.

The stake of £50 for this contest was relatively modest in comparison with the previous century when large sums of money were wagered on cricket, providing a high level of competition and financial investment that drove other crucial developments in the game. Members of the social elite who were increasingly drawn to the game possessed considerable financial resources. So as high stakes depended on the outcome of matches, providing payments to ensure the services of leading players from the game's traditional rural heartland was a logical progression. Initially these men were employed through a form of 'retained' or 'indentured' professionalism, and while occupying token jobs on the estates of aristocratic cricket patrons they spent the summer months playing cricket. Thomas Waymark, one of the earliest known professional cricketers, worked as a footman for the Duke of Richmond during the 1720s while men such as James Ayleward and George and John Ring were employed as bailiff, huntsman, and whipper-in by Sir Horatio Mann in the 1770s and 1780s.[31]

By the middle decades of the nineteenth century, however, a new form of independent professionalism had emerged which reflected the growing number of opportunities that were being provided by the game. Players began to receive payment for the individual contests in which they took part and in 1745 the Duke of Richmond's accounts included payments of £37 and 16 shillings 'to 12 gamesters at the artillery ground and Moulsey Hurst at 3 guineas each' and £10 and 10 shillings 'to ten gamesters on Bury Hill, 9th Sept'.[32] The introduction of match payments also reflected a shift in the economic background of some professionals. Many were skilled tradesmen or farmers who would not give up their occupations for more menial jobs on the aristocratic estates. For example, Richard Newland, who is regarded by many as the leading player of this period, was a yeoman farmer, as were his brothers who played alongside him in the Slindon team, which was backed by the Duke of Richmond.[33]

The geographic and social origins of these players also reinforced the link between the growing aristocratic game and cricket's popular rural roots. During the eighteenth century, professionals increasingly dominated the Great Matches and, as William Beldham later explained, became 'the pride and honour in the parishes that sent them up'.[34] Beldham was one of the most celebrated men to make the transition from rural cricket to the elite game. A farmer from Farnham in Surrey, he became widely recognised as the leading batsman in the game during the last quarter of the eighteenth century and played regularly at Lord's for the famous Hambledon club as well as various other teams.

Indeed, the Hambledon club with which Beldham became most notably associated provides perhaps the clearest illustration of how the synthesis between aristocratic enthusiasm and the game's rural roots shaped the development of cricket during this period. The great Hambledon teams of this time consisted mainly of professionals who were backed to play in big-money challenge matches by the club's wealthy aristocratic members. They included leading players from the surrounding area who were paid 'four shillings if winners and three shillings if losers' on practice days which took place on a regular basis. The investment was well rewarded as it has been estimated that between 1770 and 1790 Hambledon teams made a profit of £12,467 in stake money for their backers.[35] But through its success the club also provides a profound illustration of how a compelling sense of local identity could be invested in cricket in this context which was vividly brought to life by John Nyren's famous reminiscence that,

> There was high feasting on Broadhalfpenny during the solemnity of one of our grand matches. Oh it was a heart-stirring sight to witness the multitude forming a complete and dense circle round that noble green. Half the county would be present, and all their hearts with us – Little Hambledon, pitted against all England was a proud thought for the Hampshire men. Defeat was glory in a struggle-victory, indeed, made us 'a little lower than angels'.[36]

As the number of Great Matches in which the game's leading players took part increased during the second half of the nineteenth century, important advancements in playing technique and equipment manufacture were also made. In some ways they resulted from a process that reflected established principles in craft apprenticeships. Knowledge and skills were handed on from established players and developed further by the new generation of cricketers. For example, Richard Nyren and then David Harris developed the practice of length-bowling, which exploited the irregular bounce of uneven pitches. To counter this, John Small and then William Beldham pioneered the straight-bat technique. Indeed, Beldham later described how these changes took place and explained,

> I believe that Walker, Fennex, and myself first opened the old players' eyes to what could be done with the bat; Walker by cutting, and Fennex and I by forward play: but all improvement was owing to David Harris's bowling. His bowling rose almost perpendicular; it was once pronounced a jerk; it was altogether most extraordinary.[37]

He also paid tribute to the pioneering influence of Small who was a bat-maker and, in addition to changing 'the crooked bat of his day for a straight bat',

Beldham described him as being the first man to have '"found out cricket", or brought play to any degree of perfection'.[38]

As a consequence of the prominent position they occupied in the game, many of these professional players became leading attractions in the commercialised context of cricket in London. As David Underdown has shown, by the middle decades of the nineteenth century, cricket had become absorbed into the thriving commercial leisure culture of the capital where matches were staged at venues run by commercial entrepreneurs. Along with other sporting events such as foot-races and prize-fights, cricket was promoted to attract a large paying audience and advertisements appeared regularly in the press. The first important commercial venue for cricket was the Artillery Ground in Finsbury which, like many other sites of popular entertainment, was run by a landlord, in this case the proprietor of the adjacent Pyed Horse Inn. By the middle of the next decade it was staging matches such as the one in 1744 between the County of Kent and All-England which the *Country Journal or The Craftsman* billed as 'the greatest Cricket-Match ever known'.[39]

The increasing commercialisation of the game built on cricket's growing popularity and large crowds were not uncommon at major matches as it became firmly rooted in the popular culture of London and other parts of south-east England during the eighteenth century. According to a letter protesting about a recent increase in admission charges during 1746, 7,000 to 8,000 people regularly attended matches at the Artillery Ground at this time and in 1738, 1743 and 1751 estimated crowds of 10,000 were recorded.[40] Large gatherings at popular events were a common phenomenon during the eighteenth century.

As the eighteenth century came to a close, however, the social, economic and cultural relations that had shaped cricket's rapid development began to change fundamentally. Perhaps most importantly, the social inclusivity and common recreational culture which played a pivotal role in the synthesis between aristocratic interests, commercialism and the popular rural game were eroded. Social relations began to change significantly in the aftermath of the French Revolution and as further popular unrest grew from the human consequences of economic restructure in both industry and agriculture. Consequently, the aristocracy largely withdrew from public life and social elite involvement in cricket became centred on exclusive clubs such as the MCC, while Lord's increasingly became the focal point for major matches. The popular rural game in south-east England suffered most from these changes. Aristocratic patronage of cricket decreased at a time when a considerable reduction in work and wages exacerbated the migratory trend from country to town, causing many communities to fall into decline. So in stark contrast to the way cricket had regularly brought members of the Georgian aristocracy into contact with the lower classes, by 1844 it was with some surprise that Baron Alderson recounted how he went out into the country and had the pleasure of seeing a match of cricket, in which a Noble Earl, the Lord Lieutenant of his county, was playing with tradesmen, the labourers, and all around him; and I believe he lost no respect from that course; they loved him better, but they did not respect him less. I believe that if they themselves associated more with the lower classes of society, the kingdom of England would be in a far safer, and society in a far sounder condition.[41]

A changing context

The changing economic context also offered new possibilities for cricket. Despite its remarkable progress throughout the eighteenth century, the game remained constrained by the limitations of pre-modern society. The synthesis between popular interest, commercial investment and aristocratic involvement which pushed cricket forward during the period was only possible in London and the south-eastern counties of England where economic and demographic growth were heavily concentrated. These conditions were changed significantly by the increasing spread of capitalist industrial society during the first half of the nineteenth century and circumstances which could support the game's development in other parts of England being created.

Cricket's emergence as a game of genuinely national dimensions, therefore, took place during a transitional period in British society. As the capitalist economic system spread, the gathering pace of urban industrialisation had a profound impact upon work and leisure. The informal patterns of pre-modern recreation were not compatible with the increasingly regulated structure of work for those lower down the social order while its profligate and excessive culture conflicted fundamentally with the new roles which were ascribed to both the working classes and the gentry. Consequently, leisure became a key issue and new social and cultural ideas were developed through a growing body of rhetoric which promoted values that underscored the new structure, such as Muscular Christianity, rational recreation and the concept of the Gentleman Amateur. According to Robert Malcolmson, the strengthening of opposition to the old recreational culture combined with the new demands of working life meant that 'the foundations of many traditional practices were relentlessly swept away, leaving a vacuum which would be only gradually reoccupied, and then of necessity by novel or radically revamped forms of diversion'.[42]

Cricket was a symbolic focal point for the new approach to sport and leisure as writers such as Pycroft and Thomas Hughes began to ascribe a new moral purity to the game which opposed the pursuit of self-interest and placed a new emphasis upon fair play, physical exercise and the team ethic. These new sporting values contrasted fundamentally with the popular traditions which had driven the game's remarkable development during the eighteenth century and became a central component in the influential culture of the rapidly expanding middle classes. Key elements of popular recreational culture, such as professionalism, gambling and the traditional role of cricket as a form of entertainment, came under attack in a way which reflected the social divisions that grew out of the new economic system.

However, the process of change was far less comprehensive than early social historians suggested and, as new attitudes towards leisure were spread, the kind of cultural contestation which Peter Bailey has highlighted took place. Bailey argues that 'leisure was one of the major frontiers of social change in the nineteenth century, and like most frontiers it was disputed territory'.[43] The compelling culture and structure of sport that characterised cricket's pre-modern growth continued to play a key role as the game spread beyond its traditional boundaries to the expanding urban industrial regions of the north and Midlands. Major new venues that mirrored the commercial model which had been developed by George Smith were established at Darnall in Sheffield during the 1820s and Trent Bridge, Nottingham, in 1843.

The economic structure of both these rapidly expanding towns was centred upon industries in which independent trades and small-scale production continued well into the second half of the nineteenth century. Consequently, a considerable proportion of the labour force was free to determine its own patterns of work and leisure and set time aside for watching and playing sport. Both consequently became important centres for producing professional players and also enjoyed a significant market for commercial cricket matches. So high-stake contests between teams of professional players were staged and in 1824 an estimated crowd of 20,000 people were present at Darnall on the Friday of a match between Sheffield and Leicester for 200 sovereigns. The increasing spread of large-scale production and factory discipline saw crowds decline during the next few decades, but sufficient demand for commercial cricket remained in these areas and in 1845 a match between eleven of All-England and fourteen of Nottingham for 200 sovereigns took place at William Clarke's recently opened Trent Bridge ground 'in front of thousands' of spectators.[44]

Commercial venues for cricket also continued to operate in south-eastern England. Daniel Day was the proprietor of various cricket grounds during the middle decades of the nineteenth century, including one in Southampton which he ran from the adjacent Antelope Inn during the 1840s. Ireland's Royal Pleasure Gardens in Brighton also had a cricket ground. It was run from the Hannover Arms Inn which was taken over by George Brown, the famous bowler in the 1830s, before Thomas Box, the Hampshire, Surrey, All-England and MCC wicketkeeper, became the proprietor in the 1840s. Although run on a commercial basis, these venues were aimed more at providing facilities for local teams and clubs to hire than staging the major matches for stake money in order to attract large crowds. But in July 1827 the Royal Ground in Brighton staged a match between All-England and Sussex in the last of a three-match series for a stake of 1,000 sovereigns. A crowd of between 3,000 and 6,000 spectators attended the event which was held to test experimental laws allowing round-arm bowling.

Despite claims to the contrary, gambling also continued to have a significant presence in cricket throughout the first half of the nineteenth century. Even at Lord's where following a series of match-fixing allegations the expulsion of bookmakers is widely quoted to have taken place in the 1820s, betting continued to be a feature of cricket matches during this period.[45] When 'seventeen gentlemen members of the Mary-la-bonne Club and eleven professors, [were] selected from all the great players in England' in 1827, the kind of socially mixed crowd that marked eighteenth-century major matches was in attendance and *Bell's Life* explained,

> The match was made principally by Mr Aislabie, who backed the eleven players. Very heavy sums were dependent upon the event, and we never witnessed a struggle of this, or any other kind, which gave greater satisfaction: persons from all parts of the Kingdom were attracted by it, and we observed upon the ground sporting characters of all ranks and descriptions, from the high flying *fishmonger* down to the well known *baker*.[46]

Indeed, as late as 1848, when the Gentlemen recorded a rare victory over the players before a crowd of around 5,000, *Bell's Life* told readers how 'large sums of money changed hands, and the result of the game drew forth large cheers from the takers of the odds'.[47]

Cricket's continued growth throughout Britain during the first half of the nineteenth century was greatly assisted by the expansion of local and national newspapers. Stamp duty and other forms of taxation, which had been raised to discourage sedition during the French Revolutionary Wars, were reduced in the 1830s before being abolished in the 1850s and the growing economic and civic status of many provincial centres resulted in a number of new publications being founded. At local level, newspapers provided a means of organising and publicising the game. Some clubs issued challenges to local rivals through the press and in 1836 a letter from 'One Of The Poole Eleven', which appeared in the *Hampshire Advertiser*, announced that,

> The Poole Club are willing and ready to play the Christchurch at any time or place as may be agreed on and for any stakes from one sovereign to twenty two.[48]

But more often, local newspapers featured reports which reflected the increasing importance of the growing number of local clubs that were formed as social institutions for the expanding middle classes during this period. Social activities continued to feature prominently in the activities of these organisations and in 1840 the *Leicester Chronicle* reported that a

Return Match between the Northampton and Harborough clubs was played on the Harborough Cricket Ground on Wednesday last. Mr Packwood, George Hotel, provided a very excellent dinner of which upwards of fifty gentlemen partook.[49]

Most of these organisations maintained a degree of social exclusivity by charging subscription fees that prevented working-class membership. For example, in the 1830s, the fee to join the Todmorden club was 2s 6d, which when combined with a further 1s per month subscription charge, made an annual cost of 14s 6d, more than the weekly wage of a local weaver.[50] But in July 1852 the *Essex Standard and General Advertiser for the Eastern Counties* reported on a match that involved a new form of organisation which, as we shall see, was to play an important role in the large-scale development of the game during the last third of the nineteenth century. The match in question was played between Colchester Mechanics Institution and West Bergholt and the home club was an early example of the way in which cricket came to be seen as a means to promote the growing movement to reform the recreational habits of those lower down the social scale.[51]

But perhaps the clearest indication of cricket's spreading popularity and the diverse range of meanings which were being represented through the game during this period can be found in the pages of *Bell's Life*. As Adrian Harvey identi-fied, during the first half of the nineteenth century *Bell's Life* played an increasingly important role in the emergence of a national structure for sport in Britain. The publication provided a range of services which included helping to arrange and promote matches as well as report on them, while for a time the editor also adjudicated on disputes between competitors.[52]

Cricket was at the forefront of these developments and as the first half of the nineteenth century drew to a close the diverse array of meanings which were present during this transitional period in the game's history was clearly visible in the contents of each single edition of *Bell's Life*. On 28 June 1846, for example, *Bell's Life* included details of over eighty matches which either had been played or were arranged to take place in the next few weeks. The teams involved repre-sented counties, provincial towns, rural villages, schools and universities from across the country. They included the MCC, Surrey, Norwich, Stowmarket in Suffolk, Horsham in Kent, Eton College, Wadham College, Oxford. But clubs from the new industrial conurbations in the north and the boroughs of inner London such as Manchester, Tower Hamlets, Sheffield, Putney and Islington were also well represented.[53]

The influence of cricket's pre-modern past clearly still resonated throughout the game during this period. On some occasions socially mixed teams could still be found and working-class professionals were employed to play alongside members of the social elite in a forthcoming match between Manchester and Sheffield at the Hyde Park ground in which each side was to field 'six gentlemen and five players'. Gambling also continued to retain a significant presence. A notice announced that 'Sam Baldwinson and Tom Hunt, both of Manchester, can be backed to play a single wicket match, home and home, for £25 or £50 against any two of the northern counties eleven that played at Lord's Ground this year'. The two players who issued this challenge were leading professionals, but single-wicket matches could also be found in much less likely settings. Details were published of a contest at Hurstbourne Tarrant in Hampshire 'between four crack hands of that place for £20 [sic] which excited the praise and admiration of a numerous assembly'. Perhaps more surprising, however, was the report of a challenge which had appeared in the *Brighton Gazette* for local professional George Picknall of Sussex to play the famous Kent amateur Alfred Mynn. It stated, 'We have no doubt that Mr Mynn can find plenty of backers; and it now remains for Sussex to wrest the laurels from Kent. Let the match be made for £100 a side, to be played in Box's ground.'[54]

Yet the majority of the matches which were featured in this edition of *Bell's Life* reflected the way in which new meanings were becoming increasingly influential in cricket. Most of the matches that were featured did not take place for stake money and a notice from the Blackheath Eagle club suggests further that the competitive traditions of the game were being eroded. It explained that the club 'would be glad to make a friendly match with any eleven from within ten miles of Blackheath'. An even more casual form of the game was being pioneered by the recently formed I Zingari club whose match at Newport Pagnell was the subject of a detailed report. This socially exclusive organisation had been formed among the alumni of leading public schools and universities and refused to employ professionals in its matches which took place against leading provincial clubs or at country houses. In a similar vein, a match at Lord's between the Gentlemen of Kent and the Gentlemen of All-England was also reported on at length.

Despite the way cricket was being increasingly influenced by the new social, economic and cultural relations, however, as we shall see, the next major phase in the game's development was a reflection of its commercial traditions. Towards the end of the 1846 season, William Clarke began touring the British Isles with a team which consisted mainly of leading professionals and is widely regarded as having been pivotal to cricket becoming a sport of truly national dimensions. As we have seen, Clarke's background in cricket lay in the commercial stake money matches which had dominated the sport over the previous century. He was a publican, professional cricketer, and entrepreneurial promoter in the style of George Smith and his All-England eleven mostly played exhibition odds matches against local teams, in which their opponents fielded between sixteen and twenty-two players.

Notes

1 See P.E. Razzell and R.W. Wainwright, *The Victorian Working Class: Selections from the 'Morning Chronicle'* (London, Frank Cass, 1973), p. 302.

2 T. Collins, J. Martin and W. Vamplew (eds), *Encyclopedia of Traditional British Rural Sports* (London, Routledge, 2005), p. 116.

3 See C. Brookes, *English Cricket: The Game and its Players through the Ages* (Exeter, Weidenfield and Nicholson, 1978), p. 34.

4 See Rev. R.S. Holmes, *The History of Yorkshire County Cricket 1833–1903* (London, Archibald Constable and Co, 1904), p. 11.

5 See A.W. Pullin ('Old Ebor'), *Talks with Old Yorkshire Cricketers*, Leeds, reprinted from the *Yorkshire Evening Post*, 1898, p.114.

6 See Holmes, *History of Yorkshire County Cricket*, pp. 10–11.

7 See *Leeds Times*, 5 Jun 1841.

8 See *Sheffield Independent*, 27 Oct 1827.

9 See 'Old Ebor', *Talks with Old Yorkshire Cricketers*, pp. 41–2.

10 See A.G. Steele and R.H. Lyttelton, *Cricket: With Contributions by A. Lang, W.G. Grace, R.A.H. Mitchell and F. Gale* (London, The Badminton Library of Sports and Pastimes, 1888), p. 1.

11 See Rev. J. Pycroft, *The Cricket Field or The History and the Science of the Game of Cricket* (Longman, Brown, Green and Longmans, Second Edition, 1854); H.S. Altham and E.W. Swanton, *A History of Cricket* (London, George Allen and Unwin, 1947); D. Birley, *A Social History of English Cricket* (London, Aurum Press, 1999); R. Bowen, *Cricket: A History of its Growth and Development Throughout the World* (London, Eyre and Spottiswoode, 1970); J. Major, *More than a Game: The Story of Cricket's Early Years* (London, HarperPress, 2007); and C. Box, *The English Game of Cricket* (London, The Field Office, 1877).

12 See D. Underdown, *Start of Play: Cricket and Culture in Eighteenth-Century England* (London, Penguin, 2000), p.3.

13 Pyecroft, *The Cricket Field*, quoted in Birley, *A Social History of English Cricket*, p. 94.

14 See Pyecroft, *The Cricket Field*, p.16.

15 See C. Box, *The English Game of Cricket*, p. iii.

16 Examples of such prosecutions can be found at Ruckinge in Kent in 1629 and Boxgrove in Sussex in 1622; see Underdown, *Start of Play*, pp. 11–12.

17 See *St James's Evening Post*, 7 Apr 1733.

18 See the *British Journal*, 11 Apr 1730.

19 See P. Clarke, *British Clubs and Societies 1580–1800: The Origins of an Associational World*, Oxford, OUP, 2000.

20 See *Weekly Journal or British Gazetteer*, 21 Jul 1722.

21 See Clarke, *British Clubs and Societies 1580–1800*, p. 446.

22 See Underdown, *Start of Play*, pp. 130–4.

23 See *Country Journal or The Craftsman*, 28 Aug 1731.

24 See Underdown, *Start of Play*, p. 24.

25 See ibid., p. 38.

26 See *Old Whig or The Constant Protestant*, 24 Jul 1735.

27 A. Mote, *Cricket's Glory Days The Extraordinary Story of Braodhappeny Down* (London, Robson Books, 1997), pp. 182, 188.

28 See *Gazetteer and Daily London Advertiser*, 4 Sep 1756.

29 See Mote, *Cricket's Glory Days*, p. 169.

30 See *Bell's Life in London*, 22 Jun 1828.

31 See Underdown, *Start of Play*, pp. 69–70 and Brookes, *English Cricket*, p. 61.

32 See Major, *More than a Game*, p. 58.

33 See Underdown, *Start of Play*, p. 94 and Brookes, *English Cricket*, p. 62.

34 See Pycroft, *The Cricket Field*, p. 138.

35 See K.A.P. Sandiford, *Cricket and the Victorians* (London, Ashgate, 1994), p. 26.

36 See A. Mote (ed.), John Nyren's The Cricketers of my Time (London, Robson Books, 1998), p. 71.

37 See Pycroft, The Cricket Field, p 55.

38 See E.V. Lucas, The Hambledon Men (London, Henry Frowde, 1907), pp. 140–1.

39 See Country Journal or the Craftsman, 23 Jun 1744 and the General Advertiser, 18 Jul 1746.

40 See Brookes, English Cricket, p. 49, Underdown, Start of Play, p. 84 and Westminster Journal or New Weekly Miscellany, 16 Jul 1743.

41 See Berrow's Worcester Journal, 22 Aug 1844.

42 See R. Malcolmson, Popular Recreations in English Society, 1700–1850 (Cambridge, Cambridge University Press 1973), p. 170.

43 See P. Bailey, Leisure and Class in Victorian England: Rational Recreation and the Contest for Control (London, Routledge and Kegan Paul, 1978), p. 5.

44 See The Era, 14 Sep 1845.

45 See Underdown, Start of Play, p. 165, J. Ford, Cricket – A Social History 1700–1835 (Newton Abbot, David and Charles, 1972), pp. 101–02, and P. Wynne-Thomas, The History of Cricket: from the Weald to the World (Norwich, The Stationery Office, 1997), p. 56.

46 See Bell's Life, 1 Jul 1827.

47 See Bell's Life, 6 Aug 1848.

48 See Hampshire Advertiser & Salisbury Guardian Royal Yacht Club Gazette, Southampton Town and County Herald, Isle of Wight Journal, Winchester Chronicle and General Reporter, 8 Oct 1836.

49 See The Leicester Chronicle, 15 Aug 1840.

50 See E., M. and B. Heywood, Cloth Caps and Cricket Crazy: Todmorden and Cricket 1835–1896 (Todmorden, Upper Calder Valley Publications, 2004), p. 2.

51 See The Essex Standard and General Advertiser for the Eastern Counties, 30 Jul 1852.

52 See A. Harvey, The Beginnings of a Commercial Sporting Culture in Britain, 1793–1850 (London, Ashgate, 2004), pp. 31–62.

53 See Bell's Life, 28 Jun 1846.

54 Box's ground was a commercial venue.

2 Origins of clubs

In his work on sport and leisure, Jeff Hill has identified 'voluntary association' as a 'classic British cultural form'. He cites a 1996 report which stated that there were between 200,000 and 240,000 voluntary bodies in Britain, involving around 21 million people, with 14 per cent of these organisations being linked to sport. He also quotes a House of Lords report from 1973 which stated that voluntary clubs were the 'lifeblood' of sports provision in Britain.[1] This is interesting evidence from the modern era and will give us some necessary perspective.

We have identified a number of key issues which contributed to the growing organisation of sport during the eighteenth and nineteenth centuries. Now we are going to look more closely at one of the most important aspects of this process: the growth of clubs.

The prevalence of gambling and the informal nature of sport during the eighteenth century had an important impact upon the way in which early organisational structures in sport emerged during this period. These characteristics had a strong influence upon the existence, and in many cases the absence of, organised clubs in cricket's formative years.

Another prominent theme has been the impact of changes in the social, cultural and economic landscape that took place during the nineteenth century. This had an equally profound effect upon the widespread growth of formalised cricket clubs. But before we look closely at these issues it will be useful to identify some of the key resources required to form and run a formalised sporting organisation such as a cricket club.

Perhaps the most basic of these was regular access to free time, which was needed in order for members to meet with a frequency that made this kind of formal organisation sustainable. As we have seen, the economic constraints that led to the sport's early informality were strongly linked to this issue. Available leisure time for the lower classes was largely intermittent and spread around the feasts and fairs of the agricultural and religious calendars. So before the middle years of the nineteenth century, regular free time was only available to the gentry.

The greater access to leisure time which was enjoyed by members of the gentry clearly stemmed from their financial independence. A certain degree of expendable income was clearly required to set up and maintain such organisations, as well as to participate in their social activities, which in many cases could be rather substantial. Therefore, equipment, such as bats and balls, would be needed along with a ground on which to play.

This brings us to the necessity of a suitable space on which to play cricket regularly and develop permanent facilities. As we shall see, finding available land was often a major problem for fledgling clubs. Land ownership was, and to some extent remains, centred among a small section of the population, with the gentry and the church particularly prominent. Consequently, many early informal matches were played on common land.

Education was also essential as, along with managing funds, the ability to arrange fixtures and other social activities was clearly fundamental to the efficient running of a club. Along with written rules, financial and administrative records are vital. These tasks clearly require a degree of education that has not always been available to all sections of society.

References to matches involving teams which claimed some form of communal identity can be found as early as the beginning of the eighteenth century. In 1705, the *Postman* gave notice of 'a match at cricket' that was to be played between 'eleven Gentlemen of a west part of the county of Kent, against as many of Chatham, for eleven guineas a man'.[2] As the language of the notice suggests, it is likely that these opponents were groups of players who had been assembled to play in this specific match, rather than any kind of organised cricket club.

As well as such matches involving the gentry, David Underdown has uncovered that regular cricket matches were also played between the rural communities of south-east England during this period. Between 1717 and 1727 the diary of Thomas Marchant, a farmer from Huntspierpoint in Sussex, refers to matches in which 'our parish' played against teams from other local villages such as Henfield, Cowfold, Steyning and Newick. But here again there is little evidence to suggest that any kind of formal cricket club existed.[3]

Underdown alludes to the loose arrangement of cricket teams during this period through details from the diary of Thomas Turner, who was an East Hoathly shopkeeper in the 1750s and 1760s. Matches were played on East Hoathly Common, which hosted a number of diverse teams rather than ones linked to any singular organisation. In 1756, Turner played for the 'Street' quarter of the Parish against the 'Nursery' quarter, 'each time paying his due as a 'gamester' … in this case a shilling a match'.[4] Turner also reveals that there were 'matches between farmers and tradesmen, between married men and bachelors, and one between an eleven of men named John and the rest of the Parish'.[5]

References which distinguish between early cricket teams and cricket clubs are scarce, but by the time Turner was enjoying playing cricket, formal clubs had begun to appear elsewhere in the south-east. Not surprisingly the earliest references to 'cricket clubs' are found among groups of the London gentry, and they seem to have first developed as an offshoot of gentlemen's clubs in the capital. In the 1730s and 40s, a 'London Club' featured strongly in matches at the Artillery Ground. This organisation drew up the 1744 laws of cricket, which were published eight years later under the auspices of the 'Cricket Club'. It had strong links to the Star and Garter, a gentlemen's club in Pall Mall, where in the 1750s the Jockey Club was formed. By 1774, a cricket club bearing the Star and Garter name was in existence and it revised and published the laws of cricket in that year.

The London gentry were a social group with the time, money and education to form cricket clubs. In the case of the Star and Garter CC, the motivation to form an organised body seems to have been provided by gambling. As we have seen, the club's willingness to draw up a set of arbitrary regulations was strongly linked to stake-match challenges.

Access to necessary land on which to play was also an important advantage for this social group. In 1787, the most famous of all cricket clubs, the MCC, was formed when members of the White Conduit club, another of London's gentlemen's clubs, provided Thomas Lord with the necessary funds to open a new cricket ground.

These early clubs also served a social function and matches between groups of members were often played. This was the motivation behind the formation of a club in York in 1784. The rules for this organisation stated that members should meet

> upon Heworth Moor every Tuesday and Friday morning at four 'o'clock until the fifth day of September next for the purpose of playing Cricket, to play for one penny a game and to fine three pence if not within sight of the wickets each morning before the Minster strikes five 'o'clock, every person hereafter to be admitted a member to pay one shilling.[6]

The relatively high financial demands upon members ensured a degree of social exclusivity, which naturally meant that they spent their leisure time with men of similar status.

Although few details have survived, it is almost certain that other similar clubs were formed in the region during the first half of the nineteenth century. Intriguingly, 1826 saw matches involving Huddersfield Old Club, which played and beat Manchester New Club, and Huddersfield New Club, which played and lost to Halifax New Club on Skircoat Moor.

Quite often these early clubs existed for only a few years before folding or being replaced by new organisations. A club in Sowerby Bridge was formed in the 1840s and in 1852 published a set of written rules which stated that 'any

Gentleman desiring to join this club, shall communicate his intention in writing'. This early club had folded before the current organisation was formed in 1877, but in 1853 the *Halifax Courier* reported that,

> The club at Sowerby Bridge ... now numbers about 50 members, is well patronised by the gentry and mill owners of the neighbourhood, and though comparatively in its infancy, is in a very flourishing position.[7]

The Heywoods' work on cricket in Todmorden has shown that a socially exclusive early club was formed in the town during the late 1830s. Research relating to the social background of the players who took part in the club's first recorded match, in 1838, shows that they were either employers of labour or self-employed. This conclusion is supported by a subscription charge of 2s 6d to join the club and a further 1s per month, which would have excluded working-class membership. In 1841 this club also folded and a more socially inclusive body was formed in 1850.

Modern cricket clubs

While this early type of cricket club was clearly in decline during the second quarter of the nineteenth century, a new form of more democratic and socially inclusive club was beginning to emerge. These organisations were run by democratically elected officials and committees, and did not discriminate against lower economic groups by charging high membership fees. Consequently, their emergence was strongly linked to a number of key social and economic developments.

The early examples of these clubs also reinforce the theme of interchange between old and new social and economic forces that we have identified elsewhere. In the West Riding of Yorkshire, the two most prominent early clubs were formed in the handloom weaving villages of Lascelles Hall and Dalton. The leisure opportunities which could be offered by one of the last processes in the textile industry to be mechanised and rationalised have already been discussed. Both clubs also owed their early success to gambling and stake-match challenges. These matches provided funding, attracted a following of supporters and gave the players the opportunity to cover any loss of earnings. They also provided the possibility of employment as professional cricketers elsewhere, and many players who made their names at these clubs found positions with other clubs.

However, regular leisure time still remained scarce for most working people in the first half of the nineteenth century. The clubs at Dalton and Lascelles Hall were clearly exceptional, both in the circumstances which enabled them to be formed and in the wonderful successes they enjoyed. While other new clubs began to appear during this period, unlike Dalton and Lascelles Hall, details about them are scarce.

For cricket in England the 1860s was the pivotal decade in which, according to Keith Sandiford, a 'great cricket explosion' took place.[8] The West Riding was one of the key areas for this rapid expansion of the game. In 1856, the *Leeds Intelligencer* gave the scores of forty-four matches during the whole of the summer. Four years later, the number of fixtures mentioned in the press had shown only a modest increase and the *Leeds Times* included thirty-two matches in June 1860, which featured fifty different teams. But by 1865 the same newspaper was giving the scores of ninety-eight matches that had taken place across the West Riding in that month alone.

This rapid expansion of cricket reflected a more general extension of leisure opportunities further down the social scale. It was made possible by a combination of social and economic developments. These decades had seen a steady improvement in travel and communications, while greater economic stability had made more money available for leisure.

However, specific circumstances in the 1860s suggest that the greater availability of leisure time was crucial to the rapid expansion of cricket as a participation sport. The combination of various factory acts and changes in working practices meant that most industries established the Saturday half-day holiday during the 1860s. This provided a regular weekly period of time away from work in which cricket could be played.

Even so, while the greater availability of leisure time enabled many people to now play in regular formal cricket matches, it did not necessarily lead to the formation of cricket clubs. Like their predecessors in the south-east of England during the eighteenth century, some of the new participants in cricket matches were little more than cricket teams that came together for occasional matches. They were assembled under a variety of different identities and, at best, appear in the press for a few years before disappearing. In 1866, the *Huddersfield Examiner* included matches which involved long-lost clubs such as:

Batley Canada
Batley Young Victoria
Birkby Lee Head
Chickenley Young England
Clough House 'Amateur Casuals'
Dewsbury Perseverence
Folly Hall Standard
Heartshead Royal Blue
Lockwood Rehoboth Church Choir
Mirfield Rifles Club
Mirfield Young Alma
Nine Gimcrack Club
Nine West End Boys
Queen Street Academy

Taylor Hall
Westown Mutual

Education, organisation and the space to play cricket also had to be found
before formalised clubs could be established. This meant that in virtually every
case, some form of outside agency was involved with the formation of new mid-
nineteenth-century cricket clubs. This support was given in two ways: either by
a formal relationship in which the club adopted the identity of a parent organisation, or an informal relationship in which an organisation gave support to a
club which represented the local community.

As outside help was needed to form the new cricket clubs, their growth in
number during the 1860s indicates that many sections of society were concerned
at how this newly available leisure time was to be spent, particularly by the
working classes. They can be categorised into six different groups. We will use
exemplars from Calderdale and Kirklees, in West Yorkshire, to illustrate the points
we make.

Paternalists

Many individuals and institutions have been involved in founding cricket clubs.
Some cricket clubs have benefited from the generosity of wealthy or kind-hearted
local figures. Sometimes the paternalism of local landowners has been crucial;
key individuals saw support for their local community as a duty which came with
their social status.

As in other areas of society, cricket was seen as a way of bringing
'respectability' to what had been notoriously dissolute institutions, as the
Victorians strove to educate a new breed of gentlemen fit to rule Britain's empire.
The subsequent strength of cricket in these schools led to 'alumni' or 'old boys'
clubs being formed, where institutional bonds of the school were continued; and
at the same time, social and business relationships could be forged.

These people provided the main type of informal sponsorship of new cricket
clubs, linked to the traditional paternalistic responsibilities of the gentry during
the pre-modern period. Consequently, landowners donated land to play on or
rented it out for a nominal fee, gave regular financial support to clubs and
occasionally accepted nominal positions such as president or patron.

The early formation of Lascelles Hall CC in Huddersfield resulted from this
type of paternalistic gesture. The club came into being after two local boys were
sent to the local hall having been caught playing cricket on its private land. Mrs
Walker, wife of the owner, a wool merchant from Cowersley, Huddersfield, is
reputed to have said; 'These young man seem very fond of cricket. Let them have
a playground.'

Elsewhere in Huddersfield, after previously causing the demise of the old
Slaithwaite club by taking back the ground for building purposes, Lord
Dartmouth became benefactor of the re-formed cricket club. In 1877, he gave a

subscription of £25 to the club and four years later provided land for a new ground. Furthermore, the Lepton Highlanders cricket ground lies on part of the Whitley Beaumont estate and during the 1870s Mr H. Beaumont Esq. gave a regular subscription of £1 and was one of the club's official patrons. Other interesting case studies include the following:

Todmorden CC

At a special meeting of Todmorden CC in 1841 it was passed, 'That this club be broken up'.[9] Although the demise of the early club is difficult to explain, events over the next decade were to secure the future of cricket in the town.

They revolved around the Fielden family who purchased the Eccles Holme Estate, which included Centre Vale, in 1843. The purchase was made by John Fielden who, after piloting the ten-hour bill through parliament in 1847, died in 1849.

The Fielden Estate then fell into the hands of his cricket-mad son, Samuel, who immediately set about reforming Todmorden CC. Sam Fielden's enthusiasm for cricket was quickly evident and by 1851 the new club had engaged its first professional. He was Joseph Crossland from Dalton CC, near Huddersfield.

Crossland made his name in the Dalton side which played in a number of major stake-money matches during the 1840s and 1850s. Crossland both coached and played for Todmorden and in 1851 moved to live in the town.

Triangle CC

Triangle CC was founded in 1862. It was originally attached to Triangle Reading Club, which was based at the Old White Bear Public House. 'Triangle Reading Room and Cricket Club' was the full, formal title of the organisation. Initially, the club had forty members. They played their first match on 20 October 1862 against Sowerby. Triangle scored 74 and Sowerby replied with 65.

Employers

Employers also gave informal assistance to help form cricket clubs. During the middle years of the nineteenth century, many began to recognise that the health and morale of their workforce had a strong link to its rate of productivity. Philanthropic employers began to provide better living and working conditions and some also saw the value of rational recreation. Taking an interest in the leisure activities of the workforce could also guard against traditional mores of popular pre-modern recreation, like drinking, gambling and absenteeism for unofficial holidays such as St Monday.

Support was often given to a club bearing the name of the local community. Cricket in the Armitage Bridge area of Huddersfield had been linked to various branches of the Brookes family since its early years in the 1830s. But in 1876, when the family provided the club with its current ground, a close relationship was formed with Messrs John Brooke and Sons who owned the family's mill in the village. At Booth CC, near Halifax, this type of philanthropy helped resurrect the club after its original ground had been ploughed for food production during the Second World War. In 1946, Mr Ronald Murgatroyd, a local mill owner, provided a new ground at Broadfold. He also became president of the club in the same year and occupied the position until his death in 1974.

A competitive element was also involved and if the club was successful this reflected well on the business. In some cases, money was provided to develop facilities or to pay players. This was sometimes done by forming a club which retained the identity of the company involved, like Hunsworth Mills CC, the forerunner of Cleckheaton CC (near Dewsbury), which was formed in 1864 and remained as a works club until 1885.

Mill owners and other employers were often part of the non-secular movement for social reform through sport and recreation. Along with the drinking and gambling that were associated with many traditional forms of recreation, absenteeism for events which were held on spontaneous holidays, like St Monday, was clearly damaging to production. Similarly, recreational activities improved the general health and morale of employees, which was also beneficial, and employers sponsored cricket clubs in both a formal and informal way.

In some cases teams were started through the business, and bore its name, although prominent businessmen were also known to provide a ground at a peppercorn rent or sell land cheaply to the local club or provide it with general financial backing. But the competitive imperatives of traditional sport could also be at the forefront of an employer's involvement in cricket. As in business, the drive for status and success motivated investment. This meant that in some cases money was provided to develop facilities and to pay players, or jobs were offered to prominent players who were then required to play for the local team. Good examples include the following:

Bridgeholme CC

The club originated directly from local industry. The cricket teams from J.J. Tatham Ltd, Nanholme Mills, and Moss Brothers, Bridgeroyd Mills joined forces to form one club in 1950. The name 'Bridgeholme' was invented by combining 'Nanholme' and 'Bridgeroyd'. These two mills still exist today, although Nanholme is now re-named Springholme and is owned by Pickwell-Arnold. Prime movers in the amalgamation were Mr R. Tatham of Nanholme Mills and Mr Percy Sowden of Moss Brothers, who was also Chairman of the West Riding Education Committee.

Initially, players had to be employees of the two companies, but qualification was extended during Bridgeholme's period in the Hebden Bridge & District League between 1952 and 1955. This league was founded as a subsidiary of the Calder Valley Cricket League in 1893 amid the rush to create leagues in cricket, football and rugby across the industrial north and Midlands. These two local leagues continued to thrive through the first half of the twentieth century but by the early 1950s their future was bleak. The advent of alternative entertainments, facilitated by the development of the television and motor car (among others), caused a decline in the amount of cricket played across England.

The survival of a new club was remarkable when Todmorden was home to so many teams. The club had no ground during its first season in 1951 – its only year in the Todmorden & District League – and played all matches away. In 1952, Hill House, the Cross Stone ground, was rented for the club's first season in the Hebden Bridge League and by early 1953 the Eastwood ground, next door to one used from the 1890s to 1930s by Eastwood CC, was ready. Bridgeholme moved still further a field in 1956, joining the Halifax League. Since then the club has played continuously in either the Halifax League or the Halifax Association.

Sowerby Bridge United CC

In Sowerby Bridge, a group which was 'composed in the main of manufacturers' sons and of the gentry in the neighbourhood … played the game on land in the vicinity of the present Willow Park'.[10] This team was known as Sowerby Bridge United, but was also given the nickname the 'shirtneck lot' because of their social status.

Religious groups

Religious groups of all denominations were involved in forming cricket clubs during the second half of the nineteenth century. In the West Riding of Yorkshire, Mytholmroyd Methodist CC was formed in 1894, while Almondbury Zion CC was active until just before the Great War, and when hostilities ceased it became Almondbury Wesleyans CC. At Rastrick, the New Road Sunday School CC was formed in the 1880s.

As the nineteenth century progressed, it became common for religious bodies of most denominations to provide recreational opportunities for their congregations. This is often seen as showing a resolve to improve the health of the body, as well as of the mind, by promoting 'rational recreation'. It was part of a general movement to reform traditional working-class leisure habits, which were increasingly seen as incompatible with the values of modern society. Promoting these activities was also an effective means of encouraging church attendance.

As well as providing the crucial commodity of land on which to play, religious organisations were able to assist in the organisation and running of clubs. Church officials often took a keen interest in clubs and assumed roles such as club president. This was the case at Illingworth St Mary's CC, in Halifax, where the second inaugural rule of 1884 stated that, 'The Club be conducted by a President (the Vicar of Illingworth)'.[11]

This type of church sponsorship of cricket was also an effective way of encouraging church or chapel attendance, and new clubs were often only available to members of the congregation. The third inaugural rule at Illingworth St. Mary's decreed that 'no person be admitted as a member of the Club unless he be a teacher or scholar in St.Mary's Sunday School or a member of the Congregation of that Church'.[12] Key case studies include the following:

Almondbury Wesleyans CC

This club, successor to Almondbury Zion CC, was founded in November 1920, and 1921 was their first full season. Cricketers from opposing teams are always interested in the club's Methodist links. Keith Crawshaw, club secretary, explains: 'In the early days there was a strong connection between the club and the local Wesleyan church. Most of the cricket team were regular attenders – in fact, they were actually obliged to go to church a certain number of times each month. Today, the situation is different, with only a few club members still having links with the church. But that said, we're very proud of the connection and we're pleased that the minister at the church still holds the position of club president.'[13]

Crossbank Methodists CC

Cross Bank Wesleyan Chapel was opened in March 1871, 'a neat and handsome' building according to the local Batley newspaper. Two years previously, the Sunday School building had been opened. Around 600 young people attended the Sunday School. The chapel building was paid for by the Brearley family (£4,000), and dedicated to the memory of Robert Brearley, the founder of the local worsted manufacturers. The first minister at the church was a Rev. Frederick Friend.

The church had been built during a boom time for Methodism in the districts of Cross Bank and Carlinghow. Before it closed down, Cross Bank Methodist Church was home to a mixed Bible class, a Ladies Fellowship, Scouts and Cubs, and a Youth Group. Little is known about the origins of Crossbank Methodist CC but 1904 is a possible date of formation. The club is proud of its heritage. The Methodist link may have disappeared – a product of various factors, including the amalgamation of local chapels – but in the words of one senior figure at The Rumbolds, the club 'will never change its name'.

Golcar CC

Golcar CC was founded as St John's Golcar CC in 1871, the name reflecting links with the nearby church. The founders of the club were T.P. Taylor, D.T. Bailey, D. Gledhill, Humphrey Dyson, James Bolton and Arthur Shaw, who went on to become one of the most influential figures in cricket across Huddersfield. Meetings were held in a conservatory in St James's Street and then in the Church School. In that first season, 1871, the team played at Scar Bottom in Scar Wood, near to the railway line.

In 1872, the club moved to Low Westwood Bottom where they rented a field for £1 15s per annum, an amount viewed as so extortionate that one of the local clergy, said to be the curate of the parish, had to become 'surety' for the rent. St John's Golcar held its first major fundraising activities in 1876, two concerts which raised £13 5s 6d in total. By the end of 1876, the club had twenty-one members and £13 (about £400 at today's values) in the bank. Confident about the future, it moved to improved surroundings at Town End (Swallow Lane) in 1877, and has played there ever since.

The club's first recorded match was against the curiously-named Milnsbridge Cold Water Army on 28 June 1873. Through the 1870s, a succession of very local teams appeared in the fixtures, including Longwood Castle (1874), Cliffe End (1875), Parkwood (1875), Golcar Liberal (1876), Golcar Church Institute (1876) and Leymoor (1878). By 1891, Golcar CC – the club dropped 'St John's' from its name in 1882 – was ready to take its place as founder members of the Huddersfield & District Cricket League.

Illingworth St Mary's CC

The club's centenary brochure refers to newspaper evidence of a team called Illingworth St Mary's playing friendly matches in 1879. The inaugural meeting was held on 22 February 22 1884 at the Illingworth Church Institute. A set of rules was drawn up, the first of which decreed 'this club be called the St Mary's Cricket Club'. The club's link to the parish was also demonstrated in the next rules.

> Rule 1: The Club be called the St Mary's Cricket Club.
>
> . . .
>
> Rule 3: That no person be admitted as a member of the Club unless he be a 'teacher or scholar in St Mary's Sunday School or a member of the Congregation of that Church'.[14]

King Cross CC

Like many clubs that began life during the second half of the nineteenth century, King Cross are strongly linked to a religious organisation. In 1878, the Young Men's Class at King Cross Wesleyan School started a cricket team which played its early matches on Savile Park Moor. According to the *Yorkshire Evening Post* in the 1930s, this club was known as King Cross Wesleyan CC. But when a new ground was rented at West View, the club was re-formed as King Cross CC.

Luddendenfoot CC

General opinion dates the formation of Luddendenfoot St Mary's CC – predecessor club of the current Luddendenfoot CC – to the 1880s. There was an obvious link with the local church, perhaps with a group of local choirboys. However, local cricket historian Andrew Hardcastle has discovered that cricket was being played in the village as early as the 1860s.

Mirfield Parish Cavaliers CC

The origins of Mirfield Parish CC are hazy, but 1880 is generally viewed as their date of formation. In 1912, they won the Dewsbury & District Junior League Shield outright and in 1919 took part in the Heavy Woollen Cup for the first time. In the early and middle decades of the twentieth century, Parish won their fair share of Dewsbury League titles at both junior and senior level.

A set of rules issued by the old Mirfield Parish CC included Rule 2: 'That the Vicar of Mirfield (if willing) be President of the Club, and the Assistant-Clergy Vice-Presidents'.[15] This confirms the club-church link, but also gives the vicar an 'opt-out' if he so desires.

Northowram Fields CC

Northowram Fields CC were formed originally as Northowram St Matthew's CC in 1907 and linked to the local parish church. St Matthew's is a Gothic church designed by J.F. Walsh, and built in September 1910. A year later, S.L. Watkinson gave £3,000 for the tower, the bells, and a clock, and the church was consecrated in 1912.

Northowram St Matthew's originally played in the Halifax & District Church (Sunday School) League. However, by 1914 they were playing in the Halifax District League.

Slaithwaite CC

Cricket was played in Slaithwaite before the present club was formed in 1873. The young men of Hill Top managed to beg or borrow the equipment from this original club and form the Slaithwaite St James CC. Although no mention is made of a link with St James's, the local Anglican Church, the club's original name leaves little doubt that one existed.

By 1877 this club was known by its current name, Slaithwaite CC. The *Huddersfield Examiner* series, 'King Willow's Haunts', published in 1932, lists the leading players from this period, who were 'Thomas and Lewis Bamforth, James Sykes, Wright Gledhill, John H. Wood, John Hopkinson, J.T. Quarmby, J.H. Dransfield, Hiram Wood, Thomas Hirst and G. Maxwell'.

In the early days, Slaithwaite often had to play 'fifteen to eighteen men ... against the first elevens of other clubs'. This type of odds match was common for much of the nineteenth century.

Southowram CC

The example of Southowram helps us to understand the role played by churches in the expansion of cricket in late Victorian England. All the village's teams had a church link. There were teams from the Methodist chapels and both Anglican churches, St Michael's at Bank Top (now demolished), and Southowram Parish, St Anne-in-the-Grove, formed their own teams. Of the various precursors to today's Southowram CC, the St Anne's Church team had the longest and most chequered history. It probably began in the 1880s and in its early years the team was sometimes referred to as 'St Anne's Church Choir' or 'Southowram Choir'.

Sowerby Bridge Church Institute (SBCI) CC

One of the earliest mentions of Sowerby Bridge Church Institute came in 1878, fifteen years before the club believes it was founded (1893 – hence the Centenary celebrations of 1993). Sowerby Bridge Church Institute CC was founded as Christ Church CC. Most players attended Christ Church and, catering for numerous leisure activities, the Institute was the church's social and sporting arm.

Sowerby St Peter's CC

The Sowerby St Peter's fixture card from 1904 shows the club's president was the Vicar of St Peter's Church, the Reverend John Walker MA. The church played a central role in the community and the village cricket team made membership of the congregation an added attraction. The tie still exists today and although the church doesn't play an active role in running the club, the present curate often visits on matchdays.

Spen Victoria CC

Although 1862 is often cited as a 'birth date', the club was formally established in 1865, by six men: George Wright, George Hardwick, Sam Haley, Alfred Starkey, James Strafford and Robert Corry. Valuable assistance was received from James Woodcock of Marsh Rolling Mills. These founding fathers were associated with Cleckheaton Wesleyan Sunday School. All members of that first inaugural team had to attend chapel regularly to play and this meant they often struggled to find a full side.

One of the club's earliest fixtures was against Hunsworth Mills, now known as Cleckheaton. In 1865, the club moved from Whitcliffe Road – its first home – to Spen Lane, where it has resided ever since. It also became known as Cleckheaton – later, Spen – Victoria (rather than Cleckheaton Wesleyans).

Stones CC

Stones CC was formed through the local Wesleyan chapel. Their first ground was situated in a field opposite the church. Some time in the 1930s the club changed names from Stones Wesleyans to Stones Methodists. Given the club is now known simply as 'Stones', this means it has had three different incarnations.

Public houses

Despite pressure for reform, the pub remained a focal point for working-class communities. This relationship traditionally included various forms of popular recreation being staged by the landlord. These activities were an important means of attracting customers.

The link between cricket and public houses had long been established, and many of the early local grounds had been set up and run by local publicans. As the nineteenth century progressed and sport became more organised, many landlords saw the commercial advantage of sponsoring a club which could bear their pub's name. In July 1834, for example, the *York Courant* reported on a match between the Leeds Union and Geldard Arms public houses.[16]

Because of the growing stigma attached to public houses, less formal relationships with cricket clubs were perhaps more common. Huddersfield club Lepton Highlanders first rented their ground from the White Horse pub. The growth of new social values also meant that informal support for a cricket club could result in contrasting interests.

Another Huddersfield club, Broad Oak, benefited from early links with a Mrs Sykes, who first rented the current ground to the club. She was a committed member of the congregation at the local Christ Church and was largely persuaded to make the offer by James Dyson and J.E. Kaye, who were both wardens at the church. However, equally concerned with the welfare of the fledgling club was Joseph Sykes, the landlord of Th'Alma public house nearby. He had previously arranged a match between married and single men and when the annual rent for the new ground was fixed at £10 he agreed to donate £5 a year.[17]

Where the involvement of factory and church in cricket clubs represented the movement for leisure reform in the nineteenth century, the public house was strongly linked to the mores of traditional leisure culture. In fact, the pub remained the focal point for most working-class communities, despite the pressure for reform. Publicans were traditionally involved in cricket and owned many early grounds, which they ran on a commercial basis.

As leisure became rationalised during the second half of the nineteenth century and permanent clubs were formed, publicans saw the social and commercial advantage of sponsoring the new organisations. Relevant case studies include the following:

Blackley CC

In the early days, Blackley's home ground was situated at the top of South Lane and was called Blackley Field. However, by the turn of the century, this venue had been sold, with developers eager to start building houses nearby. So, the club moved to what is now their current site. (In the late nineteenth century, this ground was owned by the Ainleys, a family connected with the Wappy Spring brewery). The Golden Fleece pub sits on the boundary edge today – and at one point was the club's official HQ.

Bradshaw Tavern

In 1861, a team called Bradshaw Golden Fleece played Queenshead United. Bradshaw CC was formed in 1923 during a meeting at the Bradshaw Tavern, the pub that still overlooks the ground. The image of a white castle now dominates the Bradshaw crest – due recognition of the fact that White Castle Breweries owned the Bradshaw Lane ground in yesteryear.

Greetland CC

By 1864, a team called Greetland Royal Albert was playing matches, and in that year they met West Vale United. In 1869, another local derby saw Greetland Victoria meet Greetland New Delight. These matches were often casual affairs, played by occasional teams rather than formal, early 'clubs' with links to the present Greetland CC. However, Greetland New Delight had been in existence for some time, having met Sowerby Bridge Victoria seven years earlier in 1862.

Halifax Association

Many teams in the now defunct Halifax Association were connected with local pubs. In fact, West End CC, Stirk Bridge CC, and others, actually originated in pubs, and it was natural for these clubs to take on the name of their home hostelries. Not surprisingly, Calderdale's *Pub Paper* featured regular updates of Association news.

Leymoor CC

Leymoor's ground on Parkwood Road, Huddersfield, is celebrated for one thing: the proximity of the Walkers Arms, the local pub. Club secretary Graham Parr explains the situation: 'Our ground is linked to the pub because the brewery – Punch Taverns, and before that Bass North – own the cricket field. We have a great relationship with the current landlords, who help us tremendously. Recent summers have been so good, weather-wise, that on some Sundays the playing area is virtually ringed by sunbathers – folk who had popped into the pub and who had ended up at the cricket. The pub also has an Evening League side, which plays its home games at Parkwood Road on Monday nights.'[18]

Shepley CC

Shepley CC was formed at a meeting in the Black Bull Inn on 21 July 1871. This makes it the oldest sporting organisation in the village. We are told that Mr Kaye Armitage – a local mill owner – 'played a prominent and active part in the club's formation'.

It was eventually resolved that: 'We have a Cricket Club to be called "The

Shepley Cricket Club" and that we have the Laithe Croft of Mr Senior's subject to conditions named and the rent to be £5, a year paid in advance.'[19] Shepley employed their first professional player in 1874. A cricketer by the name of R. Crooks received 35s per week for his services.

There are many other cricket-pub links too. For example, local brewery Websters used to have their own side. In addition, there are clubs situated close to pubs (eg. Rastrick, Round Hill) and clubs with 'official' watering holes (Norwood Green, Pear Tree Inn, and Sowerby St Peter's, Rushcart Inn).

Schools

In the 1840s and 1850s the public school system was reformed. New subjects were introduced along with a milder disciplinary code after violence and bullying had become commonplace. Sport became an integral feature of the new curriculum, with cricket at the forefront. It was seen as a 'respectable' pastime, suitable for educating the new breed of gentlemen needed to run Britain's expanding empire. As the game's popularity grew, 'old boys' teams were formed. These allowed members to retain a connection with their school and to forge social and business relationships.

The old boys cricket clubs first became popular at public schools in the south of England and clubs like Harrow Wanderers and Eton Ramblers were formed during the second half of the nineteenth century. Interesting case studies include the following:

Old Almondburians CC

Schools cricket has been played at Arkenley Lane, Almondbury, Huddersfield since 1884. King James's School, Almondbury, dates from 1608. It was established as a special 'royal school' after one Thomas Beaumont rode to London to petition King James I on behalf of the 'gentlemen of Almondbury'. Beaumont succeeded in his mission and the school has traded on its royal connections ever since. In 1958, a pavilion building was built at Arkenley Lane to commemorate the 350th anniversary of the founding of the school.

Old Almondburians CC was founded in 1976. Today, they play in the Huddersfield Central League. As their website says: 'The Old Almondburians' Society is a fellowship of past pupils and staff of King James's School in Almondbury, Huddersfield. Membership is currently around 700 and the Society's affairs are administered by an Executive Committee which meets monthly.' The Society has two stated objectives: (1) To uphold the honour and status of the school. (2) To provide a means of contact between members, one with another and the school. Membership ranges from those who joined the school in 1920 to present-day school-leavers.

Old Crossleyans CC

Old Crossleyans is a relatively young cricket club, formed in 1976. It has a historic link with what is now the Crossley Heath School, located close by. The Crossley Heath School is the product of a 1985 merger between Crossley & Porter School and Heath Grammar School. In January 2005, it was named as the best state-funded school in Yorkshire.

Crossley & Porter School was originally the Crossley Orphanage and became a secondary school in 1919. Heath Grammar School had been founded by Dr John Favour in 1600. Boarders at the school previously resided at Standeven House, Broomfield Avenue. What is now the function room and bar used to be the schoolboys' library.

Even though the boarders have long since gone, the school still uses the arena for sports fixtures. Old Crossleyans CC also play their home fixtures at Broomfield Avenue.

Social reform groups

The non-secular movement for social reform was carried out by a number of organisations. Among others, these included working men's clubs, mechanics institutes and YMCAs. Many of these organisations saw cricket clubs as a means through which their ideas could be spread. Consequently, in the West Riding of Yorkshire, clubs like the forerunner of Bradley Mills CC, Bradley Mills School Working Men's Club (also known as the 'Pop and Pasty Club'), was formed in 1875. The current Brighouse CC came about following a merger between the old Brighouse Alexandra Club and the Town's Working Men's Institute in 1873.

Here again, providing organised sport in this way was seen as a means of maintaining membership. The 1863 Yorkshire Mechanics' Union reported upon a number of clubs where,

> The cricket field is governed by the committee, and great decorum and a fair reason-able amount of restraint exercised. It certainly seems unwise that the members of the village institutions should discontinue their acquaintance during the summer, or only maintain it by meetings at street corners. A certain large amount of labour is necessary to reenlist the members when the winter sets in and the institution reopened to full activity, and a considerable amount of effort is lost which would be very valuable and more profitably expended on the working of the society.[20]

Many successful cricket clubs were subsequently formed through mechanics' institutes. Two relevant examples are as follows:

Marsden Mechanics' Institute CC

This club was formed in 1865, the organisation proving crucial after the club lost the use of its ground in the 1870s. In 1879, the *Huddersfield Daily Examiner* reported on a match against Lascelles Hall to mark the opening of a new ground. It stated that, 'The committee of the M.M.I.C.C. have been very active of late superintending the formation of a new ground for the club'.[21]

Triangle CC

Triangle CC, near Halifax, came into being as the Triangle Reading Room CC in 1862. This club also decreed that 'none can be members who are not also members of the Triangle Reading Room'.[22]

Independence and community pride

It is clear from the examples quoted that while most cricket clubs were formed through a formal link with some type of existing agency, many subsequently became separate independent organisations. In many cases, motivation for this move came from a strong sense of community pride which saw clubs take on the identity of their village or town. It also reflected a longstanding desire to compete with clubs representing neighbouring communities.

As we have already identified, a strong sense of competition was maintained in many areas throughout the nineteenth century. The consequences of this competitive culture is best demonstrated by the cricket clubs which were formed through religious organisations. As these clubs became established, many found that the rules limiting membership to congregation members only were restricting their ability to compete with local rivals. This was the case when Huddersfield-based Honley St Mary's CC became Honley CC in 1879. The press report of the meeting at which the decision was taken explained that,

> On reviewing the old rules it was found that, to improve the efficiency of the club, some changes were necessary among which the most important were that the title should be altered to that of 'The Honley Cricket Club' and that the club should be open to anyone subject to the approval of the committee.' This, it was hoped, 'will give the Club a better chance of competing with its neighbours and 'Honley in this respect may not be behind the neighbouring villages.[23]

Illingworth St Mary's CC in Halifax relaxed their rules on membership at their AGM of 1887. Non-congregational members were allowed to join, but they could 'not at any time exceed in number one fourth of the whole club including themselves.'

Then, following the end of the Great War, the club decided:

> That the time is now opportune for reconstruction of Cricket and we as a Club of the district make application to play in the Yorkshire Cricket Council. The reasons are as follows:
>
> 1 To provide Cricket in the District of the highest class possible.
> 2 That the District is not represented by such Cricket.
> 3 Being very central to the villages of Ovenden, Bradshaw, Mixenden and Holmfield.

4 That the Illingworth Club being one of the oldest in the Borough of Halifax (if not the oldest) look upon it as their duty to take this action.

An application for admittance to the 'Yorkshire Cricket Council' has been accepted on condition that we alter our ground and dressing accommodation which will entail an outlay of upwards of £200.[24]

In true Victorian style, the dynamics of competition and community pride led to a strong desire among clubs to improve themselves away from the field of play. Securing a suitable permanent ground was usually the crucial step and this often provided the basis from which facilities like new pavilions and scoreboards were built. In the late nineteenth century, the re-formed Slaithwaite CC, in Huddersfield, first used what it could of the equipment that had been passed on from the previous organisation. This included 'an old army bell tent' which was used as a 'dressing tent'. The club played at Old White Royd and Meal Hill Lane before its current Hill Top ground was secured in 1881. While at Meal Hill, the club began to improve its facilities as 'the old tent was considered unsuitable and a wood tent erected'. To buy the necessary wood for the new building, 'six of the members contribute £1 each as a loan to the club'. Following the move to Hill Top, an extension to the ground was secured in 1886 and after fundraising bazaars in 1884 and 1887 had raised over £120, work on a new pavilion and clubhouse began in 1901.[25]

Clubs in the larger towns were able to draw upon greater resources and in many cases set their sights higher. As well as providing the highest possible standard of cricket for their members, they also strove to stage the type of major cricket events that had been common in the region since the 1820s. As the number of touring professional elevens increased, they played in many towns across the West Riding of Yorkshire such as Batley, Mirfield, Huddersfield and Halifax.

These early events were not commonly staged by an individual local club, but Todmorden began hosting regular major matches in the 1860s. In 1864, the United England XI visited Centre Vale, and in 1868 the All-England XI played against a local twenty-two-man side. Six years later, in 1874, one of the annual fixtures between the United North of England and the United South, who included W.G. Grace, was staged by the club. (Vamplew argues that the one-sided nature of most of these games led to the County Championship – where games were more competitive – having an increased appeal among spectators.[26])

Later that decade, Elland CC also began staging major matches and in 1878 the Australian touring side came to Hullen Edge. Regular games were held by the club in the next decade against the Parsees in 1886 and Casey's Clown Cricketers in 1880. Clown cricketers were evidently a popular draw during the 1870s and 1880s and such teams also visited Todmorden, Hanging Heaton and Hebden Bridge in the 1870s. The *Halifax Courier* gave a brief description of events at Elland:

One of the players, Dugwar, is a juggler and equilibrist: the rest of the Clowns do not play cricket but greatly amuse the spectators between the innings and as the game proceeds with jokes, acrobatic feats and whimsicalities.[27]

These developments were taken furthest by clubs in the major towns of the West Riding. One principal club emerged in places such as Leeds, Bradford, Sheffield, Huddersfield, Halifax and Dewsbury, and grew rapidly to become a kind of civic institution in its own right. Competition among these clubs grew to reflect similar economic and civic rivalries which saw the construction of increasingly grand public buildings, such as town halls and libraries. Sports clubs became a similar source of civic pride and as well as competing on the field of play the leading cricket clubs strove to develop bigger and better facilities. The main goal of all these clubs was, once again, to stage major matches, but now these were the home fixtures of Yorkshire CCC in the expanding county circuit of the 1870s and 1880s.

Many of the major cricket clubs began as relatively modest organisations before developing rapidly. The principal club in Huddersfield was founded in 1866 as Huddersfield St John's, the initiative of Rev. W.E. Owen of St John's Church. After leasing the Fartown ground in 1868, the next decade saw a series of major developments. In 1872 the first ground had been enclosed and a second ground leased. The club also played fixtures against Yorkshire in 1873, Parr's All-England XI in 1874, and staged a north versus south match, featuring E.M. and W.G. Grace, in 1875.

Like most other similar clubs, Huddersfield St John's then increased its membership and profile by merging with other sporting organisations to become Huddersfield Cricket, Football and Athletic Club in 1876. This type of multi-sports organisation became a common development – in the West Riding it occurred in Batley in 1880 and Dewsbury in 1887.

The growth in sports and members required a similar increase in facilities. At Fartown, Huddersfield, these initially included a new football pitch and bowling green at a cost of £1,440. But the major period of development came after the club became a joint stock company in 1879. A new pavilion was erected in 1884 at a cost of £1,250, and in 1886 spectator accommodation was increased through the erection of a permanent grandstand which cost £1,200. Five years later, in 1891, a further £8,600 was spent on new facilities and when they were opened, with an American athletics event, a crowd of 14,500 was able to assemble in the ground. Elsewhere, Halifax Cricket and Football Club was established in 1888 after spending £5,000 on a new pavilion at Thrum Hall.

It is clear that the rapid growth in cricket clubs during the second half of the nineteenth century was made possible by the rise of new social and economic forces. The key resources of time, space, money and organisation only became available through continued economic growth and the development of new social ideas. However, the cultural identity of these new West Riding clubs still retained important characteristics of pre-modern cricket.

Vamplew identifies a major expansion in cricket in the 1860s and associates this with the middle classes and the cult of athleticism. He argues that the consequence of this was the establishment of clubs throughout the north and Midlands.[28] At the same time, as the nineteenth century progressed, he argues, there was progressively less aristocratic patronage of the game.[29]

The rapid growth of cricket in the 1860s indicates that it was already a well-known popular sport. During the previous two decades, the professional touring elevens had been playing an increasing number of matches in the region, which regularly attracted large crowds. Staging this form of major spectator event quickly became an important goal for many leading clubs and remained as such until the Great War. More importantly, the desire to develop facilities and host the leading teams was driven by the continuing importance of competition. To many clubs the impulse of community pride and the desire to compete with rival local clubs surpassed the social and economic interests that had assisted their formation.

Notes

1 J. Hill, *Sport, Leisure and Culture in Twentieth-Century Britain* (Basingstoke, Palgrave, 2002), p. 130.

2 See C. Brookes, *English Cricket: The Game and its Players through the Ages* (Newton Abbot, Readers Union, 1978), p. 25.

3 See D. Underdown, *Start of Play: Cricket and Culture in Eighteenth-Century England* (London, Penguin, 2000), pp. 36–7.

4 Ibid., p. 38.

5 Ibid., p. 38.

6 See Rev. R.S. Holmes, *The History of Yorkshire County Cricket 1833–1903* (London, Archibald Constable and Co, 1904), illustration facing p. 11.

7 See www.ckcricketheritage.org.uk/calderdale/sowerbybridge/clubhome.htm (last accessed 15 Mar 2012) and *Halifax Courier*, 21 May 1853.

8 See K.A.P. Sandiford, *Cricket and the Victorians* (London, Ashgate, 1994), pp. 53–80.

9 See www.ckcricketheritage.org.uk/calderdale/todmorden/clubhome.htm (last accessed 24 May 2012).

10 See www.ckcricketheritage.org.uk/calderdale/sowerbybridge/clubhome.htm.

11 See Illingworth St Mary's CC minute book 1884 at www.ckcricketheritage.org.uk/calderdale/illingworth/archive/arcgallery2.htm (last accessed 15 Mar 2012).

12 See Illingworth St Mary's C. C. minute book 1884 at www.ckcricketheritage.org.uk/calderdale/illingworth/archive/arcgallery2.htm (last accessed 15 Mar 2012).

13 www.ckcricketheritage.org.uk/southkirklees/almondburywes/clubhome.htm (last accessed 15 Mar 2012).

14 www.ckcricketheritage.org.uk/calderdale/illingworth/clubhome.htm (last accessed 15 Mar 2012).

15 www.ckcricketheritage.org.uk/northkirklees/mirfieldparish/clubhome.htm (last accessed 15 Mar 2012).

16 See *York Courant*, 17 Jul 1834.

17 See *From Little Acorns: A Centenary of Cricket at Broad Oak 1880–1980*, Huddersfield, 1980.

18 Personal communication.

19 www.ckcricketheritage.org.uk/southkirklees/shepley/clubhome.htm (last accessed 15 Mar 2012).
20 See the Twenty-Sixth Report of the Yorkshire Union of Mechanics' Institutes, Yorkshire Union of Mechanics' Institutes, Yorkshire, 1863.
21 See www.ckcricketheritage.org.uk/southkirklees/marsden/archive/arcgallery2. htm (last accessed 15 Mar 2012).
22 See *The Sowerby Magazine*, Aug 1862.
23 See newspaper cutting in Honley CC Committee Minute Book 1879–93, held by the West Yorkshire Archive Service, Ref WYK1268/1/1, also available at www.ck cricketheritage.org.uk/southkirklees/honley/archive/arcgallery1.htm (last accessed 15 Mar 2012).
24 See www.ckcricketheritage.org.uk/calderdale/illingworth/archive/arcgallery11.htm and www.ckcricketheritage.org.uk/calderdale/illingworth/archive/arcgallery12. htm (last accessed 15 Mar 2012).
25 See 'Brief History of the Club' article in Slaithwaite Cricket and Athletic Club committee meeting minute book 1922–28, available at West Yorkshire Archive Service, ref. WYK1278/1/1, and also at www.ckcricketheritage.org.uk/south kirklees/slaithwaite/archive/arcgallery53.htm (last accessed 15 Mar 2012).
26 W. Vamplew, *Pay Up and Play the Game* (Cambridge, Cambridge University Press, 2004), p. 57.
27 See *Halifax Courier*, 7 Aug 1880.
28 Vamplew, *Pay Up and Play the Game*, p. 58.
29 *Ibid.*, p. 184.

3   Organised competition

In Chapter 1 we talked about some of the key characteristics of pre-modern sport and how they were closely linked to the social, economic and cultural structure of contemporary society. Many of these characteristics disappeared as sport was transformed by the fundamental changes that took place in British society during the nineteenth century. This transformation was driven by the spread of economic reorganisation, which increasingly broke down the old social, economic and cultural relations. But this process took place over a number of years and during that time there was some crossover between aspects of the early pre-modern sporting culture and the social, cultural and economic components of change.

We also mentioned that this period of transition, which roughly encompassed the middle decades of the nineteenth century, coincided with the formative development of cricket as a sport. Consequently, the interchange between old and new cultural dynamics in cricket played a particularly important role and this is best viewed through the prolonged importance of challenge and stake matches.

Throughout the nineteenth century, local and national newspapers carried information about such matches. As a prelude to our discussion, let us note the following excerpts from local and national newspapers:

THE WETHERBY CRICKET CLUB hereby Challenge the HAREWOOD CLUB to Play them a Match and Return Match at Cricket on Neutral Ground, for any Sum not less than Twenty-five Guineas, and not exceeding One Thousand Guineas.
  NICHOLAS LAMBERT
  President to the Club

Wetherby, Sept 11, 1810[1]

****

A cricket match for ten guineas a side was played on Hunslet-Moor, last Monday, between the Leeds and Armley clubs, when the former won the match by 126 notches:

First innings – Leeds 80

Armley 36

Second innings – Leeds 135

Armley 53

Two of the best players belonging to the Leeds club were barred by their competitor.[2]

****

To the EDITOR of the LEEDS MERCURY

SIR, – Observing a Paragraph in the Intelligencer of last Monday, stating that a *Challenge has been given to the Leeds Cricket Players, by the Boroughbridge Club, and has not been accepted* – If you can spare a Corner in your paper, you will oblige us by inserting, *that we have received no Challenge either direct or indirect from the Boroughbridge Club*; we will allow, that One of the Players, in the Match lately played at Harrogate, came forwards individually to say, with a little warmth, being rather chagrined at the decision of the Game, that the Boroughbridge should play the same Eleven of Leeds, that had been then playing, when he was told with that candour which we hope will always mark the Leeds Players, whether successful or not, that we had no objections to meet the Boroughbridge, yet we could not think of being tied exactly to the same Eleven then present ...[3]

****

The second meeting of our rival Cricket Clubs took place on Wednesday last, on Woodhouse-moor, to decide which was to be the 'Champion' Club; much skill was displayed on the occasion, particularly by the 'Old Oncs' who acquitted themselves with great *éclat*, and gained the match in style, they having eight wickets to go down.

Leeds New Club,	1st Innings .... 83 Notches	
	2d Do .... 14 Do.	
	-------97	
Old Club,	1st Innings .... 78 Notches	
	2d Do .... 20 Do	
	-------98[4]	

****

Cricket Match at Darnall for 200 Sovereigns

Between 6 of Sheffield, with 5 of Leicester given, against 11 of Nottingham on the New Ground at Darnall, on Monday, Tuesday & Wednesday, July 21, 23 and 26 1826.

Nottingham first innings
Barker 9 bowled by Rollings
Jervis 3 caught by Owston
Clark 5 bowled by Marsden
Jervis 20 caught by Rollins
Smith 6 run out ...[5]

****

BICESTER AGAINST OXFORD

The match between Eleven Members of the Oxford Club and Eleven of the Bicester Club was decided on Tuesday, the 27th ultimo, at Bicester, in favour of the latter, at one innings, and two runs to spare, as follows:-

BICESTER	1st Inn	OXFORD	1st Inn	2nd de
Mr. H. Painter	15	Mr. R. Preston	4	15
- J. Painter	3	- J. Preston	2	3
- Jones	0	- Archer	2	3
- T. Phillips	0	- Bradfield	2	4
- G. Painter	1	- Evans	0	0
- Hall	19	- Hedges	3	2
- Maley	0	- Silver	0	0
- Blackwell	10	- Burrin	0	0
- W. Phillips	0	- Hooper	1	0
- Paxton	6	- Allen	0	0
- Harris	2	- West	1	10
Byes	3	Byes	0	5
Total	-59	Total	-15	-42

The return match will be played at Oxford, on the 15th of July.[6]

****

... the small parish of Duneton this season, they have played several matches in Goodwood Park with the young Earl of March and his party, and, owing to the success which has attended them, were induced to challenge Brighton. The match came off on Monday and Tuesday at Brown's grounds, Brighton, in the presence of a considerable concourse of spectators, among whom we noticed Sir John Byng and the Earl of Westmoreland, who appeared to watch the progress of the game with considerable interest. The result was as follows:-

BRIGHTON		DUNETON	
First innings	59	First innings	17
Second ditto	52	Second ditto	91
	----		----
Total	111		108

The Duneton players are not a match for Brighton, and it was only by extraordinary good luck, at the very close of the game, that they made so even a match of it ...[7]

****

CHALLENGE – The Members of the Britannia Cricket Club will Play the Dexterity Club the GAME of CRICKET, a full Field, on the 14th of May next, for £11 a side. The Money is now ready at Mr Mitchell's, Druid's Arms, Huddersfield – May 9, 1835.[8]

****

THE CRICKETERS OF DALTON will play those of Bradford for £50 a side, or they will play them on the Victoria Ground for £1 per man, at any time they may appoint. Direct to H.Crosland, secretary of the Dalton Club.[9]

****

CHALLENGES – The Halifax Junior Cricketers will choose eleven out of the twenty-two who have already played the Heckmondwike Club (and allow them the same privilege), and will play them for £10 a side, on the Leeds Ground; each club choosing its umpire from the Leeds Victoria Club – Eight of the Halifax Clarence Club will play any eleven bona fide residents of Heckmondwike, and members of the Heckmondwike Club, for £50 a side.[10]

****

HOVINGHAM v RIPON CLUBS – The Hovingham Club have accepted a challenge from the city of Ripon Club, to play a home and home game, for 11 ovs a-side. The first game to come off at Hovingham, to-morrow (Monday).

The return match between the Cheltenham and Gloucester Clubs will take place to-morrow at the Town Ham, Gloucester.

****

TO THE EDITOR OF THE ERA

Sir, – A few weeks ago I was challenged, through the medium of BELL'S LIFE, to play a game of single wicket, for £25 a-side, by Mr. George Chatterton, of Sheffield, to which I answered by return of post, that I was quite willing to play him but not for so large a sum; after waiting some time for an answer and receiving none, I wrote back to BELL'S LIFE, saying I would meet him where he liked to make a deposit, but the letter never aappeared ... I am still open to play Chatterton, or any other resident player in Yorkshire, for any reasonable sum, not exceeding £50. Hoping you will give insertion to the above,

I am, Sir, yours respectfully
THOMAS HUNT
Chesterfield, July 25, 1843[12]

In many ways the challenge dominated pre-modern sport. On one level it was a practical means of organising cricket in this period. The unregulated working week prevented a structure of sporting fixtures from being planned. Matches had to be arranged in an ad hoc fashion to fit around the availability of those involved. The issue and acceptance of a challenge to play on a certain day at a specified venue and time served this function well.

But more importantly, the challenge gave sport a distinctive meaning which was built around the key role of competition. The challenge was a means of playing out the rivalries that existed between villages, parishes and personalities (i.e. nobility). The concept of sport being played purely for its own sake came through the development of amateur values in the mid-nineteenth century. Before this, as Brailsford points out, the sporting contest began 'in defence of honour in the combat sports, spread to other forms of competition, and was cemented in by centuries of playing for stake money'.[13] Gambling heightened the sense of competition for obvious reasons and played a crucial role in the emergence of the large-scale and relatively sophisticated popular sporting events which we have identified.

This had a particularly profound effect upon cricket as, unlike most other sports, cricket developed many of its modern characteristics during the pre-modern period. We'll look at this process next, but to illustrate the way in which the combination of the challenge and the stake increasingly dominated the sport in England before the middle of the nineteenth century here are examples of three different types of cricket match which all show the widespread importance of the challenge and the stake. The first is from Joseph Lawson who describes the early informal matches that took place in Pudsey:

> It was some time before the new style of cricket was played with the order and decorum we see today. When it first came into vogue village clanship was rife. Money was mostly played for, and frequent uproar, confusion and even fighting took place.[14]

The second refers to a match played on 8 October 1786: 'On Monday ... a grand cricket match was played upon Pigbourn Lees between the gentlemen of Doncaster and the gentlemen of York for a hundred guineas.'[15] And in 1826 the *Sheffield Independent* reported on 'The Great Cricket Match at Leicester for 400 guineas a side between Eleven best of All-England and Twenty two of the Sheffield and Leicester Clubs'.[16]

The challenge and the early development of cricket

Between 1700 and 1850, stake-match challenges drove the development of cricket in four distinctive areas:

Rules and laws

Perhaps the most celebrated of these developments was the early appearance of laws. Most other sports were first codified during the second half of the nineteenth century. For example, the two forms of football established written rules after their respective governing bodies had been formed: the Football Association in 1863 and the Rugby Football Union in 1871. However, cricket was first codified in the middle years of the eighteenth century. Ironically, this came through the need to clarify the terms of each contest and prevent disputes in matches which often carried considerable wagers, and not to reinforce the principles of sportsmanship and fair play.

Specific parameters for each contest were agreed through the issue and acceptance of the challenge and these often came in the form of 'Articles of Agreement'. In the earliest known instance, sixteen 'Articles of Agreement' were drawn up for two matches between the Duke of Richmond and Mr Alan Broderick in 1727. These included the length of the pitch, twenty-three yards, the jurisdiction of the umpires – from which the two gentlemen protagonists were naturally excluded – and rules for the qualification of players.

In 1752, the first attempt to standardise a set of regulations for the game was made when the 'cricket club', who played at the Artillery Ground in London, published the 'laws' by which they had been playing since 1744 in the *New Universal Magazine*. Further notable amendments were made in 1771, 1774 and 1788, when the first MCC laws were published. By this time the no ball, short run and the dismissals of hit wicket and a prototype LBW law, termed 'standing unfair to strike', had all been introduced, along with regulations for the size of the stumps, bails, ball, and bat and the addition of a third stump.

A degree of flexibility still remained and this usually related to the requirements of gambling. As we saw in the previous chapters, the variations often concerned the eligibility of players, or specific terms to even out the sides, such as given men or an increased number of players on one side.

Despite the existence of written MCC laws, the continued importance of gambling in cricket during the 1840s was demonstrated by the function of *Bell's Life* newspaper, which acted as arbiter for disputes. On 21 August 1841, the *Halifax Guardian and Huddersfield and Bradford Advertiser* published the 'final decision of *Bell's Life*' which stated that,

> In the match between the Bradford and Leeds Victoria clubs, the batter was bound to go out in accordance with the decision of the umpire. The former club wins, and the bets go with the stakes.[17]

The development of cricket techniques and equipment

During the first half of the eighteenth century, matchplay teams, which featured the best cricketers of the day, were assembled by wealthy backers to play stake-match challenges. The famous Hambledon club marked the climax of this period of the development in cricket which had been made possible by the great patrons' investment in the sport. Backed by a group of wealthy gentlemen, which included at various times Rev. Charles Powlett, Sir Horace Mann, the Earls of Tankerville and Winchilsea and the Duke of Dorset, the Hambledon club assembled a stable of professionals from an increasingly wide area.

The greatness of the club, and the level of gambling in the game at its highest level at this time, is reflected in the calculation, from surviving records, that between 1770 and 1790 Hambledon played for £32,527 in stake money and won £22,497. (It must also be noted that advertised stakes, which could top £1,000, were not always accurate.)

The increased number of professional players and matchplay teams also improved and developed techniques and playing equipment. The Hambledon players were paid to attend practice sessions and competed in a regular programme of stake-match challenges. This meant that elite cricket players were competing against each other on a regular basis. Practice sessions would have had a competitive character through the economic necessity of selection for the Great Matches and the skills of the Hambledon players were developed, perhaps not from formal teaching, but by a process of watching and doing as crafts were traditionally learned.

Consequently, as the Rev. John Mitford identified in an 1833 edition of The Gentleman's Magazine, it was on 'the down of Broad Halfpenny' where,

> ... somewhere between the years 1770 and 1780, that a great decisive improvement took place and that cricket first began to assume that truly skilful and scientific character which it now possesses.[18]

These developments in technique were also transferred to the manufacture of cricket equipment. As Hambledon players Richard Nyren and then David Harris perfected length-bowling, which exploited the irregular bounce of uneven pitches, John Small, and then 'Silver' Billy Beldham, adopted the straight-bat approach, which encompassed forward play and playing down the line of the ball. Consequently, to compliment the new technique, Small, who was also a master bat-maker, first changed the shape of the cricket bat from its original curved form to one similar to that which is used today.

Developing the profile and facilities of cricket through private and commercial investment

The success of the Hambledon club shows the immense popularity of cricket within the rural communities of south-eastern England, with estimated crowds of 20,000 being reported at a number of their fixtures in the region. Although still mainly confined to London and the south-east, this growing prominence of cricket meant that the game began to attract commercial investment during the eighteenth century. It came mainly in the form of proprietor-owned grounds, which were mentioned in Chapter 1, and their early development owed much to the game's popularity in London. The capital's most important early venue was the Artillery Ground, by the 1740s managed by George Smith, the landlord of the nearby Pyed Horse public house. He also owned the catering and drinks concession, and for some time had used ropes to mark the boundary of the 'civil ring' which distinguished those spectators who had paid from those who had not. In 1746, Smith incurred the disdain of many spectators by raising the admission charge at the ground, after which it was reported that,

> The small appearance of the company is plain proof of the resentment of the public to any imposition, for the price of going in being raised from two pence to sixpence, it is not thought that there were 200 persons present when before there used to be 7000 to 8000.[19]

The spread of cricket as a recreational pastime

Before the rise of amateur values during the middle years of the nineteenth century, it seems that sport was rarely played for purely recreational purposes. It's clear from the diverse type of matches which were played for stakes that this, in conjunction with the challenge, provided a reason for people to play cricket. This was the case for both the locals who played informal ad hoc matches in the lanes of Pudsey and the gentlemen who met to play on Chapeltown Moor in 1776.

The challenge and early cricket

Let us take Yorkshire as a case study. By the 1820s, when cricket in Yorkshire first developed a national reputation, the period of aristocratic domination of the sport had come to an end. However, the game's introduction into developing urban industrial regions gave cricket challenges new life. Instead of aristocratic rivalries, major challenge matches now reflected competition between the new expanding towns and villages of the rapidly expanding industrial capitalist economy.

The first great rivalry to involve a side from Yorkshire was between Sheffield and Nottingham. Teams representing the two towns had been playing occasional stake matches since the 1770s. But it was following the establishment of 'big match' cricket at Darnall in the 1820s that regular stake matches were played. This rivalry had probably reached its highest point in 1828 when the following notice appeared in *Bell's Life* in London:

THE SHEFFIELD AND NOTTINGHAM CLUBS.
To the Editor of 'Bell's Life in London.'

Sir - Observing in your last publication a challenge from Sheffield to meet Nottingham Old Cricket Club, home and home, for £500, we offer three modes of accomplishing their wish:- First, to play on the same terms as last year; or secondly, if this should be rejected, to pitch the stumps half way between Sheffield and Nottingham, each party bearing its own expense; and thirdly, if neither of the above pleases them, to meet in Lord's Cricket Ground, on the same conditions (viz, each party bearing its own expense), and for the sum which Sheffield has named.

For the Nottingham Old Cricket Club,

June 11th, 1828   WILLIAM CLARKE.[20]

Like the early stake-match challenges in London, the rapid development of cricket in Sheffield was driven by this type of fixture. The matches were staged on a commercial basis and were promoted through the press. The public nature by which challenges, such as this one, were issued and accepted was clearly also intended to capture public interest. Consequently, Darnall quickly became a venue which hosted important matches. They were watched by large crowds and raised the profile of cricket in an area that was undergoing rapid urban and economic growth.

As a result of the sport's popularity, Sheffield had assembled a matchplay team of local professional cricketers by the late 1820s. It included men such as William Woolhouse and James Dearman, as well as the most notable of Sheffield's early cricketers, Tom Marsden, who became an immensely popular figure and Yorkshire's first genuine star player.

During the 1830s, other matchplay teams from the rapidly growing towns of the West Riding textile belt had also begun to appear. By the end of that decade a regular circuit of stake-match challenges had been formed which included teams from Huddersfield, Halifax, Leeds, Heckmondwike, Keighley and Bradford.

In the Huddersfield area, the emergence of a professional matchplay team from the handloom weaving village of Dalton reflected how the pre-modern economy still had an influence upon the sport. The relative autonomy enjoyed by men employed in this craft-specific trade meant that they could take time off to both practice and play in matches. Consequently, through the performances of men like Andrew and Joseph Crossland, John, George and Joseph Berry and George Armitage, Dalton quickly became one of the leading sides in Yorkshire.

The club was formed in 1831 and began to play stake matches against the region's leading sides at the start of the next decade. In 1841, Dalton played Leeds Victoria for £50, and also issued the following challenge in *Bell's Life*,

The cricketers of Dalton will play those of Bradford for £10 a side or they will play them on the Victoria ground for £1 per man, at any time they appoint. Direct to H Gossland Secretary of the Dalton Club.[21]

Elsewhere, Heckmondwike played Halifax Clarence for £10 in 1842, Keighley had played Halifax for 5s per man in 1839 and Halifax played Rastrick Albion for

£20 in 1843. As early as 1842 competition between these clubs had resulted in matches for an unofficial championship of Yorkshire being played and Dalton contested the title twice in that year. The first occasion was against Bradford Old Club, at Horton Lane, for £20 a side and the second against Sheffield, at Hyde Park, for £100 a side.

Despite the claims of Bradford, Huddersfield and Sheffield were the two most prominent early cricket centres in the West Riding, and a strong rivalry subsequently developed between them. The two towns provided most of the leading players in the county as first Dalton, and later Lascelles Hall, played in a number of stake matches against the South Riding side.

The high point of the West Riding challenge matches came in the early 1850s and was marked by a fixture between Dalton and Sheffield in 1851. This match deserves closer attention as it encapsulates many key characteristics of major stake-match challenges, while at the same time it demonstrates how aspects of pre-modern cricket could interchange with new developments in sport and society.

The relatively new concept of county cricket added to the importance of the match, as the *Huddersfield Chronicle* reported:

> We understand that the assumed superiority of the Sheffield players has for some time excited the ambition of the Dalton men, and repeated offers were made by them to contest it. These offers, however, were always declined until the Dalton men placed their rivals in a position from which they could not escape, by inserting a challenge in *Bells Life* for a match of £100.[22]

This quote also reveals how the growing profile of the local press, another new concept, provided a further stimulus to challenge matches in the region. A number of publications were founded in Huddersfield, Leeds, Bradford, Sheffield and Halifax during the 1830s and 1840s, and the newly established prominence of cricket in the region was reflected in their coverage of the sport. The challenge matches were promoted in these publications with pre- and post-match commentary which often provided partisan support to the clubs within the vicinity of the newspaper concerned.

In contrast to the partisan account which appeared in the *Huddersfield Chronicle*, the more impartial *Leeds Times* explained that, following Dalton's victory in the match,

> Still, we must remember that Sheffield have on many a previous occasion defeated Dalton, and we must not, therefore, conclude, that because there is a turn in such a somewhat uncertain game as the one in question, that Dalton are superior.[23]

The match was also a major sporting event which, through developments in regional and national communications, attracted widespread attention. It was staged at Old Trafford, a neutral venue, and was the subject of considerable betting which took place across and outside the region. As the *Huddersfield Chronicle* explained,

> The match excites very great interest, and many people from Yorkshire will be present. In Manchester the betting at present is about even, with the call on Dalton, but in Leeds the odds are rather in favour of Sheffield.[24]

Discussions in the press also show the major challenge matches were closely linked to the development of professionalism in the region. After the *Manchester Guardian* had expressed 'its unqualified disapprobation of matches at cricket for stakes' it was argued by the *Huddersfield Chronicle* that,

> The Dalton men occupy a position in life that prevents them from making pecuniary sacrifices such as matches purely for honour, when on a scale such as the one at present under notice, must necessarily entail, and therefore if they are to come into the field at all to contest the superiority of clubs so notorious, it can only be by the generous support of the gentry or by matches under similar arrangements as the game under notice.[25]

Away from these major matches other less significant fixtures also resulted from challenges and, during the 1830s and 40s, many carried a stake.

In 1857, a match for '£5 a side' took place between Holmfirth, who were backed by J.P. Crossland and Lockwood, who were similarly backed by C.G. Floyd.[26] Ten years earlier, in 1847, eleven moulders of Messrs Bray and Co. had played eleven engineers from the same firm with the losers to pay for a supper for the 'Whole of the hands employed by the firm'.[27]

Even when the Halifax Albion and Temperance clubs met in 1841 they retired to Wadsworth's Temperance Hotel after the match where dinner was still 'provided by the losers'.[28]

Single-wicket matches

Aside from these matches between teams which mostly represented rival communities, stake-match challenges were even more fundamental to another form of cricket contest. This was the single-wicket match, through which the most explicitly commercial form of challenge matches were played. They resembled prize-fights with backers often providing finance to make matches between opponents. In 1840, the following appeared in *Bell's Life*:

> CHALLENGE – George Carr, of Sheffield, having previously stated that he was prepared to play Harry Sampson, for £25 a side, he can now be accommodated for from £25 to £50 a side, but if he should not receive the support of his backers, Sampson will play him for £10 a side, but not less. The money is ready at Mr Dawson's, the Wicker.[29]

Single-wicket matches also reflected the variety and informality of pre-modern sport. As well as the stake, the terms of each contest were often negotiable and, as we saw through the match between John Thewlis and eleven landlords residing within a mile of Chickenley, designed to even out the contest. Other bizarre contests also took place and Andrew Crossland, the famous Dalton player, once played against Bendingo, the prize pugilist.

The prominence of single-wicket matches during the first half of the nineteenth century led to an unofficial championship of England being established. In 1828, Tom Marsden placed a notice in the *Sheffield Independent* which read:

> Sir, - Will you please to state in your next paper that my friends are ready to back me to play any man in England a match at single wicket for the sum of £50.[30]

Eventually his challenge resulted in two games against Fuller Pilch, from Norfolk, which ended in defeat for Marsden. However, they were not played until 1833, by which time Marsden was past his best.

By the 1860s, many of the components which were to characterise leisure in modern society had begun to take shape. The rationalised working week had been shortened in most industries, and a regular Saturday half-day holiday was established, around which a programme of regular pre-arranged fixtures could be formed. New social and economic demands were also conspiring against traditional pre-modern forms of recreation. Social reformers, like the rational recreation movement, had begun to encourage the replacement of traditional pastimes such as drinking and gambling with leisure pursuits which aimed to cleanse the mind and body. In sport, the new concept of 'amateurism' was preaching a similar doctrine. Many now viewed that the true value of participation was simply for the sake of the game itself, rather than any glory or gain that was linked to winning. Consequently, although some single-wicket matches were still being played, the stake-matches had all but died out by the 1860s.

One of the last major challenge matches to be played involved Lascelles Hall and Sheffield, for £100, and resulted from the deep rivalry that remained between what were still the two strongest cricket centres in Yorkshire. By this time, the type of big-match cricket which was first provided by the stake-match challenges had moved forward. Events elsewhere in cricket had prompted teams of professional touring elevens to begin travelling the country in the late 1840s, playing exhibition matches against local teams. These were still in the form of odds matches that were played against eighteens, twenties or twenty-twos and, in the early years, were occasionally contested for stake money. Over the next two decades, the touring eleven matches increasingly became the dominant form of major cricket event in Britain. But in the 1870s they too were superseded by the growing popularity of matches between elevens of the county cricket clubs, and the link between big-match cricket and the informal pre-modern format of the sport was ended.

However, the legacy of the challenge survived the demise of the stake matches and these other characteristics of pre-modern sport. Even though it was now possible to pre-arrange a programme of fixtures by 1860, many notices such as this appeared in the local press:

> CHALLENGE – The Red House Cricket Club would be glad to arrange matches with the following clubs.- Corduroy, Bradford Moor, Shipley Utd, Low Moor Royal Blues, Low Moor Perseverance, Address Red House Inn, Barkerend Road, Bradford.[31]

More importantly, two decades later, the West Riding of Yorkshire had emerged as one of the regions in which cricket's competitive traditions were shaped to complement the new society. During the 1880s cup knockout competitions were inaugurated across the region and this was followed by the spread of the league format in the next decade. The initial rush to form and join these modern types of organised competitions, and their continued success, saw the sport in Yorkshire, and other parts of the north and Midlands, stand apart from the more general shape of English cricket. A glance at the broader developments in British sport also suggests the legacy of the challenge has remained embedded in the more general collective sporting psyche. Two of the most prestigious domestic competitions in British, if not world, sport owe their origin and identity to the concept, as 'challenge' cups continue to be the most important knockout competitions in both Association and Rugby League Football.

Competition

Competition has been a key issue in the growth of cricket so far. It was largely through the traditional competitive impulse of sport that early contests were staged and shaped to fit around the constraints of pre-modern social and economic demands. The informal character of early sport was also linked to the need for an even contest, while, more specifically, gambling and the competitive implications of the challenges drove many of the early developments in cricket. These competitive traditions were also strongly evident as the character of modern cricket began to take shape. The profusion of new clubs that were formed in the West Riding during the second half of the nineteenth century were often driven towards their eventual character by a strong sense of local pride and the impulse to compete with similar organisations in rival communities. This last phenomenon can be seen to show how the pre-modern competitive tradition was re-shaped by the demands of modern capitalist industrial society.

It would be clearly wrong to say that competition in the pre-modern period was not organised. As we have seen, the challenge developed a relatively sophisticated framework from which the early versions of generally accepted laws in cricket were to emerge. However, the social and economic landscape of pre-modern England was not compatible with the type of rationalised programme of competitive sport that came later.

The birth of rationalised organisational frameworks in sport followed general social and economic trends towards similar types of extensive formal administrative structures. Among other things, unregulated urban and economic growth had led to chronic health and social problems during the first half of the nineteenth century. Consequently, governmental apparatus was increased to implement new legislation at local and national levels, as well as to satisfy the needs of extended political participation.

The new institutions, which were often run by elected committees and officials, also spread to leisure activities and a diverse range of voluntary associations sprang up in the middle years of the nineteenth century. As early as 1818 a Philosophical and Literary Society was formed in Leeds, and a variety of other organisations were later established, ranging from mechanics institutes to the volunteer corps.

These organisations were almost always formed by the middle classes and this was the case with the early governing bodies in sport. The class distinction was particularly pronounced in athletics. The Amateur Athletic Club was formed in 1866 to regulate the sport. For the fourteen years before this body became the Amateur Athletics Association, in 1880, 'anyone who was a mechanic, artisan or labourer' was excluded from its events.[32]

The governing bodies in football and rugby had a similar social origin. The inaugural meeting of the Football Association was attended by representatives of a small number of mainly middle-class clubs from the London suburbs and some public school old boys' clubs. Their intention was to devise a generally accepted set of rules from the various versions of the game that were played in the public schools.

However, social exclusivity was not to occur in these sports which originated from the popular participation game of folk football. In similar fashion to cricket, the new style, democratic and socially inclusive clubs spread rapidly in both codes with the assistance of outside social, religious and economic groups playing a key role. Eight years after the Football Association had been formed in 1863, the organisation had fifty affiliated clubs, but by 1888 the number had risen to 1,000. In Lancashire and Yorkshire especially, similar organisations were also established on a rapid scale in rugby.

This also meant that the competitive traditions of pre-modern sport were upheld in both codes, especially in the new urban industrial regions. Ironically, the inaugural FA Cup competition was based on the 'cock house' knockout competition that was held at Harrow. It was given a lukewarm reception by the still predominantly middle-class members of the FA and only fifteen of the fifty affiliated clubs entered the inaugural competition in 1871. However, the huge influx of new, socially inclusive clubs saw the competition take off during the 1880s. The watershed came in 1883 when Blackburn Olympic became the first predominantly working-class team to win the trophy. The event illustrated the cultural sea-change, as excitement in the town was so great that every few minutes the score was relayed by telegram to the Cotton Tree Inn, where it was displayed before an expectant crowd.

By the 1880s local cricket associations had also begun to be formed. But while Keith Sandiford has noted that these organisations flourished everywhere in England, they did not become commonplace in the West Riding of Yorkshire. One exception was the Huddersfield Cricket Association which was formed after the following advertisement was placed in the *Huddersfield Examiner* by Mr A. Mayall, secretary of Cliffe End Cricket Club:

> Wanted, a meeting of the secretaries of the local clubs in the Huddersfield District, to meet at the Paragon Inn on Tuesday the 3rd of August 1886 to arrange matches for next season, and to take into consideration the question of neutral umpires for purely local matches.[33]

While other similar organisations were formed to administer cricket in the West Riding they were usually linked to the emergence of cup knockout competitions. A Heavy Woollen & District Challenge Cup Committee was formed in Batley at the end of the 1882 season and met for the first time at the Royal Hotel to draw the inaugural ties. In a 1897 article on the origins of the Halifax Parish Cup, the *Halifax Courier* recalled how,

> The first move towards the introduction of a trophy was made by a party of local enthusiasts, who formed themselves into a sort of guarantee association …[34]

Neither were competitive issues totally absent when the Huddersfield Cricket Association was formed. The need to address the question of neutral umpires was an important concern and the *Huddersfield Examiner* commented,

> … all will admit that the decisions given by unprejudiced umpires must necessarily be more satisfactory to all concerned than those of partisans of the clubs engaged … The one practical objection to this arrangement would be the difficulty of getting a sufficient number of disinterested umpires to forego the pleasure of following the fortunes of the clubs in which they were most particularly interested.[35]

Moreover, just a few weeks later, at the Association's inaugural dinner on 6 November 1886, Mr Edward Lumb offered to donate a challenge cup to be competed for by the member clubs. The offer was accepted and the competition – the Lumb Cup – began in the following year.

Elsewhere, challenge cup knockout competitions were formed throughout the West Riding in a variety of sports during the 1880s. They followed on from the success of similar competitions in the two codes of football. In line with the growing popularity of the FA Cup, the concept gained momentum locally in rugby with the formation of a Yorkshire Cup competition which began in 1878. In cricket, a seemingly one-off cup knockout competition had been organised by local publicans in the Silkstone area as early as 1867. But the first regular major cup competitions in the region began in 1880. They were formed in the two largest towns: Leeds, where Councillor Emsley of Hunslet donated a fifty-guinea challenge cup, and Sheffield, where another fifty-guinea challenge cup was given by Mr W.R. Wake esq. Three years later the most famous and oldest of the surviving cup competitions, the Heavy Woollen Cup, was established in and around Batley. Elsewhere, the Halifax Parish Cup, the Airedale Challenge Cup, the South Leeds & District Challenge Cup and the Craven Cricket Union Cup were among a number of other knockout competitions to begin before the end of the decade.

We will look closely at the impact of these cup knockouts next, but their immediate success saw the concept of rationalised competition in sport taken to a new level in the next decade. League competitions were formed with equal if not greater gusto across the region in the 1890s. Association Football had again shown the way, but this time cricket in other similar urban industrial regions was also at the forefront of the new initiative. As well as the Football League, the Birmingham League and Bolton & District Association were formed in 1888. Other cricket leagues followed in North Staffordshire in 1889, and in North East Lancashire, later the Lancashire League, in 1890. In February 1891, another meeting of cricket clubs was called in Huddersfield. This time the formation of a local cricket league was the main focus of attention and a further gathering of club officials later in the year passed the motion that, 'A cricket league be formed for the Huddersfield and District'.[36]

The inaugural season of the Huddersfield & District League took place in 1892 and, by the middle years of the 1890s, a further eight leagues were in operation within the locality of the town. These included the Huddersfield Combination and Alliance leagues, which provided league cricket to member clubs of the Huddersfield Cricket Association who had not been asked to join the initial competition. Elsewhere in the district, the Huddersfield & District Junior Alliance League, the Lockwood & District Junior Alliance League, the Colne Valley League, the Colne Valley Junior Alliance League, and the Sheepridge & District League all came into being.

In Halifax, a similar profusion of leagues quickly appeared. The first of these was the Calder Valley League in 1891 and it was quickly followed in 1892 by the Halifax Amateur Cricket League. In 1894, the larger clubs in and around Halifax formed the Halifax & District Cricket League, while the Todmorden and Hebden Bridge leagues also came into being. In the following year, the trend of localised competitions continued and the Spen and Calder Valley League, the Ovenden & District League, the Sowerby Division and the Brighouse Cricket League were established.

Similar events took place elsewhere in the West Riding as competitions were also formed among teams with more specific common links. In Leeds, where the Leeds League had commenced its first season in 1892, a number of church leagues were quickly formed. These included the Leeds Church League, the Leeds & District Primitive Methodist League, the Leeds Wesleyan League and the Leeds & District United Methodist Free Church League. A number of contrasting competitions were also begun in Halifax during the first decade of the twentieth century. The inaugural season of the shortlived Halifax Licensed Victuallers League took place in 1905 and this was followed by the formation of the Halifax & District Church Sunday School League in 1907 and the Halifax & District Nonconformist League in 1908. In 1895, just three seasons after the first major league competition had been staged in the region, the *Yorkshire Post* reported regularly on events in twenty-three different leagues.

The impact of cups and leagues

From their inception, league and cup competitions captured the collective imagination in local communities. In almost every case, the inauguration of these new competitions represented a combined sense of civic pride, individual status and community identity. This was strongly reflected in the tone of reportage in the press. On 5 May 1880, *Athletic News* announced, in an article headed 'The Yorkshire Challenge Cup', that,

> The first ties for the 50 guinea challenge cup, offered by Mr W.R. Wake esq., of Sheffield, for competition amongst Yorkshire Cricket Clubs (the first ever presented in the county) were played on Saturday. No fewer than 34 of the most prominent clubs have entered, and many of the chief professionals have been engaged, an extraordinary amount of interest was manifested in the result of the various contests [sic] ... and at nearly all there were large attendances.

The *Halifax Courier's* description of how the Halifax Parish Cup came into being carried similar aggrandised sentiments:

> ... after a lot of preliminaries the summer of 1888 found the principal clubs in this, the largest parish in England, competing for a piece of the silversmith's art, in the shape of the magnificent challenge cup.[37]

In a similar way to stake-match challenges, the cost of these trophies demonstrated the importance of the competition. Usually the cups were donated by leading local dignitaries, and they sought to gain prestige from the scale of their generosity. Another £50 cup was donated in Leeds, by Councillor Emsley of Hunslet, Mr Walter Morrison, of Malham Tarn, gave a cup to the Craven Cricket Union, and Mr Edward Lumb provided the Huddersfield Cricket Association with its impressive first trophy.

The cup committees and member clubs were also keen to promote good relations and raise the profile of their organisations within the local community. Considerable sums of money were often raised at cup finals and a charitable donation was common, with local hospitals usually the chief beneficiaries. Proceeds from Lumb Cup finals were donated to Huddersfield Royal Infirmary and at the 1887 final £61 9s 6d was raised. In Leeds, as the trophy was being presented after the second Emsley Cup final, Mr Emsley remarked that 'he did not think the committee could do better than present the money taken at the gate during the two days' match to the various Leeds charities'.[38]

Popular interest in these competitions was also considerable. The finals were regularly attended by large crowds. In 1889, the Lumb Cup final recorded gate receipts of £51 11s as a crowd of around 3,500 spectators gathered at Armitage Bridge, while the first Heavy Woollen Cup final attracted a crowd of around 5,000 people.

However, the impact of these events is best shown in the celebrations that followed for the victorious sides and the strong sense of local identity that they expressed. After Birstall had beaten Batley in the 1892 Heavy Woollen Cup final, a local newspaper reported that:

> The members of the respective teams mounted their wagonnettes, Mr Ackroyd with the cup in his hands taking up a position in the box of the Birstall conveyance. Headed by the Birstall Brass Band they then proceeded through Batley. Having made one or two calls *en route*, the players, with a few of their friends … made their way to the Coach and Six Inn, the headquarters, in front of which were gathered, despite the heavy downpour of rain, about 1,000 people who gave lusty cheers as the captain Mr Ackroyd, and his men, stepped from the wagonnettes bearing the trophy aloft.[39]

Similar scenes were encountered in Greetland after the local club had broken the initial stranglehold that Halifax and Elland held over the Halifax Parish Cup. One of the district's two leading clubs had won the competition in each of its previous six years before Greetland defeated Sowerby Bridge in 1894. The *Halifax Courier* described how,

> The Greetland eleven, accompanied by Mr J.E. Eastwood, the president of the club, reached West Vale in a waggonnette at dusk. A large crowd were awaiting their arrival and cheered vigorously when the team came in sight.[40]

Scenes like this were common as victorious sides returned home after finals. One particularly euphoric homecoming followed the 1923 Sykes Cup final. This trophy was donated by Sir Charles Sykes in 1920 and was competed for by the Huddersfield & District League clubs. Paddock won the third final and the *Huddersfield Examiner* vividly described how,

> A huge crowd awaited the arrival of the Charabanc at Longroyd Bridge, and to the martial strains of 'See the Conquering Hero Comes', played 'con brio' by the Milnsbridge Socialist Band, the party proceeded up the village. The crowd increased as the procession went along and no road vehicle could stay its progress. The Tramcar was compelled to creep sedately behind, and even the Golcar bus had to run out of

its orthodox track at a later stage. The effects of all this upon the smaller inhabitants of Paddock was similar to the music of the Pied Piper of Hamlin and it is doubtful that he had more children following him than the Paddock team ... After all winning a cup is a thirsty job, and it was not surprising that a further halt was called at Paddock Head, to the great confusion of the Golcar bus service. By this time the crowd was tremendous, and the general enthusiasm, to which was added the merriment of the team's mascot donkey, which can both eat ice cream and ride a bicycle, will cause Paddockers to remember for a long time the occasion when their cricket team won 't' cup.[41]

The rush to form new leagues in the 1890s was met with similar enthusiasm. In 1892, the *Yorkshire Post* anticipated the first season of the Leeds League by commenting that,

At no time has club cricket in Leeds caused more interest or counted more adherents, and the public interest in it is distinctly on the increase. This is more especially the case in Leeds and district, where the outlook is more promising than it has been for years.[42]

The article went on to proclaim,

The success of the Huddersfield League has also justified its inception. Already membership is large, and on all hands there is a visible spirit of emulation to qualify for its ranks. This latter indeed is likely to be one of its main functions, as it is also the case of the various Challenge Cup competitions – the exciting of our players to greater endeavour by providing a goal for their ambition.[43]

These observations were endorsed further in the following year, when the clamour to form new competitions elsewhere in the region gained momentum. The Yorkshire Post again captured the mood, noting that,

League contests there are in abundance, and although it may be possible at some future date to overdo them they are at present necessary for the good of the game by bringing out that perfection of talent to the attainment of which every earnest eleven must strive.[44]

In most cases, league cricket was also successful in capturing the support of the West Riding public. Indeed by June 1894 the league concept had engulfed followers of the sport in the region to such an extent that, with regard to a friendly fixture, the *Yorkshire Owl* saw fit to comment that the

Sheepscar men took matters far too easily on Saturday, and it seems that if a match is not a league one, the animation in the affair is entirely lacking. There would not be above fifty people on the leather men's ground to witness the match in question.[45]

This atmosphere of general apathy was in stark contrast to events at a Leeds League match at Holbeck's ground in July 1894 when there was

... a big crowd at the Recreation Ground to witness the match between Holbeck and Leeds, and excitement ran high, including two or three fights.[46]

In similar fashion to the cup final wins, league successes also often brought euphoric celebrations. When Todmorden won the Central Lancashire League in 1896 around 1,300 away spectators swelled the crowd to 4,000 as the Centre Vale side visited Rochdale with two victories needed to secure the title. Three weeks later, when the victories had been gained, the celebrations took place and the sense of civic pride was appropriately enhanced as festivities were also staged to mark the town's new status as an independent borough. An 8,000-strong Charter Day procession was held which included a wagonette carrying the players and the cup, and a second vehicle which carried the club's committee. Fittingly, the celebrations continued into the night with fireworks and dancing to music from the brass bands.

The league concept reached its most ambitious point in the region with the formation of the West Riding League in 1893. *Athletic News* described this competition as 'the chief organisation of its kind in the county'. Its formation followed very closely parallel events in rugby and the Yorkshire Rugby Union's first Yorkshire Senior Competition began in September of the same year. Both competitions were entered by leading clubs from the major towns. The first West Riding Cricket League competition included Leeds, Huddersfield, Bradford, Sheffield, Dewsbury, Keighley, Barnsley, Brighouse and Halifax, with the football sections of Halifax, Bradford, Huddersfield and Dewsbury also entering the Yorkshire Senior Competition.

There were interesting similarities between sports. In 1885, professionalism had been accepted in Association Football following the sport's rapid growth in the urban industrial regions and the competitive implications of the new cup knockouts. Although the Rugby Football Union remained staunchly amateur, similar events in rugby union caused increasing conflict before the sport's 1895 split and the formation of the Northern Rugby Football Union. Professionals had also been an integral part of cricket for over 100 years. But in all three of these major sports, regulations were brought in to control the payment of players. Most of the new cricket league competitions also had concerns about professionalism. Many, like the Halifax Amateur Cricket Association League, specifically avoided the payment of players, while others placed limits on the number of professionals in each team. In the Leeds League, clubs were limited to one paid player, and listed in the 'objects' of the Huddersfield League was, 'The controlling of professionalism'. The West Riding League also allowed limited professionalism, with a maximum of three paid players per team. However, the league went further than most other organisations by making an allowance for broken-time payments, the issue which caused particular conflict in rugby. Its rules decreed that,

An amateur shall be defined as one who does not receive any money over and above expenses actually out of pocket and an exact equivalent for the loss of his wages accruing from his usual occupation.[47]

The subject of professionalism in the new cup and league competitions was behind most of the criticism that their rapid rise attracted. On 12 May 1882, *Cricket Magazine*, a national publication, included an article that warned of the potential for corruption which was offered by Challenge Cups in football and cricket. Interestingly, on 22 June 1882 the same publication also expressed concern ... that cricket might be made a profitable commercial speculation; and, for the first time in the history of the game, the question of gate money was made a matter of primary importance.[48]

Predictably, this view was more fervently expressed in rugby and in 1882 Rowland Hill, the secretary of the RFU, wrote that cup ties 'caused an evil spirit to arise, and that sometimes men are influenced more by the desire to win rather than to play the game in the true spirit.'

In elite cricket, the structure of the County Championship avoided this type of direct competition. Although, as early as the 1860s, a championship title was awarded to the side which lost the least number of matches in a season, it was given by the press and not the governing body. An MCC attempt to introduce a formalised knockout competition in 1873 was rejected by the counties, with only Kent and Sussex accepting the invitation to participate. Even after the Championship was officially inaugurated in 1890 the competition retained a loosely arranged structure. As late as 1912, the title was decided on a points percentage basis and while the champions, Yorkshire, played twenty-eight matches, second-placed Northamptonshire played only eighteen times.

This attitude was clearly in stark contrast to the way the new competitions had been embraced at club level in the West Riding. While a number of the early competitions were shortlived, the concept remained popular among local clubs. A period of restructuring followed the initial boom in league cricket and following the Great War, an era of stability was reached which lasted in many places into the 1990s. By this time, for example, where the Huddersfield area had initially seen eight leagues in operation during the 1890s, a similar number of clubs were grouped into three main league competitions. These were the Huddersfield & District League, which had two divisions, the Huddersfield Association Cricket League and the Huddersfield Central Cricket League.

The ambitious West Riding League was one of the short-lived competitions and its demise in 1899 reflected both the strengths and weaknesses of league cricket in the region. The West Riding League can be seen as an attempt to form a regional cricket competition along the lines of the Football League and especially the later Northern Rugby Football Union. Many members of the West Riding Cricket League were in fact sections of the same organisations that formed the Northern Rugby Union in 1895. They developed a limited commercial business ethos which embraced such things as limited liability and expenditure on spectator facilities. In terms of professionalism, although clearly falling short of its prevalence in the Association Football competition, the West Riding League went further than the initial rules of the Northern Rugby Union. Player payments in the new code of rugby were limited to broken time, while the West Riding League allowed both this form of remuneration and limited open professionalism.

However, league cricket on the geographical scale of the West Riding League failed to capture the public imagination in the same way as the two football competitions. The financial implications of poor attendances were the main cause of its demise, and most clubs that were able had to use revenue from football to meet their cricketing expenses. Consequently, in 1899, the West Riding League was replaced by the Yorkshire Cricket Council. This new structure for the leading clubs in the county initially represented a total reversal from the ambitions of the West Riding League. It was formed as an administrative organisation in the fashion of the cricket associations, 'for the purpose of providing neutral umpires and insisting on punctuality'.[49] This ideological reversal was reinforced on 20 April 1899 by the *Yorkshire Post* which commented that, 'Club cricket in Yorkshire may be said to be once more clothed in its right mind'.[50] The organisation subsequently evaded calls for a championship to be awarded until 1904 as, 'this was a reversal of the principles on which the Council was formed'.[51] Even when it relented to pressure from the clubs, a championship system that was based on the 'counties' championship' was adopted for the 1904 season.

The strength of the league concept in West Riding cricket clearly lay in the flourishing local competitions. This was highlighted by the events which followed the formation of the Bradford League in 1903. In the space of twelve years, the competition had taken the league concept to a new level by gaining national prominence and enjoying record crowds during the Great War. Its rise was enhanced by the cessation of county cricket which enabled Bradford League clubs to sign a host of first-class and Test cricketers, such as Jack Hobbs and Sydney Barnes. The continued success of the Bradford League demonstrated that a high level of league competition could be successful in the region if it retained a local complexion. Unlike rugby and especially Association Football, the game had an elite domestic tier, through county cricket, before the league emerged. Consequently, little space remained between the high-level local leagues and the County Championship for the type of more expansive domestic competitions that existed in the football codes to be successful.

Competition had been crucial to the way cricket and other sports developed in the West Riding and other urban industrial regions of Britain. The rapid rise of popular sport was largely built upon traditional rivalries that existed both within and between communities. Its rise ran parallel with the period of not only rapid urban growth, but also dramatic change, as many people's lives were transformed by the spread of the capitalist industrial system. Sport became a key means through which collective identities were built in what were essentially new communities, and competition enabled them to be fully expressed. The leagues and cup knockouts reinforced this process, by providing forms of rationalised competition through which the traditional expression of rivalry and identity was successfully translated into modern industrial society.

Notes

1 *Leeds Mercury*, 15 Sep 1810.
2 *Leeds Mercury*, 9 Aug 1817.
3 *Leeds Mercury*, 24 Oct 1818.
4 *Leeds Mercury*, 23 Oct 1824.
5 1826 handbill.
6 *Bell's Life*, 8 Jun 1828.
7 *Morning Post*, 9 Oct 1834.
8 R. Light, *The Other Face of English Cricket: The Origins of League Cricket in the West Riding of Yorkshire* (Huddersfield, Cricket Heritage Publications, 2008).
9 *Bell's Life*, 22 Aug 1841.
10 *Bell's Life*, 5 Sep 1841.
11 *The Era*, 30 Jul 1843.
12 *The Era*, 30 Jul 1843.
13 See D. Brailsford, *Sport, Time and Society: British at Play* (London, Routledge, 1991), p. 14.
14 See J. Lawson, *Progress in Pudsey* (Sussex, Caliban Books, 1978 (first published 1887)), p. 82.
15 See Rev. R.S. Holmes, *The History of Yorkshire County Cricket 1833–1903* (London, Archibald Constable and Co., 1904), p. 11.
16 See *Sheffield Independent*, 2 Sep 1826.
17 See *Halifax Guardian and Huddersfield and Bradford Advertiser*, 21 Aug 1841.
18 See D. Birley, *A Social History of English Cricket* (London, Aurum Press, 1999), p. 34.
19 G.P. Buckley, 'Fresh Light on Pre-Victorian Cricket, 1937', in Birley, *A Social History of English Cricket*, p. 50.
20 See *Bell's Life*, 15 Jun 1828.
21 See *Bell's Life*, 22 Aug 1841.
22 See *Huddersfield Chronicle*, 4 Oct 1851.
23 See *Leeds Times*, 4 Oct 1851.
24 See *Huddersfield Chronicle*, 27 Sep 1851.
25 See *Huddersfield Chronicle and West Yorkshire Advertiser*, 4 Oct 1851.
26 See *Leeds Times*, 7 Oct 1843, *Huddersfield Examiner*, 19 Sep 1857. Also see *Leeds Intelligencer*, 28 Jun 1856 – Aberford v Boston Spa for £1 2s and a new ball.
27 See *Leeds Times*, 28 Aug 1847.
28 See *Leeds Times*, 18 Sep 1841.
29 See *Bell's Life*, 31 May 1840.
30 See Holmes, *Yorkshire County Cricket*, p. 27.
31 See *Leeds Times*, 9 Jun 1860. For other examples, see similar lists from Yeadon, *Leeds Times*, 15 Mar 1862 and 11 Apr 1863.
32 www.englandathletics.org (last accessed 16 Mar 2012).
33 See T. Walton, *One Hundred Partnership: A History of the Huddersfield & District Cricket Association* (Huddersfield, Huddersfield & District Cricket Association, 1986).
34 See www.ckcricketheritage.org.uk/docs/0830081897CUPFINALSPCW.pdf (last accessed 16 Mar 2012).
35 See Walton, *One Hundred Partnership*.

36 See A. Lodge, *Drakes Huddersfield Cricket League Official Souvenir of the Centenary of the League* (Huddersfield, Huddersfield & District Cricket League), p. 13.

37 See *Athletic News*, 5 May 1880.

38 See *Leeds Times*, 9 Sep 1882.

39 See *Batley News*, 2 Sep 1892.

40 www.ckcricketheritage.org.uk/calderdale/greetland/archive/arcgallery11.htm (last accessed 16 Mar 2012).

41 www.ckcricketheritage.org.uk/southkirklees/paddock/archive/arcgallery11.htm (last accessed 16 Mar 2012).

42 See *Yorkshire Post*, 2 May 1892.

43 See *Yorkshire Post*, 2 May 1892.

44 See *Yorkshire Post*, 22 Apr 1893.

45 See *Yorkshire Owl*, Vol. IV, No. 90, 27 Jun 1894.

46 Ibid.

47 See *Athletic News*, 19 Apr 1897.

48 See *Cricket*, 22 Jun 1882.

49 See *Yorkshire Post*, 20 Apr 1899.

50 Ibid.

51 Ibid.

4 The two world wars

According to Hill, the two world wars gave governments the opportunity to influence the conduct of sport, but their involvement was still tentative.[1] This should not surprise us as governments had no history of intervening in sport. For his part, Wigglesworth compares the 1914–18 and 1939–45 experiences. He argues that, 'If a discontinuation of sporting activity typified reaction to the First World War then a dogged determination to carry on regardless was the general response to the Second'.[2] He also says that because healthy volunteers were required, 'so a disproportionately high percentage of recruits were sports club members'.[3] This is interesting because it indicates the links between sport and war – the relationship was always going to be important.

The Great War

The Great War was conceived of by some in cricketing terms. Siegfried Sassoon wrote:

> I see them in foul dug-outs, gnawed by rats
> And in the ruined trenches, lashed with rain
> Dreaming of things they did with balls and bats[4]

Birley says that in general terms Sassoon displayed great nostalgia for the pre-1914 era, mainly because it was such a contrast to the period that followed.[5]

J.H. Dowd, the cartoonist, depicted a German soldier playing cricket in an unsportsmanlike fashion.[6] Another cartoon, in Punch, featured a German plane bombing an English cricket match.[7] The match continued with one of the fielders running towards the boundary to retrieve the ball. The light-hearted caption read: 'We dropped bombs on a British formation, causing the troops to disperse and run about in a panic stricken manner'. It was as if nothing could disrupt English people from playing cricket – and this became a point of contention. Even the Batley News talked about 'our brave boys playing the greatest of games'.[8]

Should cricket go on – or should it not? Was sport a useful distraction from war, an 'alternative' that could soak up people's need, or even thirst, for activity, physical exercise, teamwork and recreation? Or was it the case that cricketers – because of their training and outlook – would make good soldiers?

The relationship between sport and war has attracted much historical attention. In 2004–05, the Imperial War Museum put on an exhibition entitled 'The Greater Game'. The subtext was that war could be conceptualised in terms of sport and competition. It was a 'game' of sorts.[9] George Orwell, famously, described sport as 'war minus the shooting', and this theme was taken up by one of the most acclaimed modern cricket writers, Mike Marqusee.[10]

We should not forget either that some of the most famous sporting encounters took place on the frontline. At Christmas 1914, French and German soldiers engaged in an impromptu game of football in the trenches and a trophy was awarded at the end of the match.[11]

In England, war was popular with the aristocracy, who viewed military combat as a kind of competition. Some cricket people – like Lord Hawke, Gilbert Jessop and Plum Warner – became associated with 'war work' and military recruitment. For their part, *The Times* stopped printing county scores – as if to say that sport was a triviality in a time of war.[12]

Sir Arthur Conan Doyle, most famous for creating Sherlock Holmes and writing the Sherlock Holmes stories, was used to help recruit men to the army. On 6 September 1914 he said: 'There was a time for games, there was a time for business, there was a time for domestic life … but there is only time for one thing now, and that thing is war. If the cricketer had a straight eye let him look along the barrel of a rifle. If a footballer had strength of limb let them serve and march in the field of battle.'[13] Also, Dickie Bond, Bradford City's famous England international winger, was used to encourage supporters to recruit for the army during the last match of the season on 28 April 1915 when Bradford City visited Bradford Park Avenue. At half-time, he donned his corporal's uniform and walked round the pitch appealing for volunteers.

How did ordinary cricket clubs function during the war? Club minute books help us in this regard. At Armitage Bridge, in Huddersfield, we encounter the following minute:

Annual Report 1917/8 – Owing to the prolongation of the war and, mainly, the calling up to the Colours of still more men, the difficulties of the Club existing in its playing sense were greater than at any other previous time. However, the remaining clubs of the Central League desired every club to continue playing and so we decided to try our utmost to keep the game on till the War was over … We also let the ground for use of the Military Hospital cricket matches from time to time and so we managed to keep the Club going through one of the most trying times in the career of the Club's history.[14]

Following on from the disastrous effects the war had on the club, it was decided to hold a concert in the Co-op Hall on Saturday 1 February 1919, admission 1s6d and 1s. The concert realised a sum of £20 for club funds.

Exeter's ground rent was reduced from £25 to £20 in 1914 and scrapped for the rest of the war.[15] Another interesting case study is Burnley. On 2 July 1916, the *Burnley Express* reported that the previous day had been the town's bleakest with 200 local men killed in the war. The club cancelled all cricket in 1917 and 1918 and issued a circular letter which said: 'The club is in danger of having to close down unless something is done in the matter of continuation. The present committee find themselves unequal to the task of building up the club as, owing to the lack of public support and the loss of members, they have not the initiative where-with to see their way to continue.' Tony Lister's research has shown that the club emerged from the war with a deficit of £225 and a dilapidated ground. A public meeting, chaired by the mayor, was held on 13 March 1919 and a twelve-man committee set to work on 're-founding' the club. The main problem was financial – it became apparent that the club would have to purchase its ground for more than £4,000 from the neighbouring football club or lose it completely. Public appeals were launched and by 1925 – seven years on from the end of the war – the ground had been secured.[16]

So, war was a traumatic experience and local clubs responded in a variety of ways. They raised money, they fulfilled their duties with regard to the war tax, and they signed up local professionals. They also saw their playing strength diminish as cricketers died on the frontline.

Clubs' central dilemma

Wigglesworth is certain that, 'The First World War, The Great War, the War to end all Wars, had as one might imagine an enormous effect upon English sport at every level'.[17] It is difficult to disagree with this assertion.

On 6 August 1914, the MCC stated that 'no good purpose can be saved at the moment by cancelling matches'. But a week later, on 13 August, they said that, 'owing to the war', all matches scheduled for Lord's in September were not to take place. Later, the Scarborough Festival had to be abandoned, with one local paper commenting: 'It means much to the townspeople in Scarborough just at their best time, but that the decision is wise in view of this morning's definite news as to British losses is the opinion generally held here.' And commenting on the situation at Hove, where Sussex were playing Yorkshire, the paper declared: 'The weather down here is wonderfully fine, and very hot, with no sign of rain. The sands were crowded this morning, and the sea was full of bathers, but even so the war interest predominated, and the match opened before a mere handful of spectators.'[18] By the end of the month, the MCC had announced that 'first-class cricket is hurtful to the feelings of a section of the public'.[19]

But at a local level, competition continued. The Halifax Parish Cup was won by Mytholmroyd in 1915, King Cross in 1916, Elland in 1917 and Brighouse in 1918. The Huddersfield Central League actually welcomed five new member clubs in 1915: Holmbridge, Leymoor, Meltham, Scholes and Thongsbridge. The first-named was immediately active in the corridors of power, as the minutes of Central League committee meetings make plain: '4 November 1915, Holmbridge moved that the matter of playing without professionals be considered 12 months hence but received no support.'[20] This shows that amid the gloom and tragedy of war, some clubs were still interested in the trivialities of sport.

Many clubs soldiered on. At Harrow, matches 'continued to take place irregularly on Saturdays'.[21] And at Turnham Green in London, in 1915,

> Permission was granted from the Council for the Club to erect posts and chains around their pitch on Turnham Green 'subject to the same being removed if and when the ground was required for recruiting parades' ... During the First World War, the club was hard put to keep it going. Matches became less frequent as the war progressed and financially we were in very low straits. Eventually it got to the point where the treasurer had to ask members to subscribe to each expense as it arose. The club was held together during these hard times, however, and among those mainly responsible for keeping things going were P.C. Taylor, J. Wilson, F. Hufflett, F. Mears, A. Warren, J. Sutchings, R. Blackburn, W. Portch and J. Passell.[22]

In Lancashire, Walsden of the Central Lancashire League had financial problems. In addition to not being able to afford a professional, in 1916 the club asked players to forgo their usual half-pay broken-time payments for wages lost while playing. In 1917, this was extended to talent money as the club came close to winding up, at least temporarily. But, significantly, records show that the club was able to insure the pavilion, tea room and bowling green against damage by air raid.[23]

At Illingworth St Mary's in Halifax, the club minute book contained the following references to the war:

> That all officers stand ... until the April meeting, when it is thought we shall have a better idea as to who then will be at liberty to play ... It was unanimously decided that it be recorded in the minutes our extreme sympathy be extended to all our lads who have fallen in this great European War.[24]

Interestingly, the clubs at Mirfield, in Yorkshire, and Padiham, in Lancashire, survived until the end of the war, folded in 1919, but came again in the years following the Second World War.[25]

The example of the Bradford League demonstrates that cricket carried on but was also affected — in a novel way — by the war. With the County Championship abandoned, there were few opportunities for leading English players to 'keep playing'. So many took advantage of the fact that league cricket, for the most part, remained unaffected. Frank Woolley, Jack Hobbs, S.F. Barnes and others all headed for the Bradford League.

The other course of action was to stop playing — out of solidarity or necessity. Military folk were particularly outspoken on this issue. As late as 1917, a Major Norris was quoted in the *Batley News* as saying, 'We are menaced by this country being overrun with Germans and I want you, gentlemen, as leaders in Dewsbury, to let the younger men, who are able, come and drill. Never mind bowls, cricket and football. Let them come and learn to shoot, and protect their homes.'[26] As we have already noted, there was no county cricket between 1915 and 1918.

The moral argument was put forward by W.G. Grace. He argued that men who were physically fit should not be playing cricket while others were losing their limbs in the trenches. He wrote to *The Sportsman* on 27 August 1914: 'I think the time has arrived when the county cricket season should be closed, for it is not fitting at a time like this that able-bodied men should be playing cricket by day and pleasure-seekers look on. I should like to see all first-class cricketers of suitable age set a good example and come to the help of their country without delay in its hour of need.' Within a week, first-class cricket had been terminated.[27]

Some clubs were forced to disband temporarily. At Great Brickhill in Buckinghamshire, no cricket was played between 1915 and 1918.[28] Decline had set in at Henfield in Sussex before the war – in 1911 in fact, 'with not a single recorded match taking place in the four years up to the outbreak of World War I'. But the intervention of 'a cricket-loving vicar, the Rev R.J. Lea, who arrived in 1913', saved the club. 'Even during the war years, he worked hard to ensure the circumstances whereby cricket would return once peace came.' Henfield resumed playing in 1920.[29] The Aston & District club, in Cheshire, was the product of a three-way amalgamation between Combermere, Broomhall and Wrenbury, who had all played up until 1914, but not, seemingly, thereafter.[30] The St Anne's club, in Lancashire, only re-formed in 1924.[31]

Club committees had to make some tough decisions. In the West Riding of Yorkshire, Honley's annual report for the 1915 season explained that a crisis point had been reached with 'practically all the eligible players having joined the Army or Navy (to the extent of about 60)'. It was later decided, at the 1916 AGM, that 'we discontinue cricket for 1916 … write to the League Sec that we have abandoned cricket' and 'inscribe a Roll of Honour to the men who have joined the Army and Navy during the Great War'.[32] But there was good news in places. At Rodmersham in Kent, there was no 'official cricket' between 1915 and 1918. But, 'After the first post-war season of 1919, enthusiasm was high and in 1920 a second eleven was formed mainly to encourage young players'.[33] Chipping Sodbury also resumed playing in 1920, 'fixtures being arranged on a limited scale with a number of local Clubs'.[34]

The situation at Crowhurst in Sussex was also interesting. There seemed to be a club in existence between 1894 and 1912. During the war, no matches are recorded. But on 21 June 1919, the *St Leonard's Observer* reported as follows:

CRICKET CLUB REVIVED – The Crowhurst Cricket Club has been revived and a good deal of interest is being taken in it. The following officers have been appointed:- President. Lt Col P.R. Papillon D.S.O., D.L., J.P., Captain. Mr J Bye, Vice Captain. Mr N Lambrick, Secretary. Mr H Pont. Mr Lambrick has lent the club a field, which will be put in order after the haymaking. The club is in need of funds and it is hoped to hold a concert shortly to raise some of the necessary money.[35]

The re-formed club's inaugural match took place on 26 July 1919. In all, seven games were played that summer – Crowhurst winning three and losing four – and the club's 'end-of-season supper' was held at The Plough public house. At this point in their history, Crowhurst club funds amounted to £2 16s.

Broadening the debate out, it is clear that grassroots cricket was affected by the experience of war in a number of ways.

Death of cricketers in battle

The Commonwealth War Graves Commission has stated: 'Cricketers from all over the world gave up everything as they redirected their sporting qualities – passion, dedication, camaraderie – to the war effort. These men, who came from all the major cricket nations of the time, fought on the land, sea and in the air. Their tragic deaths are typical of so many, their graves and memorials looked after by the … Commission, and we will always wonder what they and their comrades would have gone on to achieve had they survived.'[36] Wigglesworth says that there were sixty pages of obituaries in the 1917 edition of *Wisden*.[37] This is a significant statistic that tells of the contribution cricket, as a sport, made to the war effort. Many first-class cricketers enlisted during the war – maybe as many as 210.[38] Some held commissions in the Territorial Army and others were volunteers.[39] Estimates put the number of first-class cricketers who died during the war at between thirty-four and seventy-seven.[40]

At a local level, many cricketers enlisted. Harry Wallace, the Slaithwaite professional, joined the Colne Valley Territorials.[41] And Percy Smith, who was a significant name in the Yorkshire Council, was a gazetted lieutenant.[42]

The war had a devastating effect. Clubs were ravaged and their playing resources severely diminished. At Stockport in Greater Manchester, a war memorial overlooks the playing area:

STOCKPORT CRICKET CLUB IN THE GREAT WAR 1914–1918

128 MEMBERS OF THIS CLUB JOINED HIS MAJESTY'S FORCES AND THE FOLLOWING MADE THE SUPREME SACRIFICE

W H BOURNE, W BROOKS, W A CRAGG, L C EMERY, E L GOODALL, H M GRANGER, J D GREEN, S HEYDON, B HORNER, J B LISTER, T H PENNY, C B SCHOFIELD, L F SHARP, G SLACK, J H STAVEACRE, W C YATES[43]

Mytholmroyd, in the West Riding of Yorkshire, produced a special memorial to mark the end of the war. It featured photographs of eleven club men who had lost their lives. The text read:

THE EUROPEAN WAR 1914 – 1918

SERVICE – SACRIFICE – FAITHFUL UNTO DEATH

HE WHO GIVES HIS LIFE FOR ANOTHER ENOBLES HIS OWN SOUL

AN EMBLEM – LEST WE FORGET – FROM THE MYTHOLMROYD WESLEYAN SUNDAY SCHOOL CRICKET CLUB[44]

Wavertree CC in Liverpool lost six players who had played for them in the 1914 season: J. Hewitt of the Royal Engineers Tunnelling Company; Robert Talbot Jones, a sergeant in the Kings Liverpool Regiment (KLR), 17th Battalion; Thomas Oakes, a rifleman in the KLR; Fred J. Roberts, a captain in the KLR, 1st Battalion; Herbert Done Roberts, a private in the KLR, 12th Battalion; and Neil John Tunnington, a corporal in the KLR. All were first eleven players except Hewitt and Tunnington.[45]

And after the war, the Reading & District League said it was proud of local cricketers' contribution to the war: 229 of its players had enlisted, 30 had lost their lives, 45 had been wounded and, in total, local cricketers had received four Military Crosses, four Military Medals and three Distinguished Service Medals. Pat Neal, Mirfield's historian, is unsure about the situation at his club: 'How many of the players were called up is unclear and on the Mirfield Roll of Honour of the dead only one name appears that could be one of the players.'[46]

So, local cricket was affected significantly by the war. Many cricketers died on the frontline and clubs worked hard to commemorate the lives of the fallen.

Disruption

On an organisational level, there was severe disruption. The Lancashire League did not function in 1917 and 1918, though its member clubs continued to play friendlies and clubs in the Rossendale Valley competed for a special trophy.[47] The Halifax & District League folded (and only re-emerged in 1921), while the Halifax & District Church (Sunday School) League disappeared for good in 1915. In 1916, the Halifax League suspended activities due to the war. This was slightly odd given that, as we have noted, the Halifax Parish Cup continued, and also that in May 1916 a local cricket correspondent stated: 'Considering the large numbers which have been drawn into the military machine, the interest in local cricket continues to be of a quite virile character.'[48]

In 1915, the Yorkshire Council said that friendly matches would replace league fixtures. In the words of one writer, 'it prohibited competitive cricket', although not all clubs agreed with this edict.[49] In 1916, it re-organised itself – the argument being that less travel was desirable during the war. One effect of this was the birth of a 'Halifax Section', which included clubs such as Sowerby

Bridge, Lightcliffe, Siddal and Clifton Britannia (with Illingworth joining in 1920). There remained a Halifax Section up to 1925. Other clubs – for example, Hanging Heaton, Gomersal and Staincliffe – acquired 'wartime membership' of the Yorkshire Council in 1916.

These examples illustrate the fluidity of the wartime situation. The birth of new competitions and the introduction of new types of membership were significant developments. Local leagues were thinking on their feet and trying to adapt to changing times.

In his work, Mike Butler has demonstrated how, and to what extent, the Heavy Woollen Cup was affected by the war. He talks about the 'half-hearted enthusiasm for cricket' and notes the tone of the local press – which seemed to accept that at such a critical time, cricket would have to take a back seat. He has also unearthed some fascinating information. For example, in 1914, the cup committee decided to drop the price of admission to the final to 3d because of the sombre international situation. But – and this is curious – gate receipts in the final actually exceeded those of the previous year by £6. Perhaps this was a statistical quirk; or it shows that the pricing policy was clever; or that the general public viewed cricket – and, in particular, a big local final – as a useful distraction from the war.

Another interesting issue emerged in late 1917. Ossett had won the trophy in both 1916 and 1917 and a hat-trick was a possibility – and it was a tradition that any club winning the cup three times in a row could keep it. This alerted the Liversedge secretary, who stated that the cup had been slightly devalued during the war because of clubs pulling out; and so, he argued, Ossett shouldn't be allowed to keep the trophy if they won it a third time. He lost the argument eventually – but the fact that he even suggested a 'wartime amendment' to the rule helps us understand the atmosphere of the time and some clubs' perceptions of 'wartime cricket'.[50]

Wartime conditions were also an opportunity. In 1915, Heckmondwike entered the Dewsbury & District League in search of a 'better class of cricket'. On the other side of the Pennines, the Lancashire & Cheshire Federation was established in 1916 with ten member clubs; but regular fixtures only commenced after the war had finished.[51] Thus, leagues and cups were affected significantly by the war. Leagues were abandoned and cup competitions were impacted upon. But at the same time, ambitious clubs could use the dislocation of war to their own advantage.

For Wigglesworth, the 'abrupt end to professional cricket was replicated in the amateur game as members took the King's Shilling in their thousands, leaving juniors and veterans to look after the interests of clubs in their absence'.[52]

Grounds put to alternative uses

At Lord's, Old Trafford, Trent Bridge, Derby and Leicester, cricket had to give way, either to military hospitals or army units.

At a local level, some clubs voluntarily turned their grounds over to other uses or had them requisitioned by the authorities. Jeffrey Stanyer says that the County Ground, Exeter, was used for a variety of purposes: soldiers were billeted there, other sports were played, and animals were allowed to graze on the outfield.[53] In Yorkshire, by 26 August 1914, 'the Leeds ground had been commandeered by the military authorities, and the devastation wrought ... was appalling. The artillery had caused deep ruts, and straw and oats were strewn about. The ground could never be made right again.'[54]

These examples illustrate the dislocation brought by war. Whether large or small, clubs owned significant areas of land. A cricket ground was a major community resource and could be put to good use.

In 1916, the Kensington Road ground in Reading was requisitioned by the War Office and used as a recreation ground by the Royal Flying Corps, but Martin Bishop argues that it was maintained to a good condition during the conflict.[55] This seemed to be a theme. In 1917, one of the local newspapers in Yorkshire commented:

> ... there will be very little outdoor sport in the coming summer, and cricket clubs will find their slender financial resources will be subjected to further financial strain. There will be general approval, in these circumstances, of a proposed arrangement between Dewsbury Town Council and the trustees of Dewsbury and Savile Cricket Club for the Corporation to take over the supervision of the cricket field for the season and to contribute towards the cost of maintenance. The Savile enclosure is an exceedingly pleasant resort for the public, and it has the advantage of being easy of access to residents in the thickly populated parts of the borough.[56]

Following the outbreak of war in 1914, Outlane, near Halifax, managed to continue throughout 1915 and for most of 1916. However, the 1917 season saw the cricket ground requisitioned for food production and, although the club committee continued to monitor the ground situation, the club effectively ceased to function. Other clubs were inventive. Primrose Hill were one of the first clubs in Huddersfield to organise workshop cricket competitions during the years 1916–17. Two local businesses represented on the cricket field were the Primrose Hotel and Broadbent & Sons. Both teams made it to the final in one year, with the Primrose Hotel just coming out on top in what was recorded as 'a very keen tussle'.[57]

All this emphasises the fact that cricket clubs were at the heart of their communities.

Charity fundraising

During the war, Lord's staged a variety of charity matches involving representative sides with many star names on view. Plum Warner was also associated with a variety of fundraising efforts.

At a local level, it is clear that clubs had a conscience. Many matches were staged with the aim of raising money for charity. In July 1918, a game between Ashton Old Boys and Police and Specials at Ashton-under-Lyne, Manchester, was organised. There was novelty about the invite:

> Members of our Town Council and others – We do hereby declare it to be our will and pleasure that on Saturday, the 20th July 1918 at 2 of ye clock p.m., prompt, the above-named well tried, true, and trusty willow wielder, skilled in the art of retrieving and despatching to its destination the sphere needed in ye olde English playe and game of 'Creequette', do present himself at Ye Arena, Reyner Lane, Sur La Mans, Assheton, to join with comrades of bye-gone days of glorious memory in engaging as 'Ye Olde Boyes of many a feat' in friendly combat with 'Ye Blue Boyes of ye heavy feet' to the intent that thereby the Prisoners of War Fund may be replenished.

The match raised £350 for the Prisoners of War Fund.[58]

In Pennine country, Walsden played rivals Todmorden to raise funds for the War Relief Fund in 1914, and in support of the Centre Vale Military Hospital in 1915 and 1916, the latter match raising more than £50 (the sum of admission fees, a collection and a donkey auction!). As added attractions in 1915, the Todmorden side included Wilfred Rhodes and Percy Holmes, while Walsden had the services of George Hirst. Walsden had three England players in their ranks in 1916, Rhodes playing alongside Lancashire opening batsman Johnny Tyldesley and Warwickshire bowler Frank Field. The Todmorden team included Hirst and double cricket and football international Jack Sharp.

It is significant that local rivals took part in specially arranged charity matches. The war was now the number-one priority and, obviously, traditional rivalries and enmities were put in the shade.

On 30 September 1915, Turnham Green in London played an Army eleven in aid of the Chiswick War Relief Fund and a band took part in a recruiting parade at the same event.[59]

In May 1916, the *Halifax Courier* spoke of 'The Military Cricket Match':

> Capt. Flanagan and Mr. H. Stocks are securing strong elevens to oppose each other in the cricket match at Thrum Hall on Thursday week, in aid of the Comforts Fund. Tickets are now ready, and can be purchased at the Drill Hall, or from several tradesmen in the town. One team will be representative of the military and the other of tradesmen. The charge for admission is only 3d, and, for so worthy a cause, it is hoped there will be a large sale prior to the day and also a big attendance for the game. Selections will be played by a military band.[60]

When the match actually took place, the *Halifax Courier* reported that copies of a poem were sold in aid of the Comforts Fund.[61] Around the same time, fixtures took place between 'the military and a team representing Lightcliffe and district' – in aid of the Courier Comforts Fund – and between the military and Leeds and district.[62]

Again, this shows that cricket clubs were integral to their communities. A significant amount of money would have been raised for a variety of wartime causes.

The inter-war years

According to Holt, there was a need for 'reassurance' in the years following the Great War, 'to know that the essence of England had survived, to forget the carnage, and enjoy English pleasures undisturbed'. He cites *The Cricket Match*, the novel written by Hugh de Selincourt in 1924, as evidence of a certain mood in the country. The book revealed the 'oddities and virtues of the English character' and implied that cricket had the ability to bring the classes together – an important task given the trauma and dislocation of the war.[63]

Wigglesworth also comments on the immediate post-war period. He talks about sports clubs being more orientated towards youth and women joining clubs in greater numbers in the post-war years – important trends that we should take note of.[64] In his study of the inter-war years, Williams explores the relationship between cricket and sportsmanship, gender, class, Christianity and commercialisation. His conclusion is that the inter-war period was crucial to cricket's development.[65] In another work, he relates the fact that between 1930 and 1936 there were 170 cricket teams in the town of Bolton, Lancashire; this being higher than the figure for 1900 (130) and 1980 (120). So we are dealing with a key period in cricket's development. But how should we go on to characterise grassroots cricket in the inter-war years?

As we have noted already, the immediate post-war years were ones of re-birth, with many clubs and leagues emerging from enforced hibernation. But it was always going to be slow. Wavertree CC in Liverpool were forced to merge with Edge Hill Congregational Church CC in an effort to boost their playing strength; and the amalgamated club played five games only in 1919. Things were slightly easier in 1920, with the club fulfilling nineteen fixtures. And in 1921, the club formed a company – The Wavertree Recreation Co. (1921) Ltd – to help it recover from 'a devastating war'.[66]

There appear to be many examples not only of clubs re-forming (this would have been natural up to a point) but also starting afresh, with new premises and positive intentions.

For the best part of forty years, Stainland, near Halifax, played at Drury Lane – a venue famous for its bandstand. In 1922, the club received their current ground, on Stainland Road, as a post-war gift. The working men of the village had a new recreation area, and the folk at the British Legion were named as trustees. Sowerby Bridge, near Halifax, moved to their current headquarters in the period immediately following the end of the Great War, and purchased it in 1936. In 1919, Liversedge, near Dewsbury, had their ground bought for them by three local men. And in 1921, a new pavilion was purchased at Thornhill, near Dewsbury.[67]

In Reading, there were a number of key events in the immediate post-war years: in February 1919, the War Office handed the Kensington Road ground back to the biscuit factory for recreational purposes (with reduced working hours after the war, employees had more time for leisure); the factory announced that it was putting out three, rather than the usual five, teams in 1919; the Reading & District League decided to run two equal divisions because officials had little knowledge of the post-war playing strength of clubs; a match between the biscuit factory and Caversham was postponed as many of the players were taking part in an event to mark the return of the 2nd Battalion of the Royal Berkshire Regiment; in 1920, inter-departmental cricket resumed at the biscuit factory; and a local letter-writer suggested that, 'After 4½ years of war and all its attendant horrors our returning athletes, aye, even the ordinary public, must have recreation to restore their minds to normal conditions'.[68]

At Weybridge in Surrey, the playing area was levelled in 1921; this was done with the help of a band of jobless ex-servicemen. And in 1924, Weybridge Albion merged with Weybridge Electric to form Weybridge CC, with a phoenix being chosen as the club symbol.[69] Committee meetings at Thorpe Arnold in Leicestershire were minuted for the first time in 1931 and the club started playing league cricket soon after – in the Melton & District League.[70] And in 1938, a full set of club rules was introduced.[73]

So, gifts, hand-backs and mergers. Clubs had a variety of experiences in the immediate post-war period. Everyone would have wanted normality to resume as soon as possible but there were also logistical considerations to take into account.

The history of leagues is also interesting. In the 1920s, the Southport & District League expanded to incorporate a fourth division (1925) and two reserve sections (1928).[72] In 1920, the AGM of the Ribblesdale League in Lancashire agreed to pool travel expenses so that clubs in outlying districts were not discriminated against. And in 1925, the Ulverston & District League in Cumberland was established to cater for 'rudimentary cricket'.[73]

How should we characterise the inter-war period? In general terms, it is important for a number of reasons. First, if there was an over-riding theme, it was consolidation. The majority of cricket clubs had survived the war; now was the time to take stock.

Second, cricket established itself as a relatively cheap form of mass entertainment. In Lancashire, 'The League cricket was tremendously popular at this time and receipts were up on most grounds. Overseas stars as professionals blended superbly with the competitive nature of the cricket.'[74] Williams in fact argues that crowds were possibly higher at club games (e.g. Lancashire and Bradford League) than at county fixtures. He also argues that general interest in the game was greater than ever.[75] Membership figures also tell an interesting story. Golcar in Huddersfield had 480 members in 1935 and 450 in 1938. These figures would seem to attest to the popularity of the club and also the lack of other forms of entertainment in the village in the 1930s.

Third, it is interesting to assess how local league cricket was affected by the Great Depression, and in particular the General Strike of 1926. Historians have argued that in Australia in the late 1920s and early 1930s, Don Bradman was a symbol of hope and his batting was able to lift the spirits of a nation that had been badly affected by the economic downturn. But what of cricket in England in the same period?

The General Strike was the biggest industrial dispute in British history. It took place between 4 and 12 May 1926 and many industries were involved. The cricket season had just begun. Having time off work meant that some people were able to attend the Test Match against Australia, which otherwise they would have not been able to.[76] Others were able to help their club. At Flockton, near Wakefield, the General Strike definitely came to the club's assistance in that their new ground at Hill Top was being prepared and many locals could help out because they had plenty of time on their hands.[76] In the Midlands, strike bulletins carried the latest cricket scores – indicating that 'normal life' continued.[78] At the Reading Biscuit Factory, 'Games at the beginning of the 1926 season were disrupted due to player availability due to the General Strike. Many had joined the voluntary services and were not available in early May.' And there is also the story of Tommy Mitchell, 'an engaging entertainer and ranked high among the exponents of artful spin between the wars. Tommy, a miner at Creswell Colliery, was spotted bowling near the pithead during the General Strike in 1926. An old cricketer, who saw Mitchell turning the ball prodigiously, at once recommended him to Derbyshire.'[79]

Another story comes from Whickham CC in the north-east:

> During the miners' strike of 1926, lads and men had a keen interest in sport. As the summer months were approaching, the Australian cricket team were touring this country. Five of our youths thought it a good idea to attend a Test Match, the nearest one being held at Leeds. Our first thought was the cash. We began to prepare weeks before the date of the match. We needed 2/6d. Entrance and at least another 2/- for sundries such as programme, pop, parkings etc. The day came to prepare to leave. Our mothers packed a large bait, enough to last two days. It consisted of a granny loaf, half a stotty loaf with jam on and finally into the haversack went a pint enamel pot. We left Whickham 10 o'clock at night on bikes, with a small paraffin lamp on one bike, down Lobley Hill, along the Coach Road, Birtley, Chester-le Street, Darlington, etc. We had to travel through towns and villages as there were no by-passes in those days. Almost all these towns and villages had a fountain or horse-trough which provided us with drinks. Arriving at Headingley, Leeds, 6am, we parked our bikes in a back yard for 3d ... I do not suppose this trip would have been thought of had it not been for the miners' strike. The five cyclists were John Copeland, George Copeland, Kit Heron, Edward Proud and Charles Lambert.[80]

For his part, Williams airs the view which says that 'sportsmanship produced a spirit of social harmony which could preserve political stability'.[81] He also quotes *The Times*, which opined that giving young working-class boys the opportunity to play cricket would, 'help in the work of moulding him, body and temperament, into a strong and happy and helpful citizen'.[82] It is interesting and significant that cricket should be used in this way – it obviously had deeper meaning than other sports.

By the end of the decade, local clubs were up against it. The Golcar centenary history stated: '1929 was a disastrous year from a financial point of view. No professional was paid – and there was not enough money to pay for the Juniors' prizes.'[83] We are also told that Wavertree CC in Liverpool had to endure 'a serious financial crisis' in 1934, with the club almost folding.[84]

Fourth, we witness the first debates about Sunday cricket. According to Bryan Griffiths, 'there was much opposition from Puritan Ministers for "profaning the Sabbath by cricket playing"; and a Bill was passed in 1625 prohibiting the playing of unlawful sports (however, this was largely ignored in the country and cricket escaped because it was not so dangerous as contact sports, such as football, which often resulted in fatalities)'.[85] The Sunday Observance Act (1780) forbade the use of premises 'for public entertainment or amusement upon any part of the Lord's day … to which persons are admitted by payment of money or by tickets sold for money'. It was repealed in 2003.[86] In 1909, Bradford Council formed a 'Sunday Observance Committee' to keep the Sabbath 'uncontaminated by organised entertainment of any kind'.[87]

At Britwell Salome in Oxfordshire, 'Early matches were played only on Saturdays because of religious objections to cricket being played on the Sabbath. This restriction was relaxed after the Second World War, but only on condition that play finished before the Evening Service commenced.'[88] Evesham CC in Worcestershire had a Sunday eleven in 1935.[89] Martin Bishop says that a Sunday team was formed at the Reading Biscuit Club in the late 1930s. He states: 'This was ground-breaking in the town where almost all club cricket up until this time had been played on Saturday or midweek (normally Wednesday). However, as more clubs (with no religious ties – either directly a Church-based club or a works side influenced by the religious beliefs of the owners) such as Reading, Wokingham etc. grew, they more frequently started to utilise Sunday as a cricket day.'[90] In 1941, Birstall, near Leeds, were weighing up whether they should play a match on a Sunday during wartime.[91]

The debates rumbled on into the 1950s. Sowerby Bridge District Council had emphatically refused to open its bowling greens for Sunday use, yet leisure was beginning to encroach the Sabbath in Britain and overseas. The Halifax League was one of the first to experiment with Sunday play and it was a success. At the Mytholmroyd CC Annual General Meeting at the White Hart Hotel, Mytholmroyd, on Monday 28 October 1957, secretary N.D. Turner commented: 'During the past season Sunday cricket has been introduced and the new venture has made a substantial increase in the club's income.'[92] By the end of that season the club had a credit balance of £133 19s 8d.

Before it was acceptable for leagues to schedule fixtures on Sundays, it was reasonably common for clubs to play friendly matches 'on the Sabbath'. Benefit and charity matches were staged, some involving first-class cricketers, and this started the ball rolling with international stars such as Peter May and Keith Miller advocating Sunday play in first-class cricket. The International Cavaliers – a wandering team of big-name players – took part in ad hoc fixtures. These games were countenanced because the cricket being played was deemed to be leisurely. But in some places things were even stricter. In the 1950s especially, the Lancashire League prohibited its member clubs from playing even friendly matches on Sundays; so when Harold Dawson raised a team to play a Sunday fixture, he had to call it the 'Harold Dawson eleven' rather than 'Todmorden'.

In 1962, the Lancashire League started scheduling Worsley Cup fixtures on Sundays (prior to this, cup ties were played on weekday evenings), and a year after, in 1963, the first league matches were taking place on Sundays (initially, two per year; by the early 1980s, most league games were being played on Sundays – mainly because gate receipts were higher). Local author Brian Heywood says: 'I remember playing Sunday games at Todmorden when the nearby church was still in use. There was a racket on the hour every hour. It really disturbed us!'[93]

Sunday play began at different times in different places. In Surrey, many prestigious club matches were moved to Sundays when the leagues started (the Surrey Championship started in 1968). All the other southern counties played their league matches on Saturdays and club matches on Sundays too. Brian Heywood remembers: 'At East Molesey I can remember playing Sunday club matches against Reading (Berkshire); Basingstoke (Hampshire); Brighton and Hove (Sussex); Bromley (Kent); Finchley (Middlesex); High Wycombe (Bucks), as well as teams from other leagues in Surrey, so the pattern was the same across the south-east. The Sunday matches remained quite high profile in the mid-1980s – there was certainly a lot of rejoicing when we beat Finchley, who were the national club champions, by over 100 runs in a Sunday club match in 1985.'[94]

In some cases, it wasn't necessarily religious authorities who opposed Sunday play. When Holmbridge in Huddersfield leased their ground from a local mill owner, the club was not allowed to play after 6pm on a Sunday, such was the bond that existed between their landlord and nearby St David's Parish Church. Meanwhile, some clubs with church connections were forced to play all their Sunday games away from home.[95] When Holmbridge came into ownership of the ground (in the 1960s and 'in perpetuity', as a result of public subscription, and at a total cost of £100), it no longer had to take account of the church bells, nor had to adjourn Sunday games to Mondays. In 1969, in line with social changes and the growing commercialisation of sport, the county game embraced Sunday play with the advent of the John Player League.

What this section has demonstrated is that the inter-war period was one of great fluidity. Cricket had survived the Great War and there was now all to play for. But, as it turned out, the period 1919–39 was not an easy one to navigate. The legacy of the war was all-consuming and could not be negated. There was also a severe economic downturn which affected all sectors of society. Sport could not but be affected.

The Second World War

Predictably perhaps, cricket metaphors were employed in some quarters to explain the Second World War. The *Evening Standard* featured a cartoon of Neville Chamberlain (the batsman) about to receive a delivery from Hitler and Mussolini (the bowlers) – with a grenade for the ball.[96] In *The Cricketer*, Sir Home Gordon stated that, 'England has now begun the grim Test match against Germany … we do not wish merely to win the ashes of civilisation. We want to win a lasting peace with honour and prosperity to us all.'[97] Meanwhile, Yorkshire and England opening batsman Herbert Sutcliffe commented, 'It is a pity Hitler was not educated in Yorkshire for I feel sure that if he had been he would have learned the principles of sportsmanship and what it is to play a straight bat'.[98] Others tried to put things in perspective. One of the most famous comments about cricket and war came from Australian all-rounder Keith Miller. When asked about pressure in cricket, he replied: 'Pressure is a Messerschmitt up your arse, playing cricket is not.'[99]

According to Wigglesworth, as far as sport was concerned, there was a significant difference between the two world wars. He argues that between 1939 and 1945 the powers-that-be were favourable to the notion that sport could aid morale. This, he implies, was different from the Great War. He goes on to assert that this attitude helped to 'democratise sport' after the Second World War.[100]

In this section we will evaluate the relationship between sport and war. In what ways, if any, was the 1939–45 experience different from that of 1914–18? As such, the chapter will deal with the quandaries faced by ordinary cricketers – were they the same as during the Great War? It will also assess the logistical impact of the war on local league cricket. The first thing to say is that there was not such a dilemma about whether to volunteer this time: conscription for men aged over twenty began in the third week of April 1939, four months before war was declared.

Many cricketers served their country. Brian Sellars, captain of Yorkshire, was a lieutenant.[101] Fred Howden, a fast bowler with Batley, worked for the Military Police.[102] William Murphy of Birstall joined the RAF.[103] One of the most famous stories of the war relates to cricket writer E.W. 'Jim' Swanton. He was held captive in a Japanese prisoner-of-war camp but was sustained by a copy of *Wisden* he had in his possession.[104] The most high-profile casualty of the war was Hedley Verity of Yorkshire and England. He played in forty Test Matches, taking 144 wickets, and all told captured 1,956 wickets in his first-class career.

No Test cricket was played during the war and the County Championship was abandoned (although some thought had been given to staging a limited competition in 1940). Nevertheless, a variety of events were staged at Lord's, including schools fixtures, invitation games and matches involving the armed services, the British Empire eleven, National Fire Service, London Counties and branches of the Civil Defence. Here, Pelham Warner was a key driving force.

There were interesting developments. The BBC stopped all coverage of cricket during the war. Twenty-over-a-side matches were organised for air-raid wardens in the West Riding of Yorkshire.[105] Hundreds of Boys Brigade members in London were invited by the headmaster of Eton to camp at Agar's Plough to avoid the Blitz – and the young lads were allowed to play cricket on Eton's famous ground. Evesham played matches against RAF Gloucester, RAF Cheltenham, Army Long Marston and the BBC club at Wood Norton Hall.[106]

Around the world there were other indicators. There was cricket in India, where the Ranji Trophy was not affected and a full first-class programme resumed in 1943–44; likewise in the West Indies, where first-class cricket continued but the Inter-colonial Tournament was put on hold. And at Todmorden in the Lancashire League, the figure for average runs per wicket fell from 20.54 in 1939 to 9.94 in 1944, indicating that the quality of pitches had declined during the war and also that, as more and more men were required for war service, the quality of batsmanship declined.[107]

At a local level, clubs 'did their bit' for the war effort. Menston in Leeds supplied twenty-seven men – three were taken prisoner of war and four eventually lost their lives. Chipping Sodbury lost three players, including Tom Phipps, killed on 27 February 1941.[108] Wavertree in Liverpool lost three members: J. Kynaston, W. O'Donnell and W.M. Roberts.[109] E.G. Righton Jnr of Evesham, 'returned from the war with a distinguished military record, culminating with the award of the MC in Italy'.[110]

Cricket carried on in Guildford, with the Bedser twins, among others, making guest appearances in the town.[111] Things were also thriving at Upton on the Wirral. The club moved into the Merseyside Cricket Competition and entered a ground-sharing agreement with another local sports organisation, Upton Ladies Hockey Club.[112]

Jeffrey Stanyer says that at Exeter, cricket was 'improvised',[113] and this is a helpful observation. It could almost apply everywhere. In Yorkshire, a variety of fixtures were put on. At Batley, Hanging Heaton second eleven entertained the Royal Corps of Signals and Batley Air Raid Wardens were also playing games.[114] Walsden of the Central Lancashire League hosted fixtures involving the Home Guard, Air Raid Precautions and Air Training Corps and the club provided a 'Don Bradman bat' to be raffled as part of the 'Todmorden Wings for Victory Week'. A

Table 4.1   *Number and type of teams put out by the Reading Biscuit Factory, 1939–45*

	Senior teams	Junior teams	Women's teams
1939	4	1	0
1940	3	1	1
1941	2	1	0
1942	2	1	0
1943	2	1	0
1944	1	1	0
1945	1	1	0

minute for 25 March 1946 states: 'That the secretary write [to] the Borough Surveyor re. seating from air raid shelters.'[115]

Dilemmas for clubs

The dilemma that clubs faced during the Great War resurfaced in the period 1939–45. Play on out of solidarity with those on the frontline – or stop playing as a mark of respect? This again was a tortuous dilemma. One interesting case study was Hartshead Moor in the Bradford League. In 1941, the club joined the Bradford Section of the Yorkshire Council. Success came immediately as Moor secured the section title after beating a Salts side that included Yorkshire and England star Len Hutton. During the war, the club made every effort to support members who had been called up to active service. In 1940, a photograph of the first eleven in the form of a greetings card was sent to all those who had donned military colours, with a postal order also included. The club reported that in 1941: 'We [were still] not feeling any serious effects of the War in personnel and were still able to field a useful side.'[116]

Another interesting example is Reading. As early as 12 May 1939, a writer on the *Reading Chronicle* was opining:

> This season I imagine that quite a number of local Cricket Clubs will have their usual plans somewhat altered owing to the demands of National Service. What with members' service at weekends in Territorial Units and others being called upon for regular military duties, there may seem to be a shortage of players. Yet all this may provide a blessing in disguise, inasmuch as a local Cricket Club no longer is able to rely regularly upon just a few talented cricketers.[117]

Martin Bishop's work on the Reading Biscuit Factory casts light on the situation. He says that the club struggled on – the 'club would carry on as if there was no war'[118] – whereas during the Great War it shut down completely (he also notes the gradual decrease in media coverage of local cricket). Table 4.1 summarises his findings regarding the number and type of teams put out by the Biscuit Factory during the war.

Interestingly, Bishop says that the Reading club was able to field its three teams (Saturday first eleven and second eleven and Sunday eleven) throughout the war and host matches involving services sides, London Counties eleven and Colonial Forces eleven. He also states that the Biscuit Factory's two grounds were both 'maintained' during the war and that some inter-departmental cricket was played – which seems to suggest that cricket was valued as a 'distraction' from the hardships of war.[119] The same seemed to be true at Exeter. Jeffrey Stanyer calculates that the club played eleven games in 1940, twenty-seven in 1941, nineteen in 1942, nineteen in 1943 and five in late 1945 – and also played games in 1944 and early 1945 but he is unable to deduce how many because the relevant scorebooks have been lost.[120]

We have to remember that cricket clubs were, and are, amateur bodies. They are voluntary associations of like-minded people and negotiating the reality of war would have been a major challenge. The dilemmas they faced were real ones and often tortuous. They had to do the 'right thing' for their country but also for their members. In many cases, the decision about carrying on or not would have been forced on them by the reality of the situation around them.

Dislocation and change

The war brought huge dislocation. Leagues and clubs faced many difficulties. Large numbers of able-bodied men had signed up to fight and many grounds were requisitioned for alternative usage.

Local leagues were affected in different ways. Batley 'temporarily transferred from the Yorkshire Central League to the Yorkshire Council so that proper fixtures may be arranged'.[121] The Ulverston & District League was established in Cumberland in 1925 but was not able to survive the war. The last champions were Leven Valley.[122]

The Hebden Bridge & District League faced major problems. In 1940, the league was reduced to one division of ten clubs and by June so many players had been called up that the committee 'resolved that men from the press be allowed to play for any team in the league for this season'. Local journalists present to report a game were likely to find themselves playing for any team with an unexpected shortfall. To make best use of players before they were called up, fixtures for 24 August 1940 were brought forward to the July holiday break and the play-off semi-finals brought forward to 24 August and the league limped through to September. The AGM in January 1941 was adjourned until player availability was clearer and in March it was 'resolved that owing to the small number of clubs who can raise teams for this season we do not run a league'.[123] The league was in abeyance for over five years.

The next meeting was held on 3 December 1946, when the teams represented were Birchcliffe, Hebden Bridge Salem, Heptonstall Slack 'A' and 'B', Lumbutts, and Old Town 'A' and 'B'. These seven teams contested the 1947 season and in November of that year advertisements for new clubs appeared in the local press. Initially, new teams were attracted, including the first and second elevens of Mytholmroyd Methodists and Todmorden's third eleven. In 1949, there were twelve teams competing and in 1950 the league again ran two divisions. That was the peak of the post-war boom. After that, clubs were lost and advertising for new clubs became an annual ritual.

This seems to be a stark example of how leagues were affected by the war. The rule about journalists seems to be illustrative. With regular cricketers in short supply, the net was widened and pressmen were allowed to step into the breach. It was all very ad hoc but those in charge felt it was appropriate given the circumstances.

Some leagues were rejuvenated. In *Cricket's Wartime Sanctuary: The First-Class Flight to Bradford*, Tony Barker explains how around a hundred first-class cricketers made their way to the Bradford League, including Learie Constantine, Len Hutton and Eddie Paynter. Barker's view is that these big-name professionals faced significant travel problems and had little opportunity for practice, but played a major part in raising morale on the home front.[124]

The Heavy Woollen Cup – centred on Batley and Dewsbury – is an interesting case study. In 1942, the committee decided to use only one new ball (rather than two) per game because of the difficulty of getting balls. There were also eligibility problems. The famous Dewsbury & Savile Club announced that it was not going to play any more competitive fixtures while the war continued, and a year later the railings at the Savile Ground were requisitioned by the authorities with the war effort in mind. But in 1945, the final of the competition raised £150 in receipts. This was the highest figure since 1921 and was probably due, in part, to the ending of the war. Mike Butler writes: 'While celebrating Heckmondwike's victory [local dignitary and chairman of the cup committee, Mr F. Auty] said it was important not to forget the recent sacrifices of so many young men on the various battlefields throughout the world. Rather more controversially, Mr Auty then continued to say that the Germans lacked games of sport and because of this they were not sports themselves and because they were not sports they had lost the war.'[125]

We shouldn't be surprised by the changes and dislocation that war brought. It was inevitable that local sport would be affected by world war and the dislocation that it brought. Competitions were always going to be affected and in many ways it is amazing that so many clubs either kept on playing or were in a position to resume their activities after the war.

To fold or not to fold?

On 20 April 1940, the *Batley News* offered readers a round-up of pre-season cricket news:

> Practices began at Staincliffe last Saturday, about a dozen players turning out. So far the club has not been seriously affected by calling up. Only three of the team –

Chapman, Kaye and Stone – are with the Services. As in previous seasons, Staincliffe will have an amateur eleven. Heckmondwike held their first practice also last Saturday and, so far as can be seen, will lose the services of one first eleven player – Jarrett, a capable batsman. Holmes, Newton, White and Trevitt, all bowlers, will again be the club's professionals.[126]

Many clubs were forced to fold. Rodmersham in Kent ceased playing for the duration of the war and the 'club's minute book was actually used for the minutes and records of The Local Home Guard detachment'.[127] Potterne, a club based in Wiltshire, disbanded in 1939 and re-formed in 1947.[128] Others just hung on. It was a cleric who set the tone in Batley: 'VICAR OF BATLEY WILLING TO PLAY CRICKET. PARISH CHURCH CLUB TO CONTINUE. At a special meeting of Batley Parish Church cricket club members last night it was decided to run a team this season … The Vicar, Rev W.A. Taylor, who presided, said he was willing to play.'[129]

Cumberworth in Huddersfield were forced to cut costs. In 1937 it was announced that players would be allowed 8d (3p) each for fares; but this was rescinded in 1941 when players once again had to pay their own fares to and from matches. But in spite of the effects of the war, the club AGM decided 'that we carry on for 1942'.[130] Cumberworth put out a single side; after the conflict, they returned to running both a first eleven and second eleven. For their part, Kirkheaton – where Wilfred Rhodes and George Herbert Hirst played their early cricket – were forced to make a public appeal:

Dear Sir

At a Special General Meeting held at the Conservative Club in March, 1942, to discuss the financial position of the Cricket Club, it was decided to make an appeal to all members and sportsmen, and to the village as a whole for financial help … Our Cricket Club holds a unique position in the village, it is almost a village institution – offering sports facilities to young and old alike. It is because of this position that we feel we are right in making this appeal. YOU can help in numerous ways. If you are a member, remember the subscription rates are the minimum and an extra shilling or two from each member would go a long way towards clearing off the old debts. If you are not a member, why not join NOW?

Respectfully yours, THE COMMITTEE[131]

Surrey club Weighbridge were able to carry on, even though eighteen club members were called up. As the club itself states: '[We] survived this period intact and with the arrival of the Hurdle family, a great deal of voluntary labour and a wonderful Club spirit, Victory Year in 1945 provided one of the best season's cricket in the Club's short life. With the return of nearly all the members who were in the services it was found possible to field two sides on at least one day each weekend from 1946.'[132] Wavertree in Liverpool were indebted to individuals such as Bob Dempster, Reg Fawcett, Bill Marsden, Frank Wilkinson, Arthur Hooton, Bill Rushworth and Don Walker. 'If it had not been for the efforts of these members, the ground and wicket may never have been properly recovered.'[133]

The Turnham Green club in London also clung on valiantly. Their official history records:

> 1939 – The season was brought to an abrupt close by the outbreak of World War II
> …
>
> 1940 – Many club members served in the Armed Forces and many others had Civil Defence duties to carry out …
>
> 1943 – …As a wartime measure, the railings around the green had been removed and although wear and tear on the playing square was kept in check, the outfield became extremely rough …
>
> 1945 – Members began returning again after the end of the war in Europe and this year became an excellent season for the club …[134]

What this demonstrates is the tenacity of local clubs. Of course, there were the casualties – the clubs that simply could not overcome the barriers put in their way – but there was also plenty of invention, ingenuity and sheer bloody-mindedness. Sport, and cricket in particular, meant a lot to people and it wouldn't be sacrificed without a fight.

The dislocation of war also resulted in various ground switches. Lydney in Gloucestershire played on the Lydney Park Estate for sixty-four years up to 1939. But after the war they relocated to Bathurst Park in Lydney Town and then, in 1949, to Lydney Recreation Ground.[135]

Likewise, there was great fluidity as regards league membership. In Yorkshire, Spofforth flitted between the Wetherby League and Harrogate League.[136] Settle played in the Craven League during the war but returned to the Ribblesdale League in 1946 (but their second eleven stayed in the Craven League). In Lancashire, Blackburn St James were invited to join the Senior League when the war created vacancies in this competition. They had been a successful side in the Junior League and became Blackburn Northern in 1945.[137]

The evidence presented, therefore, is mixed. A proportion of clubs survived and a proportion also folded. Clubs swapped grounds and also leagues. Overall, it was a period of change and fluidity. But perhaps we shouldn't be surprised. This was a world war and the effects on domestic sport were bound to be great. How could they not be? Many clubs were affected directly by the war; others, indirectly and tangentially.

Use of grounds

In a time of war, cricket clubs possessed valuable resources: primarily, young able-bodied men and spacious premises. As we have seen, many clubs were decimated by call-ups and found it hard to keep on fulfilling fixtures. Others had to fall in line with the demands of government or local authorities.

Some clubs had their grounds requisitioned by the government. At Exeter, the Air Ministry and the Army Searchlight Company moved in and the Royal Army Pay Corps took over the sports tenancy.[138] German prisoners of war worked on local farms at Stone in Worcestershire and some of them lived in the cricket club pavilion.[139] At Wavertree in Liverpool, the ground was occupied by the military and actually suffered bomb damage.[140] The home of Cockney in Nottinghamshire, 'was taken over by the Army, who installed a searchlight and anti-aircraft battery'.[141]

Walton Street, home of Sowerby Bridge, was used by the War Office as a prisoner-of-war camp. One barracks official remembers: 'During the war I was stationed at the detention centre, where the cricket ground is now. The ground itself was tarmaced for a parade ground, and two mills on either side of the entrance housed the gym, workshop, sleeping quarters and sergeant's mess.'[142] Approximately two hundred soldiers were held there. One morning one of them broke away and swam across the river and escaped. Someone went after him and caught up with him at the Friendly Pub. As such, the club had to find an alternative venue for its wartime fixtures, and so it lodged temporarily at Sowerby St Peter's, up the hill in Sowerby village. Because of the 'merging' of the two clubs between 1939 and 1945, when the war finally ended, some Sowerby Bridge players switched to the St Peter's club and some players from St Peter's moved in the opposite direction.

Boxted in Suffolk also had to fall in line. In 1938, the local council gifted them a patch of land on Cage Lane, which they shared with the local football team. But when war broke out they were exiled from their new ground. The club website records that, 'Some of the field was ploughed up to grow wartime crops, though we believe our cricket square was spared this humiliation. On the cessation of hostilities, the field was restored and we returned to our sedate friendly cricket.'[142] At Oakham, Rutland, the cricket ground went under the plough and was 'used for agricultural purposes'. In 1946, club members, led by stalwart groundsman Len Tucker, worked on 'ploughing, re-seeding and rolling the ground and fixtures were arranged for the 1947 season'.[144]

After the war, at Himbleton in Worcestershire, 'The secretary pointed out that the club could have the use of the field at Court Farm again "but that the pitch would need a lot of work put into it". This proved to be a masterly understatement. Only with great difficulty could players find the "square". Eventually it was discovered by lining up a particular tree and after much effort fixtures were resumed.'[145] Lowdham in Nottinghamshire lost their home at Brakes Farm at the start of the war. 'Flat land was to be used for agriculture, and so Brakes Farm was conscripted. The new field [at Lodge Farm], which included a pond, a flat square and sharply sloping outfield was used during the War. The changing room was a double decker bus.'[146]

Cricket grounds were obviously key local resources. Some might be uncared for but in a wartime context they had the potential to be used for a variety of purposes. Some were inhabited by the military, others by prisoners. Some were turned over to agricultural use so as to assist the overall war effort. What we see in general is a sport that, whether it liked it or not, was instrumental to the war effort at a local level.

Charity and solidarity

During the war, the MCC staged a number of fundraising games at Lord's. Local clubs also arranged, and took part in, a variety of charity matches. Starting in 1940, Sheffield Collegiate organised special fixtures at Abbeydale Park. In June 1941, an RAF eleven (including Cyril Washbrook in its ranks) took on The Army (including Maurice Leyland) at the Niagra Sports Ground, Sheffield, 'on behalf of the Benevolent Funds of the Services'.[147] In the same month, 'For war charities, Mr Jack Appleyard's (Leeds) eleven played Ardsley at East Ardsley on Wednesday evening, scoring 137 for 6 wickets.'[148] In July 1941, a match between the Birstall section of the Special Constabulary and Batley AFS (Auxiliary Fire Service) Section C (Birstall) took place, each side batting for 75 minutes, with more than £5 being raised for charity.[149]

Many matches were played in support of the Red Cross and local comforts funds. In September 1940, Birstall first eleven played the club's second eleven – with the first-teamers winning by 76 runs – in a match for the Red Cross.[150] In July 1941, Mr J. Appleyard's (Leeds) eleven also played the Octurians in a 'Red Cross cricket match'.[151] Upper Hopton, near Dewsbury, were involved in charity matches against Mirfield Parish Church and Whitley Lower to raise money for the Red Cross. In the Holme Valley, the Lancaster Cup raised money for the same organisation. The third Geneva Convention, signed in 1929, gave the Red Cross a higher profile in the Second World War than it had during the Great War. During the 1939-45 conflict, it, 'carried out extensive services for the sick and wounded, for prisoners of war and for civilians needing relief as a result of enemy action, at home and abroad'.[152]

Golcar in Huddersfield raised money for the Golcar Comforts Fund, with money being sent to servicemen abroad. Those serving overseas were also granted free membership of the club. Thongsbridge in Holmfirth lost some of their greatest players in the war. In support of their efforts, the remaining players organised, and then played in, a special benefit match to help raise money for Christmas gifts to be sent to seventy to eighty local men fighting in the war.

The same pattern was evident elsewhere. In June 1940, a benefit match took place between R. Dewhurst and Co. Brookroyd Printworks and Birstall Town, raising £7 7s 9d for soldiers' comforts.[153] In July 1940, the *Batley News* reported on a 'War Comforts Fund match' between Birstall Tradesmen and Birstall Carpet Co. A week later, it stated: 'A match for soldiers' comforts at Staincliffe on Wednesday, each side batting one hour, resulted in defeat for Staincliffe CC by a Common Road Club team. Common Road made 109 for seven, and Staincliffe's reply was 102 for six. A good crowd present saw Whitaker (Spen) make a dashing

68 and witnessed 'Teddy' Hirst take three wickets for two runs.'[154] In September 1940, 'A cricket match in aid of Messrs. M.Oldroyd and Son's soldiers' and sailors' comforts at Staincliffe cricket ground ... realised £6 10s. The firm's warpers and tuners opposed the willeyers and yard men.'[155]

In May 1941, the *Batley News* noted an AFS inter-station match at Birstall – with Section D (Batley Carr) defeating Section C (Birstall) – in aid of the AFS 'and Home Guard Comforts'. A game was also planned between the Birstall Section of the Home Guard and a local AFS side.[156] In July 1941, an Edwin St. Hill eleven played a Heavy Woollen eleven, 'in aid of Birstall Cricket Club and Birstall Town Football Club Soldiers' Comforts Fund'.[157]

The Comforts Fund – an amalgam of many local funds – played a crucial role during the war. Money raised by local communities was put towards various 'comforts' for the troops: clothes, food, tobacco, newspapers, goodwill messages, writing materials, playing cards, and other gifts. The fund is generally viewed as being instrumental in maintaining the morale of the troops on the frontline.

So cricket did its bit. As a community sport – perhaps the best example of such – it was at the forefront of local, charitable efforts.

After the war

Wigglesworth has assessed the significance of the Second World War for sport in Britain. He argues that the war, and victory in it, increased the confidence of the 'public school establishment', and thus, their 'Corinthian emphasis on team games' was enhanced.[158] In a different sense, he also claims that the war led to a 'democratisation of leisure activities' through improved communications after the war and the birth of bodies such as the Sports Development Council.[159]

In his book, *The Evolution of English Sport*, Wigglesworth also focuses on other legacies of the 1939–45 war. He argues, for example, that the conflict had a significant legacy as regards Britain's sporting prowess. He writes: 'The war, national service and rationing all had a part to play in explaining Britain's continuing lack of international sporting success and the Labour government certainly had different priorities, notably welfareism, housing and education, with sport only being officially considered as an educational issue.'[160] By contrast, he argues, sport also had the potential to 'provide a boost for morale' in peacetime – and he cites the fact that attendances at football matches rose in the late 1940s as evidence of this.[161]

The war could not but have significant consequences for sport, and cricket in particular. Obviously, for six years, men had been recruited to fight and local amenities, such as cricket grounds, had been put to the service of the war effort. Clubs were naturally affected adversely. However, at the same time, there were glimmers of light. While many clubs had to fold, at least temporarily, other clubs were able to carry on. Sport was important to people, it was part of their lives, and many would have felt that carrying on playing was the right thing to do.

The evidence was varied. In the post-war era, London club Winchmore Hill seemed to benefit from its exertions during the conflict. 'Cricket continued through the Second World War to provide recreation and social functions for members of the services on leave and following the war many charity fundraising matches were played. The club continued to flourish, fielding six and sometimes seven elevens through the 1950s and 60s ... After hostilities had ceased, sport flourished at Ford's Grove with many members returning from the services.'[162]

A similar situation existed at Hutton in Essex, where it has been argued that older club members, in particular, were vital to the continuation of cricket. The club, it seems, benefited from their work and grew significantly as a result in the immediate post-war period.[163]

It was conceivable that some clubs might accrue some advantage from the wartime experience. Those that were affected less by call-ups and those that had other natural advantages were in a position to grow in the immediate post-war years.

At Wavertree in Liverpool, the 1946 season was 'transitory' and in 1947, 'full power came back to the Club's arm'.[164] In Reading,

> The war years had been difficult for the Huntley and Palmers CC and had seen a gradual decline in the club's activity. The club did not have the advantage or impetus given at the start of the 1919 season (of the new ground at Kensington Road) to kick start it back into peacetime life and for the 1946 season it tentatively fielded 'A', 'B' and junior teams. Over the following few years the club gradually recovered until in 1956 it was to field four teams on Saturday, an occasional midweek team, a junior team and, for the first time in its history, a regular Sunday side which had been introduced following the war. The *First Name News* of September 1956 reported that the club had fulfilled over 100 fixtures in the season. The club maintained this level of activity into the 1960s. Interdepartmental and ladies cricket, although being played, never recovered to pre-war levels.[165]

This shows what a landmark the war was. But, even though total recovery was difficult, it was still impressive that several teams re-emerged as early as 1946.

In Gloucestershire, there was a similar story. It was a case of gradually getting back to normal:

> After seven years of inactivity ... Chipping Sodbury Cricket Club staged a modest comeback following a public meeting held at the Literary Institute at the beginning of April, 1947, when Major L. Montague Harris presided ... It was decided to operate one team only, initially, although there was plenty of enthusiasm among the players. The Club played its first match since 1939 at The Ridings on May 17th, defeating Pro-Cathedral C.C. by 90 runs ... The general feeling expressed at the annual meeting on December 5th, 1947, was that the Club had made good progress under adverse conditions during its first year of activity since the war and with increased interest much in evidence it was decided to field two teams in 1948. The Club's financial

position, however, was none too rosy as a result of abnormally heavy expenditure which included £30 on repairs to the old pavilion.[166]

There was also relief and celebration. In 1944, England played two one-day games against a Royal Australian Airforce side. A year later, when the Allies' military victory had been confirmed, England and Australia played five unofficial 'Victory' Tests, with both sides winning two matches each. The County Championship also resumed.

The homecoming accorded to Yorkshire and England bowler Bill Bowes at Menston, near Leeds, says a lot about the post-war atmosphere: 'On Whit Monday, 21st May, the 1st XI v North Leeds proudly included W.E. Bowes. What an attraction he created – like a visitor from Mars or a man with two heads – it seemed as though not only Menston, but the whole of Wharfedale came to see him. It was in fact a genuine gesture of affection and thanks-giving for the homecoming of a well loved Yorkshire and England cricketer.'[162]

There were key patterns and trends. First, it has been argued that the war and its effects were fundamental to the demise of amateurism. According to Frank Tyson, 'The social destruction wrought by the Second World War and the high level of post-war taxation killed the amateur in English county cricket stone dead. After 1945 there weren't any lilies of the cricketing field who spun not nor wove; no one had sufficient time or income to devote seven days a week playing cricket without receiving some recompense ... So it was the 'shamateur' came into being ... receiving no direct payment as a player from the county clubs, but getting instead under-the-counter rewards as a junior administrator.'[168] Many historians have studied the relationship between war and social change, and cricket was not immune.

Amateur status was finally abolished in 1962. It has been argued that, 'The underlying reason for the abolition was the tide of social change in the wake of the Second World War with the growth of both a more egalitarian society in general and a demand for dedicated professionalism in sports such as cricket and football that became increasingly conscious of their business obligations and the need to generate income through success on the field.'[169]

Second, at a local level, many clubs re-formed officially. West Bretton, near Wakefield, staged a general meeting on 22 March 1946, just seven months after the formal end of hostilities. The minute read:

18 members present. Chairman FW Middleton. Enough support was evident to enable reformation of WBCC to officially take place. Inventory of remaining equipment would occur. Scoreboard, Umpires coats, bails, scoring numbers, matting and net would have to be replaced or repaired. The 'Petroleum Board' would be approached – reference the supply of petrol for the mower. J Smith was authorised to mow the outfield (for 5 shillings) and WT Lund would undertake the duty of Groundsman. Subscription 5 shillings per player.[170]

It is noticeable how, so soon after a war had taken place, attention had turned to 'trivialities' – for example, umpires coats, bails, petrol for the mower. But this was the nature of local cricket; these were now important issues to sort out.

Himbleton in Worcestershire held their first post-war AGM on 6 May 1946, and fortuitously perhaps, the club was in the black. 'The first business ... was to confirm the minutes of the meeting presided over by Colonel Hill on April 28th 1939. After a break of six years for the war a credit balance of £18. 15s. 0d. was reported.'[171]

The cricketers of Great Brickhill, Buckinghamshire, gathered on 25 June 1946. The acting chairman is recorded as saying:

> They were meeting that evening to decide the future of Great Brickhill Cricket. They had always been very proud of their village cricket team and it would indeed be a great pity if the grand old game of cricket was not once again started on the field which they had played for so many years. He personally thought that every effort should be made to get the game re-started as soon as possible in the village. He was quite sure that there was a real keenness amongst the younger members present and he did not think there should be great difficulty in getting a really useful team in the near future.

A committee was set up and a village fête helped raise £136 12s 10d for the revived club.[172]

The formalities involved in re-starting a cricket club are in evidence here. Clubs were respected local institutions and they would have wanted to do things properly, at committee meetings, AGMs and other formal gatherings. Villagers would have been expecting official statements and announcements.

At Endon in Staffordshire, it appears that,

> the only cricket played ... after the Second World War came at the Endon Secondary Modern School sports field ... However, in 1948 a number of interested players decided to reform Endon Cricket Club. A ground was obtained on land adjoining Moss Hill Farm, near to the old Stockton Brook Tennis Courts. Games were subsequently played on this ground until 1962. In fact the then Treasurer of the Club, Reg Boote, had a house built next to the ground, so he could watch games in his retirement! A pavilion was bought from Butterton Cricket Club, but problems still existed in keeping the outfield cut and the wicket mown. The number of fixtures increased at this time, with a number of teams a distance away, which caused transport issues – for many years the team was picked on who was in possession of a car![173]

Caythorpe in Nottinghamshire re-formed in 1949. Between 1946 and 1948, many of the club's cricketers had turned out for Hoveringham and Derbyshire and Nottinghamshire Power Company, but soon the possibility of re-formation became a reality:

The village had a flourishing youth club and early in 1949 Mr. M. Archer invited P. Antcliffe, the youth club leader, together with would-be cricketers to an 'at home' social evening at which it became clear that there was a distinct possibility of re-forming Caythorpe C.C. with a blend of experienced players and interested youth club members ... An unofficial approach to the D.& N.P.Co. regarding the possibility of sharing their ground proved positive. The pre-war Treasurer, Mr. Griffiths was contacted about the monies held by him on the Club's behalf and candidates for a fund raising committee were sounded out. Meanwhile more enthusiasm was created by two very successful matches played under the name of a 'Black Horse XI' against a Notts Casuals XI and a Hoveringham Reindeer XI.[174]

The same kind of situation existed at nearby Cuckney where, 'the tennis and bowls sections were not revived, but Wilfred Hill started up the cricket club again for the benefit of returning servicemen'.[175] And at Evesham in Worcestershire, we are told of 'progress and expansion ... well in evidence in the 1950s'. On the playing front, the club was helped by the disappearance of a number of local teams due to the war.[176]

Third, it is interesting to note the number of clubs that moved into new premises. In 1946, Turnham Green in London moved from the local green to Chiswick House: 'Facilities were not as they are today, the changing rooms were two little huts (one was later used by the groundsman) and a marquee was used for teas, the latter being erected every week.'[177] In 1952, the local businessmen and councillors who were at the forefront of efforts to re-found Dewsbury-based Mirfield (the original club had disbanded in 1919) were helped by the fact that there was a 'vacancy' at the Memorial Ground – the local park. In 1951, the lease held by the Craven Gentlemen – another Mirfield-based cricket team – had run out, and new cricketing tenants were being sought. The club started playing again in 1952.[178] The pattern was the same at Padiham in Lancashire. The club folded after the Great War, but in 1947 there were moves to re-found the club. Work began on a new ground at the Arbories and when it was opened it was dedicated to the fallen of the Second World War.[179]

Fourth, there were some strange legacies of the war. In 1960, the fuselage of a Second World War glider was used as the new pavilion at Birchencliffe in Huddersfield. And at Stone in Worcestershire, a new pavilion, 'was constructed by Gino, an Italian ex P.O.W. who had previously been a carpenter in Italy before the war. He worked ... for John Green at Lower House Farm at Chaddesley Corbett. The old Nissan hut was utilised as a tea room to begin with but later a new one was constructed, again by Gino.'[180]

The last word should be left to Hill. He claims that by the 1960s central government was more involved in sport and leisure than it had ever been before.[181] This was a product of the war and the years that followed rather then being the result of any major scheme or plan. Perhaps inadvertently this was one of the most important legacies of the Second World War and the period that followed.

Notes

1 J. Hill, *Sport, Leisure and Culture in Twentieth-Century Britain* (London, Macmillan, 2002), p. 152.
2 N. Wigglesworth, *The Evolution of English Sport* (London, Routledge, 2004), p. 124.
3 *Ibid.*, p. 108.
4 S. Sassoon, *Dreamers*, 1918.
5 D. Birley, *A Social History of English Cricket* (London, Aurum Press, 2003), p. 355.
6 J.H. Dowd, *The Kaiser's Cricket*, undated.
7 http://en.wikipedia.org/wiki/Cricket_in_World_War_I (last accessed 17 Mar 2012).
8 *Batley News*, 5 May 1917.
9 www.culture24.org.uk/places+to+go/north+west/manchester/art23136 (last accessed 17 Mar 2012).
10 See M. Marqusee, *War Minus the Shooting* (London, Mandarin, 1997).
11 See http://news.bbc.co.uk/1/hi/uk/4123107.stm (last accessed 17 Mar 2012).
12 It is also worth pointing out that the notion of a 'Golden Age' in English cricket in the late nineteenth and early twentieth centuries only really came about because of the war, the dislocation that it brought, and the nostalgic feeling that, once upon a time, in a more innocent age, things had been much better.
13 www.spartacus.schoolnet.co.uk/Jconan.htm (last accessed 17 Mar 2012).
14 www.ckcricketheritage.org.uk/southkirklees/armitagebridge/clubhome.htm (last accessed 17 Mar 2012).
15 J. Stanyer, *A Great Survivor: The History of The Exeter Cricket Club in the Nineteenth and Twentieth Centuries* (Exeter, St Leonard's Press, 2000), p. 219.
16 T. Lister, *You Couldn't Make It Up! The Complete History of Burnley Cricket Club 1834–2008* (Huddersfield, Cricket Heritage Publications, 2009), p. 21.
17 Wigglesworth, *Evolution of English Sport*, p. 121.
18 *Huddersfield Daily Examiner*, 31 Aug 1914.
19 *Ibid.*
20 www.ckcricketheritage.org.uk/southkirklees/holmbridge/docs/holmbridge_theearlyyears.pdf (last accessed 17 Mar 2012).
21 www.harrowcricketclub.co.uk/history/default.aspx (last accessed 17 Mar 2012).
22 www.turnhamgreencc.org/pages/content/index.asp?PageID=101 (last accessed 17 Mar 2012).
23 www.ckcricketheritage.org.uk/docs/032108WALSDEN842WALearly.pdf (last accessed 17 Mar 2012).
24 www.ckcricketheritage.org.uk/calderdale/illingworth/clubhome.htm (last accessed 17 Mar 2012).
25 See P. Neal with J. Norbury, *Thank You, Mr Ingham: A History of Mirfield Cricket Club* (Huddersfield, Cricket Heritage Publications, 2006) and www.ribblesdale cricketleague.co.uk/Padiham.htm (last accessed 17 Mar 2012).
26 *Batley News*, 18 Aug 1917.
27 M. Williamson, www.cricinfo.com (last accessed 21 Aug 2009).
28 www.brickhillcricket.co.uk (last accessed 17 Mar 2012).
29 www.henfieldcricketclub.com/articles/history.html (last accessed 17 Mar 2012).
30 www.astoncricketclub.co.uk/club-history/4532805863 (last accessed 17 Mar 2012).
31 www.stannescricketclub.org/clubhistory.php (last accessed 17 Mar 2012).
32 www.ckcricketheritage.org.uk/southkirklees/honley/docs/honley_theearlyyears.pdf (last accessed 17 Mar 2012).

33   www.rodmershamcc.co.uk/History.htm (last accessed 17 Mar 2012).

34   www.chippingsodburycc.co.uk/cricket-history/ (last accessed 17 Mar 2012).

35   www.crowhurstcc.co.uk/history/history.htm (last accessed 17 Mar 2012).

36   www.cwgc.org/admin/files/cricket%20leaflet.pdf (last accessed 16 Oct 2011).

37   Wigglesworth, *Evolution of English Sport*, p. 110.

38   Williamson, www.cricinfo.com (last accessed 21 Aug 2009).

39   *Ibid.*

40   *Ibid.*

41   *Huddersfield Daily Examiner*, 17 Jun 1915.

42   *Batley News*, 2 Sep 1916 and 6 Apr 1918.

43   www.stockportcc.co.uk/war_memorial.htm (last accessed 17 Mar 2012).

44   www.ckcricketheritage.org.uk/calderdale/mytholmroyd/clubhome.htm   (last accessed 17 Mar 2012).

45   D. Goodall, *Wavertree Cricket Club: 151 Years of Cricket: A Written and Pictorial History* (Wakefield, Charlesworth Group, 2006), p. 37.

46   Neal, *Thank You, Mr Ingham*, p. 39.

47   C. Farnworth and S. Hall, *Bacup Cricket Club: The Authorised History* (Bacup, Bacup Cricket Club, 1999), p. 13.

48   *Halifax Courier*, 27 May 1916.

49   *Batley News*, 24 April 1915.

50   See M. Butler, *From Batley to Barnsley* (Huddersfield, Cricket Heritage Publications, 2006), Chapter 3.

51   Ashton-under-Lyne CC, *A History of Ashton-under-Lyne CC*, Ashton, p. 21.

52   Wigglesworth, *Evolution of English Sport*, p. 121.

53   Stanyer, *A Great Survivor*, pp. 218–19.

54   *Huddersfield Daily Examiner*, 26 Aug 1914.

55   M. Bishop, *Bats, Balls and Biscuits* (Huddersfield, Cricket Heritage Publications, 2008).

56   *Batley News*, 5 May 1917.

57   See www.ckcricketheritage.org.uk (last accessed 17 Mar 2012).

58   In 1918, Ashton-under-Lyne raised £350 for the POW fund – see Ashton-under-Lyne CC, *A History of Ashton-under-Lyne CC*, pp. 5, 21, 22.

59   www.turnhamgreencc.org (last accessed 17 Mar 2012).

60   *Halifax Courier*, 5 May 1916.

61   *Halifax Courier*, 19 May 1916.

62   *Halifax Courier*, 29 May 1916.

63   R. Holt, *Sport and the British* (London, Clarendon Press, 1990), p. 265.

64   Wigglesworth, *Evolution of English Sport*, p. 110.

65   J. Williams, *Cricket and England* (London, Frank Cass, 1999).

66   Goodall, *Wavertree Cricket Club*, pp. 37–8.

67   www.ckcricketheritage.org.uk (last accessed 17 Mar 2012).

68   Bishop, *Bats, Balls and Biscuits*, p. 100.

69   http://weybridgecc.co.uk/history.asp (last accessed 17 Mar 2012).

70   www.tacc.org.uk/clubhistory.asp.

71   *Ibid.*

72   www.southportcricket.co.uk/history.html (last accessed 17 Mar 2012).

73   www.cumbriaslevenvalley.co.uk/57.html (last accessed 16 Oct 2011).

74   Farnworth and Hall, *Bacup Cricket Club*, p. 23.

75   Williams, *Cricket and England*, pp. 121, 123.

76   www.webwanderers.org/02_places/whickham (last accessed 17 Mar 2012).

77   www.ckcricketheritage.org.uk/docs/101908FLOCK11CH.pdf (last accessed 17 Mar 2012).

78 www.midlandhistory.bham.ac.uk/issues/1974b/hastinrp.pdf (last accessed 16 Oct 2011).
79 www.espncricinfo.com/cricketer/content/story/261262.html (last accessed 17 Mar 2012).
80 www.webwanderers.org (last accessed 17 Mar 2012).
81 Williams, *Cricket and England*, p.124.
82 *Ibid.*
83 www.ckcricketheritage.org.uk/southkirklees/golcar/clubhome.htm (last accessed 17 Mar 2012).
84 Goodall, *Wavertree Cricket Club*, p. 44.
85 www.benefice.org.uk/the_parish_times/cricket_and_the_church.php (last accessed 17 Mar 2012).
86 T. Barker, *Cricket's Wartime Sanctuary: The First-Class Flight to Bradford* (Sussex, Association of Cricket Statisticians & Historians, 2009).
87 *Ibid.*
88 www.britwellsalomecricketclub.co.uk/content/history.htm (last accessed 17 Mar 2012).
89 B. Shaw (ed.), *A History of Evesham Cricket Club* (Evesham, Evesham Cricket Club, 2004), p. 18.
90 Bishop, *Bats, Balls and Biscuits*, p. 121.
91 On 17 May 1941, *Batley News* reported on Birstall CC weighing up whether they should play a Sunday match with first-class cricketers promised.
92 www.ckcricketheritage.org.uk/calderdale/mytholmroyd/clubhome.htm (last accessed 17 Mar 2012).
93 In Todmorden, the local council had started the ball rolling – bowling in the local park had been allowed. Interview with Brian Heywood: 6 Jul 2009.
94 *Ibid.*
95 www.ckcricketheritage.org.uk/southkirklees/holmbridge/clubhome.htm (last accessed 17 Mar 2012).
96 Cartoon by David Low.
97 See Birley, *Social History*.
98 *Rotherham Advertiser*, 22 Apr 1939
99 www.smh.com.au › Sport › Cricket (last accessed 16 Oct 2011).
100 Wigglesworth, *Evolution of English Sport*, p. 111.
101 *Batley News*, 8 May 1943.
102 *Batley News*, 20 Jul 1940.
103 *Batley News*, 19 Jul 1941.
104 www.espncricinfo.com/ci/content/story/155357.html (last accessed 17 Mar 2012).
105 *Huddersfield Daily Examiner*, 1 Apr 1940.
106 Shaw, *Evesham Cricket Club*, p. 21.
107 See research wor undertaken by Brian Heywood at Todmorden CC.
108 www.chippingsodburycc.co.uk/cricket-history/world-war-two-beckons,209.htm (last accessed 17 Mar 2012).
109 Goodall, *Wavertree Cricket Club*, p. 53.
110 Shaw, *Evesham Cricket Club*, p. 24.
111 http://guildfordcc.com/club/club_history.html (last accessed 17 Mar 2012).
112 www.upton-wirral.co.uk/upt15.php (last accessed 17 Mar 2012).
113 Stanyer, *A Great Survivor*, p.220.
114 *Batley News*, 12 Jul 1941.

115 www.ckcricketheritage.org.uk/calderdale/walsden/clubhome.htm (last accessed 17 Mar 2012).
116 www.ckcricketheritage.org.uk/northkirklees/hartsheadmoor/clubhome.htm (last accessed 17 Mar 2012).
117 Bishop, Bats, Balls and Biscuits, p. 125.
118 Ibid.
119 Ibid.
120 Stanyer, A Great Survivor, p. 220.
121 Batley News, 19 Apr 1941.
122 www.cumbriaslevenvalley.co.uk/57.html (last accessed 16 Oct 2011).
123 www.ckcricketheritage.org.uk/docs/HBLGeneral_000.pdf (last accessed 17 Mar 2012).
124 See Barker, Cricket's Wartime Sanctuary.
125 Butler, From Batley to Barnsley, p. 59.
126 Batley News, 20 Apr 1940.
127 www.rodmershamcc.co.uk (last accessed 17 Mar 2012).
128 www.potternecc.org.uk/about-us.htm (last accessed 17 Mar 2012).
129 Batley News, 20 Apr 1940.
130 www.ckcricketheritage.org.uk/southkirklees/cumberworth/clubhome.htm (last accessed 17 Mar 2012).
131 www.ckcricketheritage.org.uk/docs/051108KH2851942ApplLetter.pdf (last accessed 17 Mar 2012).
132 http://weybridgecc.co.uk/history.asp (last accessed 17 Mar 2012).
133 Goodall, Wavertree Cricket Club, p. 53.
134 www.turnhamgreencc.org/pages/content/index.asp?PageID=101 (last accessed 17 Mar 2012).
135 www.lydneycricketclub.org.uk (last accessed 17 Mar 2012).
136 www.spofforthcc.org.uk/History/History_index.htm (last accessed 17 Mar 2012).
137 www.ribblesdalecricketleague.co.uk/Blackburn%20Northern.htm (last accessed 17 Mar 2012).
138 Stanyer, A Great Survivor, pp. 219–20.
139 http://stonecc.co.uk/index.php/history-of-stone-cc/ (last accessed 17 Mar 2012).
140 Goodall, Wavertree Cricket Club, p.53.
141 www.cuckneycc.com/
142 www.ckcricketheritage.org.uk/.../Concise%20History%20of%20Club.pdf (last accessed 16 Oct 2011).
143 www.boxtedcricketclub.co.uk/boxted-cc.../4517048139 (last accessed 16 Oct 2011).
144 www.oakhamcricketclub.co.uk/history.php (last accessed 17 Mar 2012).
145 www.himbletoncc.org.uk/About%20Pages/History-Peters.html (last accessed 17 Mar 2012).
146 www.pitchero.com/clubs/lowdhamcricketclub/a/history-17514.html (last accessed 17 Mar 2012).
147 Halifax Courier, 25 Jun 1941 and 27 Jun 1941.
148 Batley News, 14 Jun 1941.
149 Batley News, 19 Jun 1941.
150 Batley News, 14 Sep 1940.
151 Batley News, 19 Jul 1941.
152 See www.redcross.org.uk/About-us/Who-we-are/History-and-origin/Second-World-War (last accessed 17 Mar 2012).
153 Batley News, 22 Jun 1940.

154 *Batley News*, 27 Jul 1940.
155 *Batley News*, 7 Sep 1940.
156 *Batley News*, 31 May 1941.
157 *Batley News*, 19 Jul 1941.
158 Wigglesworth, *Evolution of English Sport*, p. 3.
159 *Ibid.*, pp. 10–11.
160 *Ibid.*, p. 131.
161 *Ibid.*, p. 132.
162 www.wearewhcc.com/history (last accessed 17 Mar 2012).
163 http://huttoncc.hitscricket.com/history/default.aspx (last accessed 17 Mar 2012).
164 Goodall, *Wavertree Cricket Club*, pp. 57–8.
165 Bishop, *Bats, Balls and Biscuits*, p. 129.
166 www.chippingsodburycc.co.uk (last accessed 17 Mar 2012)
167 J.H. Kell, *The History of Menston Cricket Club* (Ilkley, Scolar Press, 1980), p. 20.
168 http://en.wikipedia.org/wiki/Amateur_status_in_first-class_cricket (last accessed 17 Mar 2012).
169 *Ibid.*
170 www.westbrettoncc.com (last accessed 17 Mar 2012).
171 www.himbletoncc.org.uk/About%20Pages/History-Peters.html (last accessed 17 Mar 2012).
172 www.brickhillcricket.co.uk (last accessed 17 Mar 2012).
173 http://endon.org/cricket-club (last accessed 17 Mar 2012).
174 www.caythorpecc.co.uk/history.asp (last accessed 17 Mar 2012).
175 www.cuckneycc.com/history.php (last accessed 17 Mar 2012).
176 Shaw, *Evesham Cricket Club*, pp. 22, 25.
177 www.turnhamgreencc.org/pages/content/index.asp?PageID=101 (last accessed 17 Mar 2012).
178 www.ckcricketheritage.org.uk/northkirklees/mirfield/clubhome.htm (last accessed 17 Mar 2012).
179 www.padihamcc.co.uk/1947-1949.html (last accessed 17 Mar 2012).
180 http://stonecc.co.uk/index.php/history-of-stone-cc/ (last accessed 17 Mar 2012).
181 See Hill, *Sport, Leisure and Culture*, Chapter 9.

5   Decline and renewal

In 2004, Longsight, part of Longsight & District Sports & Social Club and located three miles out of Manchester city centre, was forced to close. The area had become run down, key families had moved out, and the bowlers, snooker players and darts players who belonged to the same organisation felt that the cricket section didn't pay its way. On the field the club had been holding its own, but off the field it was being run by a small group of stalwarts. One of these, former cricket chairman Brian Collier, said: 'We had a lot of Asian players. They were very nice lads and were good cricketers, but they were reluctant to take on adminis-trative responsibilities. After 150 years, the club folded.'[1]

In the opinion of Birley, village clubs have fared slightly better than urban clubs when it comes to survival. But it is not that simple. He focuses on the example of Troon CC in Cornwall. The club has survived but there has also been decline, with many of the youngsters moving away and giving up on the club.[2] Even rural Worcestershire has not been immune. The official history of Evesham states: 'Already in 1984 the Chairman's special report to the AGM was deploring the lack of back-up work from members and appealing urgently for support.'[3]

So, a key theme in this chapter is decline. Between 1970 and 2000, this was most evident in urban settings but it affected grassroots cricket across the board. Why was this? A number of reasons can be put forward. First, cricket was inevitably affected by social and economic change. The 1970s and 1980s witnessed an economic downturn: a three-day week, inflation, recession and widespread unemployment. 'Labour isn't working' was the Conservatives' mantra in 1978; eleven years of Thatcherism was supposed to put the country back on track. But many traditional industries were on the verge of collapse – textiles and coal mining, for example. Local communities were struggling to survive. And local sport could not but be affected as towns and villages were forced to adapt and change. At Great Brickhill, 'the period between 1973 and 1977 was one of severe inflation, and the Club found its increasing funds being eroded by rising costs'.[4] In some places, the local cricket club played a key role – it was a pillar of the community. In others, it was the first casualty, and the consequences of its demise were far-reaching. This was predominantly an urban pattern. The country-side was less affected — it had other challenges to deal with.

At the same time, society was changing. Cricket clubs were in decline not because people were 'hard up' as such; rather, communities — and thus clubs — were haemorrhaging because of changing patterns of work. Large groups of men no longer worked together in factories or mines. Instead, they worked in the new service industries — in banking, sales, accountancy and marketing. The camaraderie was not the same, there was less chat about sport, less back-slapping and less overt displays of masculinity. A key issue was mobility. In the old days, local cricket was full of odd geographical rubrics. Lancashire League sides could only pick players who lived within two or three, and then five, miles of their ground. In West Yorkshire, only clubs located within a five-mile radius of Batley Town Hall could enter the Heavy Woollen Cup.[5] But in the post-war years, families might now have one or two cars, and with improvements in the network of roads and motorways there was greater potential for working away from home. Loyalties were going to be tested and ties with local clubs were going to be loosened. In fact, cricketers could now pick and choose their club; they weren't simply restricted to the 'closest' club or the club they had played their junior cricket for.

Second, there were now many more alternatives to cricket as a pastime and leisure pursuit. Television was invented in the 1950s and those who in previous decades had either played or watched cricket at weekends now had a ready-made alternative in their own front room. The leisure industry also opened up in the post-war decades. In a typical village in the inter-war and immediate post-war years the local cricket club was a focal point. There was little else to do. Men would play cricket and women would watch or make the teas. But in the 1960s and 1970s, other attractions emerged, including supermarkets, cinemas and sports centres. Later, the heritage industry developed. Suddenly, there were many and various alternatives to playing and watching local league cricket on a Saturday or Sunday afternoon.

The logical consequence was that men would find it harder to justify playing cricket (once, perhaps twice) at a weekend, especially when some leagues were so demanding in terms of commitment (for example, in 2009, in the Lancashire League, a player playing every game for a team that reached the knockout final would have played thirty-five games — with most weekends comprising double-headers). At Church in Lancashire, two players approached the club committee with a novel idea at the start of one season. Because of family commitments they wanted to play 'as one player' — a kind of job-share arrangement. One or other of them would always be available for first-team duty. They wanted to play but not all of the time, and they didn't want to miss a game and be left out in the cold.[6]

Third, cricket has had to compete with football and other sports.

Commentators have talked about 'sport space'.[7] Football came of age in the 1950s and 1960s. By 1992 and the launch of the Premier League it was undisputably the number-one sport in England. It was 'glamorous' and 'sexy', commercialised to the hilt, and awash with star names. The two seasons continued to overlap and some cricket leagues took the decision to schedule April and September fixtures on Sundays so as to avoid clashes with football.[8] As the pace of life quickened up, cricket, apart from its gradual move towards limited-overs formats, didn't seem to be changing or responding. Time was precious and sports fans wanted instant gratification, but cricket – at county level and the grassroots – had stood still. Only in 2003 with the introduction of Twenty20 cricket did the authorities make a genuine play for a new kind of audience. The fact that the England cricket team was generally quite poor in the 1970s and 1980s also had a knock-on effect. Cricket-playing youngsters had few role-models to be inspired by.

But despite its mounting problems, local cricket has renewed itself in numerous ways in the last decades of the twentieth century.

Multiculturalism: the enriching of the local game

> A group which provides support for the Asian community has received a grant to help it start its own cricket club. Following a funding boost from the National Lottery, the Blackheath Asian Forum will now be able to run a cricket club for players aged 16 and over.[9]

For the best part of a century, league cricket in England has been enhanced and enriched by the contribution of local ethnic communities. The first overseas professionals arrived in the early years of the twentieth century – New South Walian Alex Kermode (Bacup) and fellow Australian E.B. Dwyer (Rawtenstall) both signed up in 1910; it could be argued that this was a result of the increased ambition of some local clubs and improvements in international travel.

In the 1930s, Slaithwaite, in the West Riding of Yorkshire, was a grand and rather distinguished club. Its membership – playing and non-playing – would have comprised villagers, and probably only villagers: not because there was a bar on 'non-villagers' playing but because the lack of transport meant that playing for your local (e.g. nearest) club was the only option. But as clubs like Slaithwaite became more successful, they became more ambitious. Instead of hiring an English professional from Huddersfield or Bradford, why not go further afield? Why not employ somebody from another country? An overseas batsman whose talent would frustrate Huddersfield & District League bowlers or an international spin bowler whose repertoire and variation would bamboozle local batsmen?

It was into this world that individuals such as Edwin St.Hill stepped in the 1930s. Learie Constantine was a legendary West Indian cricketer and had become a huge star in league cricket circles after signing for Nelson in Lancashire. He played an exhibition match at Slaithwaite in 1933 and accompanying him was St Hill, a fellow Trinidadian, who was professional at Lowerhouse in the Lancashire League.

St Hill was almost certainly the first black player to play in the Huddersfield & District League. He was professional at Slaithwaite in 1934 and 1945. He took 152 wickets for the club in total at an average of 10.52. In his first season, the club tied with Golcar for the league championship with St Hill scoring 408 runs at an average of 20.40 and taking 87 wickets at 12.91. The Slaithwaite annual report concluded that 'the engagement of St Hill has been successful to a point, and we claim it has brought increased interest into the League'.[10]

Ashton in Manchester signed their first overseas professional in 1949.[11] Some clubs have honoured their favourite pros. At Radcliffe, near Bury, a room in the club pavilion is named after Gary Sobers. And special chapters in the authorised history of the Bacup club are dedicated to Everton Weekes, Roy Gilchrist and Roger Harper.[12]

Meanwhile, families from the Asian subcontinent and the Caribbean were encouraged to move to Britain after the Second World War. Textile barons started to recruit male Asian workers for their mills and factories, and many West Indians came to work on public transport. But immigrants arriving in England in the 1950s and 1960s were faced with many challenges. They had to adapt to a new society, earn enough money to make ends meet, and also make friends in a new environment. For many men folk, playing sport was a 'way in' to English society – and at the same time also a natural instinct. Cricket was a religion on the subcontinent and in the Caribbean, and so cricket became their number-one pastime when they arrived in Britain.

In the early days, young children would play the game, informally and spontaneously, on pavements and street corners. Gradually, the new ethnic communities began to establish their own cricket clubs. These clubs were vital to first-generation immigrants, either because they found language a barrier or encountered racial prejudice. The first Asian cricket team in the Kirklees area was formed in 1962 – Batley Muslims.[13] Solly Adam played for this team and later became a successful sports goods retailer and agent.

In 1974, seven young Asian enthusiasts got together to establish Mount CC, based in Mount Pleasant, Batley. Hanif Mayet, one of Mount's founding fathers, remembers the period well: 'There were no Asian cricketers at that time at the big local clubs. I'd go to practise and turn up at the match and I'd always be twelfth man. If they were a man short I'd be slotted in, but even though they knew I could bat, I'd go in at number 10 or 11. It was a waste of time basically, so we used to play in the street with a tennis ball. One day I thought, "This can't go on – we've got to do something about it". We went round the neighbourhood with a begging bowl – because our fathers weren't well off. They came from India with three quid in their pockets to work in the textiles.'[14] And in recent years, local Asian clubs have claimed their fair share of silverware. Mount, Dewsbury

Young Star, Warwick Youth and Savile Stars are prime examples of all-conquering outfits in the Batley-Dewsbury area.

Caribbean immigrants also formed their own teams. In Kirklees, West Indians CC won the Lumb Cup in 1963 – a landmark moment. Thereafter saw the emergence of teams such as International CC, Caribbean Youth Club CC and International Caribbean CC.

The same patterns are evident in Reading. Martin Bishop has argued that the West Indian community played a significant role in local cricket in the post-war years. The local biscuit factory, Huntley & Palmer's, employed many recently arrived immigrants. Bishop highlights the case of Darwin Crawford. Born in 1929 in the village of Biby's Lane, near Bridgetown, Barbados, he played cricket for local clubs such as Empire, Yorkshire and the Barbados Regiment. Bishop explains:

> Darwin decided that the world was larger than his Barbados homeland and that he wanted to see more and visit some of the places he had learnt and read about at school, so in June 1952 he emigrated to England, a journey that took over two weeks by steamer. Initially he lived in London but soon moved to join the growing Bajan community in Reading, where through his friends he obtained a job at Huntley and Palmers ... By 1953 he was a regular player for Huntley and Palmers CC. Matches were played mainly on Saturdays, some Sundays and occasionally on midweek afternoons; players were expected to become members of the company recreation club/cricket club and a nominal sum was deducted from Darwin's wages to cover his membership ... Darwin was a highly respected employee and member of the cricket club – there would seem to be no hint of any difficulty over his race in what we would regard now as much less enlightened times.[15]

Given this history and heritage, there is no doubt that cricket in England has been a force for good in fostering integration. And many organisations have been founded to ensure fairness and equality. One such body is the Kirklees Black and Ethnic Cricket Forum. Its aims are to: 'Recommend policy and strategy; Raise local awareness and offer advice; Suggest programmes of action and promote opportunities; Support black and ethnic minority clubs; Disseminate information.'[16] At the same time, sports development officials have worked hard to help local clubs like Mount and Savile Stars raise funds, access grants, and enhance their coaching expertise. The indicators are very positive. Yorkshire CCC recently fielded a team that included four Asian players: Ajmal Shahzad, Adil Rashid, Azeem Rafiq and overseas professional Naveed Rana.

Local Indian restaurants are among the most generous sponsors of local clubs,[18] and in summer 2005, local government authorities in West Yorkshire staged a successful Cricket Festival in Ravensknowle Park, with the accent very much on cultural exchange. It is now also commonplace for clubs' constitutions to include references to the campaign against racism.[19] For various reasons, it has, at times, also been desirable for predominantly Asian teams to establish their own leagues. The best example is the Quaid-e-Azam, established in Bradford in 1981.

Today, there are many 'ethnic' clubs in England. London Nigerians were formed in 1991. Their ethos is 'based on providing a forum for people from a Nigerian background, or with an interest in Nigeria, to come together socially and to present a positive image of the motherland in their interaction with the wider community'.[20] Likewise London Tigers, who play in the Victoria Park Community League and who in 2006 won the Lord's Taverners Inner City World Cup representing Bangladesh.[21]

Women: from tea-making to the corridors of power

Williams argues that women have traditionally watched rather than played cricket. He cites one significant statistic: in 1977, a third of all spectators at cricket matches were female.[22] We should bear this statistic in mind as our discussion ensues.

The last few decades have seen major changes in the role of women in local cricket. A hundred years ago, if a woman was involved at a local club, she was invariably the tea lady, or the scorer, or someone who, with the co-operation of her female friends (and perhaps under the aegis of the club's 'Ladies Committee'), would organise a 'clothes evening' in an effort to raise money for her club. Today, things have changed. Of course, there are still a multitude of tea ladies, and female scorers, and always willing fundraisers. But things have also moved on. Women have taken on other mantles. They have become secretaries, treasurers and chairmen on club committees, started to play or umpire, or even helped with building and property matters. Jeffrey Stanyer wrote in 2000 about his club, Exeter:

> The role of women in the Club has expanded since the DCCC General Committee resolved in 1919 'that Ladies be not allowed in the pavilion and that dogs be not allowed on the ground.' This decision was modified at the County's Annual General Meeting when, by 19 votes to 8, '[I]t was resolved that Ladies be allowed in the seats in the Pavilion, except in the top two rows.'[23]

Women have been mainly associated with tea-making. The image of the hard-working and kind-hearted tea lady is as old as organised cricket itself. However much progress there has been in society at large, and in local league cricket in particular, women are still associated mainly with cricket teas. Clubs have always looked to women to help out in the kitchen; and in doing so, they have reflected age-old stereotypes and traditions. Often, women's contribution in the kitchen has gone unrecorded. But at Woodlands in Bradford in 1905, the women of the club were asked to help with a tea party, and in 1907 a Mrs Padgett was asked 'to make 8lbs of pastry and 6lbs of Queen cakes'. In 1913, ten women were officially asked to help with the Annual Tea and Concerts; and in 1922, the shopping list for a typical Saturday included twenty-four sandwich rolls plus tea, sugar and milk.[24]

In the 1950s and 1960s (in particular), it was common for a club to have its own 'sub-group' of willing female members. More often than not, this group would be known as the ladies committee (or ladies section). Where a club had a ladies committee, it was usually semi-autonomous and devoted to fundraising and improving the general wellbeing of the club. It would organise its own events, pay in the takings to its own bank account, and then donate money back to the club as and when it was needed for specific purposes.

What did a ladies committee look like? A photograph in the 1960 Elland centenary brochure – titled 'A Section of the Ladies' Committee' – helps us in this regard. Five women are pictured sitting on a bench outside the club's pavilion: 'Mrs Crossland, Mrs Sutcliffe (secretary), Mrs Rawlinson (chairman), Mrs Sykes (treasurer), Mrs Berry'. It is significant that they are all married and – more than likely – have husbands who play or played for the club. All the women appear to be in either their sixties or seventies and all are dressed formally for the photo: they are wearing skirts or dresses and there are several overcoats (and some fur) on display. At least one is wearing a hat. The phenomenon of ladies committees begs other questions. When were they formed? Who was on them? How formal were they? How much independence did they have within the club? What were their aims? What activities did they involve themselves in? How did they use the money that they raised?

Another case study is Hanging Heaton in Batley. In 1956, club minutes record that:

> At the invitation of Mr E. Wood, the president of the Hanging Heaton Cricket Club, interested Lady Members met at the Club and on the Committee's behalf the President asked whether the ladies would be prepared to form a Committee to run a ladies section at the Club, be responsible for catering for the cricket matches throughout the summer and organise such other activities as they desired. The ladies expressed their willingness to do so and the President then retired from the meeting.[25]

The inaugural meeting of the 'Ladies Section of the Hanging Heaton Cricket Club' (its official name) took place on 9 April 1956 at 8pm. Nine women were present and two sent their apologies. A committee consisting of all eleven was elected, with Mrs P. Bailey being elected chairman and Mrs B. Ellis honorary secretary.[26] (It is significant that their meetings were minuted – a clear sign that they regarded themselves, and were regarded by the club, as a formal body).

It is interesting that women members of the club were 'invited' to the preliminary meeting (rather than organising it themselves) and were 'asked' if they would like to form a committee (rather than doing it spontaneously). The seemingly preordained role of the ladies committee was to supervise teas and arrange other events, and the evidence we have from a variety of clubs suggests that ladies sections rarely, if ever, strayed outside these parameters. A minute from Upper Hopton Club, Mirfield, illustrates this: '1990 saw the creation of a ladies committee. The ladies' effort has always been vital to the smooth running of the club catering-wise, and we must now extend our thanks for their fundraising efforts as well.'[27] This was three or four decades on from the 'heyday' of the ladies committee – and thus emphasises the unchanging nature of their *raison d'être* still further.

Ladies committees put on events all the year round. In the 1950s, the ladies section at Hanging Heaton put on a jumble sale and dances. In 1972, the SBCI ladies held an AGM, jumble sale, recipe evening, Christmas supper, a series of committee meetings and a summer trip. They also painted and cleaned the pavilion tea room: 'Several favourable comments were received. At least our paint had dried before the first match. This was not the case in the changing rooms (which the men painted) as no doubt some of you would be aware, faced with the job of removing paint from the seat of your husband's cricket flannels.'[28] It is assumed here that women do all the washing at home and there is also a hint of innocent rivalry between the two sexes. These are interesting indicators of gender roles and relations in the early 1970s. Williams, for his part, talks about ladies committees as being 'essential'. They organised teas, dances, other social events, and engaged in fundraising. He says that in Bolton women particularly enjoyed the socialising involved in belonging to a cricket club.[29]

Today, there are fewer ladies committees but women are now serving on club committees as secretaries, treasurers, welfare officers and chairs.[30] In 1999, the *Express & Chronicle* recorded a milestone in Huddersfield league cricket: 'Women are leading the way into the new century at Skelmanthorpe Cricket Club – and they've caught positions as chair and vice-chair. Margaret Dollive, a hospital worker, and Beverley Crossland, a local hairdresser, are the first female members of the committee and they've scooped the top jobs. Members say the club … is breaking new ground and it's all down to the ladies.'[31] This was a significant moment, with women being elected to the two top jobs on the Skelmanthorpe committee.

In addition to serving as tea ladies, raising money under the aegis of ladies committees, and holding positions on club committees, women have also played the game. But we should note that it has never been a major female sport. Williams makes this point – at one juncture only forty-nine clubs, twenty-two colleges and fifty-six schools were affiliated to the Women's Cricket Association (WCA).[32]

In the early twentieth century, women's teams were rare. In 1897, a 'novel cricket match' was played between two sides at Thornhill, Dewsbury: Miss A. Senior's and Miss E. Shackleton's. There were nine players in each team. It was perhaps with the intention of forming their own team that, in February 1932, the committee at Golcar, Huddersfield, proposed a Ladies Knockout tournament to be played on midweek evenings, similar to the Workshop Knockout for men. The idea was abandoned in the June and a ladies committee was formed two months later. There was, however, women's cricket on the ground in the 1930s. In June 1934, Huddersfield Ladies CC played a match there and a local ladies match was played in July 1936.

Martin Bishop has studied women's cricket in Berkshire. He has written about the Reading Biscuit Factory Recreation Club Ladies CC and located a photograph of this side dated 6 June 1919.[33] He suggests that the first recorded women's match in the town took place between the Biscuit Factory Ladies and Huntley, Boorne and Stevens Ladies on 31 July 1924. The biscuit factory also organised inter-departmental games for female employees. In this period, he notes the existence of other sides too – Aspro Ladies, Burberry's Ladies, C.W.S. Horlicks Ladies, Huntley, Boorne and Stevens Ladies, Hurst Ladies, St George's Ladies, Sherfield Ladies, Warfield Ladies – but says that local companies rarely included the details of women's games alongside men's.

There had been one or two famous women's teams in the late nineteenth century, such as the White Heather Club and the semi-professional Original English Lady Cricketers, and cricket had been played at prestigious girls' boarding schools before the Great War. However, the inter-war years witnessed a remarkable blossoming in women's cricket. The WCA was formed in 1926 and there were twenty county associations by 1937. Williams argues that the 'main strength of the WCA was in the south and midlands of England'. But in 1927, a Dearne Valley women's league (centring on Doncaster) was formed; 1930 witnessed the birth of the Keighley Ladies Cricket Competition; in 1931 the Yorkshire Women's Cricket Federation was established; and by 1932 the Yorkshire Federation had set up its own Inter-City and Towns League (Brighouse plus Bingley, Bradford, Dewsbury, Halifax, Holme Valley, Horbury, Huddersfield, Keighley, Littleborough, Liversedge, and Sowerby Bridge all entered teams at some point). In the 1930s we also come across the Bradford Women's Evening Cricket League and the Leeds & District Women's Cricket League.

Women's cricket in this period was essentially middle and upper class. Interestingly, women's cricket was also at a crossroads. An organisational structure was developing, but this was a slow and slightly haphazard process. This is reflected in a news story featured in the *Brighouse Echo* in July 1931. Under the heading, 'SCHEME TO STANDARDISE WOMEN'S CRICKET', it was reported that:

> Mr. T. Metcalfe (secretary of the Bradford Ladies Evening Cricket League) supplied a reporter with a rough outline for a suggested scheme to standardise women's cricket in the West Riding. He pointed out that at the moment the girl cricketers in various districts play under slightly varying rules from each other and in some instances with different equipment. 'For instance,' he said. 'Bradford play with standardised equipment and the regulation 22 yards' pitch, as well as playing a maximum innings of 32 overs and having 12 players a-side. Leeds play on a 21 yards' pitch and prefer

to complete their innings while Brighouse use a 20 yards' pitch and like each side to have one hour's batting.[34]

In the regional context, this appears to be a landmark, akin almost to those significant moments in the nineteenth century when new national sporting organisations emerged to unify, standardise and govern sports (for example, in another sport, soccer, the Football Association was founded in 1863 and the Football League in 1888). Officials and administrators were obviously thinking hard about how to take women's cricket forward, ironing out small inconsistencies and helping to create a level playing field (almost literally, in fact). This seems to show that prior to the 1930s the game existed only in rudimentary and embryonic form. Actually, it bore more than a passing resemblance to some sports in the medieval period, when every village had their 'local rules'.

In the post-war period, women's cricket did not take off as expected. However, in the early years of the twenty-first century, women's cricket is as popular as it has ever been. Towcester Ladies Cricket was established in 2004: 'With over twenty-five registered players of all ages we've enjoyed four successful seasons'. The club also has a five-person management committee.[35] Orpington Nomads WCC style themselves as 'the oldest women's cricket club in Kent. Originally a wandering side, we have had a permanent home at Goddington Dene for over 25 years and are now fully merged with Orpington Cricket Club.'[36] Hayes in Kent describes itself as 'one of the top women's and girl's clubs in the South East' with teams at Under-11, Under-13 and Under-15 level, plus two senior league sides.[37] And the 'first ever official game for Redruth CC Ladies' took place on Sunday 20 May 2007.[38]

At a local level, women's cricket has benefited from the encouragement of the ECB.[39] Also important has been the success of the England women's team. In 2009, a headline on the Hayes website proclaimed, 'England Win World Cup with help from Hayes!' The report began: 'Congratulations to Lydia Greenway and the England women's cricket team who won the World Cup during March in a tight final against New Zealand – Lydia has played all her cricket at Hayes and has been a regular in the England side for the past 5 years and we are all extremely proud of her achievements – an example to us all that hard work and commitment does pay-off. We look forward to welcoming Lydia and her medal back to Hayes!' Some women's clubs have even chosen to amalgamate with the local men's team.[40] And at Denstone College in Staffordshire, in 2006, a woman was appointed to the post of director of cricket for the first time.[41]

Equipment and facilities: the players and the ground

In the early twentieth century, clubs would have had a communal kit bag. Great Brickhill in Buckinghamshire ordered its equipment from Gunn and Moore of Nottingham. In 1920, the club owned: '1 cricket bag, 2 cricket balls, 3 pairs of gloves, 4 pairs of pads, 1 bat, 2 damaged bats, 1 set of stumps.'[42] As late as the 1970s, it was unusual for players to own their own kit. Brian Heywood of Todmorden remembers: 'When I played for Calderdale Schoolboys in the 1970s, I didn't own my own pads so I had to borrow some.'[43]

In the late twentieth century, players began to own their own bats and pads. This was a massive change. Now they can buy designer items via the Internet. Players at Himley in Staffordshire can purchase club kit from the 'Fearnley Website, click on image to order and view full range.' And at Caythorpe in Nottinghamshire, the following items can be purchased: Plain Gunn & Moore shirt with classic club crest, club polo shirts, maroon club shirts, adult sweaters – with classic club crest, club caps, junior Mitre shirts with laurel leaf club badge and falcon tracksuit tops with laurel leaf club badge.[44] Society at the end of the last century had become more affluent and commercialised. Cricket equipment had become more rationalised, affordable and available – even for club cricketers.

The players

In the early days, cricket was played in impromptu fashion, without specialist attire or equipment, and there was little uniformity, e.g. no club sweaters or caps. In the early eighteenth century, when cricket as a sport in England was in its infancy, equipment manufacture was a cottage industry, and it was sometimes undertaken by professional cricketers. William Lillywhite and John Wisden opened sports equipment stores in 1844 and 1850 respectively.

Cricket equipment has evolved alongside developments in the way the game has been played. Early bats were curved, like ice hockey sticks, to combat the ball when delivered in a low, skidding, underarm fashion. But as the height of the bowler's arm became more elevated, making the ball bounce higher, straight bats that could be swung in a perpendicular movement were introduced. Further developments like cork pads, cane-handled bats and protective batting or wicket-keeping gloves became necessary as the bowling arm was allowed to go higher and deliveries became faster. In the 1980s, the cricket helmet came into common use to protect batsmen against (often concerted) short-pitched bowling.

It is important to stress that over the decades the nature and character of cricket equipment has been dictated chiefly by developments in playing technique, rather than advances in industrial and manufacturing technology. That said, in the 1970s and 1980s, the advent of new technology meant that it was easier to manufacture branded clothing at an economical rate, thus making it cheaper for local cricket clubs to purchase. Shirts and jumpers emblazoned with club colours and badges became a common sight on local grounds, and in most cases, manufacturers would also have been able to act as supplier. The growth of mail-order operations and the appearance of large, warehouse-style cricket outlets also changed the face of cricket.

In the very early days, cricketers tended to wear white, but not exclusively. On the whole, the more 'serious' the team, the more coordinated would be the cricketers' clothing. Most team photographs show how whites were preferred. However, flamboyant caps and blazers become the trademark of middle-class players and public schoolboys. Also it is clear that in some cases not all players could afford whites. Some development in the style of clothing is apparent, but not perhaps as much as one would think. When George Herbert Hirst, of Yorkshire and England, recalled the kit he wore during his early years in cricket (the 1880s), he said: 'My gear was worth all of ten shillings and I carried it in a canvas bag. I wore a shilling cap, a sixpenny belt with a snake clasp and brown boots. At the Yorkshire trial I bowled in my sweater, but I was better off than Arthur Mold of Lancashire, who couldn't take his off because he had no shirt on underneath. My shirt was blue but I got a white one with my first money ...'[45]

At the outset, players would have worn non-specialist footwear for their cricketing activities: shoes they would have worn for work, or even, perhaps, clogs. Gradually a specialist 'cricket boot' was developed, and most photographs from the early twentieth century show the majority of cricketers wearing a pretty sturdy white boot. Thereafter, as the game developed, manufacturers have put a variety of cricket boots on the market: studded, non-studded, and also a kind of lightweight 'trainer' that is suitable in some ultra-dry conditions.

Some of the more flamboyant and extroverted early cricketers wore pin-stripe trousers and gentlemen's outfits. It was as if some players were trying to impress teammates, opposition players, and even spectators, with their apparel. Over the decades, though, things began to change. As society developed, and as organisations and rules were introduced into sport, there was, naturally, more of a desire for uniformity within teams. Moreover, with the birth of a predominantly amateur County Championship competition, there was extra pressure for team members to conform. Flannels came in, made out of quite heavy material, and sometimes with fashionable 'turn-ups'. In the modern era, the old-style 'whites' have been superseded by lighter, much more comfortable trousers.

Initially, players' white shirts were worn with ties and waistcoats on at least some occasions. This is evident from early team pictures, though it is doubtful whether players ever batted, bowled or fielded with their ties on. Jumpers have always been a customary part of a cricketer's uniform, if only because of the vicissitudes of the English weather. In the early days, they were generally heavy and shapeless, and almost always all-white. Colour – or put more accurately, club colours – came much later, as did the inception of the sleeveless sweater. Even today, the difference between a first eleven and a second eleven player can often be spotted in the type of jumper.

When cricketers turned up to nineteenth-century challenge or stake matches in top hats or the like, they could have been making a point about their social status or pedigree as a player. In the inter-war years, caps became the norm, and from about the 1920s onwards clubs started to produce their own range of caps, usually customised with club crest and initials. As if reflecting fashions in society at large, cricketing headgear became slightly more casual in the latter decades of the twentieth century, with sun hats and then baseball caps complementing the traditional cricket cap. Even fashion for umpires has changed over the decades: from flat caps and long, knee-length white coats, to shirt sleeves, coloured ties and natty caps.

In the very early days, in order to strike the ball effectively, the 'bat' was long and curved. Before the 1720s it was mainly referred to as a cricket 'staffe', 'stave' or 'stick'. The second half of the eighteenth century saw the first major changes in playing techniques. This was largely due to the influence of the famous Hambledon club in Hampshire. John Small, the master bat- and ball-maker, and then 'Silver' Billy Beldham adopted the 'straight bat' approach, which encompassed forward play and 'playing down the line of the ball'. Small's innovation was a literal one and he is credited with changing the shape of the bat from its original 'curved' form to a shape similar to that which is common today.

In 1853, Thomas Nixon revolutionised cricket bat design by using cane, a flexible wood, to make the already spliced handle. Spring-handled bats also emerged. In the modern era, bats have become more powerful, customised to individual cricketers' needs, and sponsored too. The rules of the game mean that there is only limited scope for experimentation in the design of bats, but even so, distinctive models have become available in recent decades, including the Gray-Nicolls 'scoop', the Slazenger V12, the Duncan Fearnley bat 'with holes', and the aluminium bat made famous by Dennis Lillee. Now we have the 'Mongoose', 'a revolutionary design to enable batsmen to hit the ball with both sides of the blade'.[46] So, innovation remains strong, and even league cricketers can now afford to purchase 'new-style' willows.[47]

At first, batsmen and wicketkeepers would not have worn any gloves. The year 1848 was a landmark – when the kit manufacturer Robert Dark, who had been apprentice to John Small and was the brother of Lord's proprietor James Dark, advertised batting gloves made with tubular Indian rubber implants and improved leg guards. There was then a slow evolution starting with 'spiked' gloves, moving onto 'sausage' gloves, the revolutionary 'smooth' gloves made famous by England captain Tony Greig in the 1970s, and finishing with the gloves used today.

In 1841, the aforementioned Nixon patented a set of cork pads. Seven years later, in 1848, kit manufacturer Robert Dark advertised improved leg guards for batsmen. In the hundred years that followed, pads for batsmen and wicketkeepers developed slowly. From being slightly cumbersome – early varieties extended up to the knee and down to the ankle – they have been refined, and are now quite flexible and malleable, especially those used by wicketkeepers, who need slightly less protection. Over the years, batsmen, wicketkeepers and fielders positioned close to the bat have worn an array of protection in the abdominal area. These have ranged from bits of cardboard to pieces of plastic, and from conventional jockstraps to all-in-one items of general 'body protection'.

World cricket in the 1970s and 1980s was dominated by the West Indies and their throng of lightning-fast bowlers intent on employing tactics of intimidation. Batsmen were thus forced to devise ways of protecting themselves from injury. The three most obvious developments were the helmet, arm guard, and thigh pad. Gradually, too, these developments filtered their way down into local league cricket. Brian Heywood remembers the 1981 season when helmets, lacrosse-style chest protectors and arm-guards made their debut in the Lancashire League (to help counter the threat of bowlers such as Andy Roberts, Michael Holding, Kapil Dev, Franklyn Stephenson and Neal Radford).[48] Things have now moved on. A recent directive from the England and Wales Cricket Board under the aegis of 'Child Protection' legislation stated that all 'junior' players (e.g. under the age of 16) must wear a helmet while batting or keeping wicket.

In the early period of the sport's development, the ball was quite literally 'bowled' underarm in a low, skimming manner, at a wicket which was wider than it was high and consisted of two stumps with forked ends and one bail. In time, the move was made to three stumps and two bails at each end of the wicket – and this has remained the norm right up until the twenty-first century. Over time, there has been little change in the appearance and shape of cricket balls. Today, the Huddersfield League stipulates that balls should be 'of a brand and grade approved by the management, and purchased from the League'.[49]

The ground

The development of ground facilities coincides with the general growth of clubs. Early pavilions were known as 'tents', probably because, in the very early years, clubs literally used tents for changing and teatime refreshments. Many clubs had some kind of wooden hut as their first pavilion. Sometimes a club would buy a hut from another club which no longer had any use for it; sometimes the hut had been used previously, but in a different way or for another function. At Stone in Worcestershire, 'The Talbot family owned Moule's Farm and in 1937 agreed to have the cricket pitch on land that adjoined the house. We had a hut to change in. This was in the corner of the field near to the bowling green at the Hare and Hounds. A pavilion was built later. On the far side towards the main road was the building where all the social events took place. This was just referred to as "The Hut". There were dances, whist drives, snooker and parties of all kinds. A room at the back was used by the tennis club which was on the same site.'[50]

For understandable reasons, purpose-built pavilions and clubhouses were rarely constructed until a permanent home had been found with some security of tenure. At Great Brickhill in Buckinghamshire, 'One of the Club's rules was that the Club tent had to be erected and dismantled at the end of matches'. By the late 1920s, club accounts show that a pavilion had been built at a cost of £35 14s 6d.[51] At Himbleton in Worcestershire, 'Preparation of the new ground took longer than anticipated, partly due to an exceptionally wet summer in 1965. The bulk of expenditure was incurred in 1965 and 1966, and in 1967 it was reported that spending on the ground to date had been £1,064. 15s. 7d. A second-hand pre-fabricated structure was acquired and erected by club members to serve as a pavilion. This has had two major extensions and several minor improvements since.'[52]

Now, in the early twenty-first century, pavilion redevelopments are relatively common due to the existence of new public-sector funding bodies such as Sport England and the National Lottery. In many cases, these organisations have assisted clubs in their first major rebuilding project since the early twentieth century. Some leagues are raising the bar even higher with the insistence that pavilions must incorporate a dedicated umpires room.[53] Fladbury of the Cotswold Hills League opened their new pavilion in 1999; they had been helped by a £100,000 grant from the National Lottery.[54] At Great Brickhill in Buckinghamshire, a new pavilion was built in 1978.

> At that time, grants from public authorities were hard to obtain, but a combination of fully documented requests and practical evidence of serious intent to erect a worthwhile building brought £100 (the maximum permitted grant) from Bucks Playing Fields Association, and a grant of £936 from the Sports Council. Even more encouraging was the fact that Aylesbury Vale District Council, with only £1,000 available for allocation to sports projects throughout the county during 1977, and despite there being six other applicants, decided to make the Club a grant of £600.

The official verdict is that this 'acted as a catalyst for increasing the interest in the Club, both from the playing and social side'.[55]

In 2002, Radcliffe-on-Trent in Nottinghamshire

> embarked on a challenging and exciting project to provide additional playing and coaching facilities at its ground off the A52, just outside the village. This involved the purchase of over five acres of farmland adjacent to the current ground, the construction of a top-grade playing surface, the placement on an artificial wicket on the new square and the construction of a two-bay practice net facility. June 2004 saw the completion of this phase of the project. In total, this phase cost £140,000 with significant funding provided by Sport England, the New Opportunities Fund, Rushcliffe Borough Council, The Foundation for Sports and the Arts, Midland Wine, Radcliffe-on-Trent Parish Council, The Lord's Taverners and The Lady Hind Trust. The club started playing on the new ground in 2005, having purchased new ground maintenance equipment and portakabins for changing facilities.[56]

Other clubs have restored buildings – for example, Evesham in Worcestershire.[57]

Once upon a time, maintenance equipment at cricket grounds was pretty rudimentary. Groundsmen had to toil hard, and machinery was either man-powered or horse-drawn. In the 1880s, a weavers' strike in the Colne Valley in the West Riding of Yorkshire provided a much-needed source of labour for ground improvements at Broad Oak and Slaithwaite. A number of clubs owned their own horses. Well into the 1930s, Golcar's ground – located close by – incorporated a stable and yard, the horse being used to pull the cutting and rolling equipment.

The dawn of mechanisation saw the horse being sold off, and in October 1934, the stable and yard were let to a Mr Firth at £4 per annum. In the 1930s and 1940s, motorised ground equipment became more commonly available. Honley of the Huddersfield League, for example, bought their first motor mower in 1949. But at Great Brickhill in Buckinghamshire, 'the club's main hurdle seemed to be the upkeep of it [sic] mowers and in 1949 it was reported that the club should collect its mower from H. Smith of Leighton Buzzard because it had been there for two years and had not been repaired. The horse drawn mower was replaced at this time by a Fordson tractor which was purchased at auction from Government surplus supplies.'[58]

The quality of pitch covers has also improved across the board. The South Yorkshire League explains that, 'Clubs must use covers to completely or partially protect the pitch during inclement weather, to allow the game to be played. Premier Division and Division One clubs must use covers if adverse weather causes a delayed start to a match or immediately there is an interruption of play. Umpires must report any club failing to do so.'[59]

Stumps have changed only slightly over the years. In the early days they looked thin and 'spindly'; there was also a phase when stumps had metal tops, so as to stop them breaking; now they are slightly 'chunkier' than they once were. In 1929, they were made larger to help address the imbalance between bat and ball. Predictably too, in the modern period, with marketing and commercialisation so all-embracing, some stumps now carry the logo of the manufacturer or a sponsor.

At some levels of cricket, there are strict stipulations about the size and quality of sightscreens. However, in some leagues the rules are more lenient. The authorities understand that small village clubs cannot afford to erect state-of-the-art 'seeing' equipment. And thus, local clubs are given room to experiment: over the years, some have used white sheeting; others have erected makeshift boards. Some have bought sightscreens 'on rollers'; others have invested in 'sliding' screens. Many clubs choose to save money and simply whitewash the dry stone walls that lie at the top and bottom ends of their ground. Some clubs have none at all. Great Brickhill in Buckinghamshire acquired their first sightscreens in 1910. The official club history records that, 'Sir E.P. Duncombe donated the timber from his estate for the members to collect and construct'.[60] In 2009, as breaking news on their website, Radway in Worcestershire announced that their new sightscreens would 'enhance playing facilities at the Tysoe Road Ground'.[61] Unfortunately, in the modern era, sightscreens have become a sitting target for local vandals.

Moving on to scoring, in the nineteenth century, scorers 'scored' not in a book but by making notches on a piece of wood. At Great Brickhill in Buckinghamshire, 'The current score hut at the far end of the field was built in 1950, by club members ... following the clearance of some timber farm buildings'.[62] Today, some leagues insist on electronic scoreboards.

Junior cricket: from under-18s to under-7s

Junior cricket is a relatively recent phenomenon. Of course, youngsters have always played cricket − whether in their back garden or the local park − but organised cricket at clubs is very much a post-war phenomenon. In the late nineteenth and early twentieth century, juniors would fill in for adults in senior sides when required but this was the limit of their involvement at clubs. They may have watched, or acted as club scorer, but there would have been huge logistical problems in organising junior sides. Anyway, many children left school at the age of fourteen and were treated as adults in the workplace. So why would there be 'junior' cricket teams?

Up until the Second World War, most cricket for children was organised by schools. The relationship between schools cricket and cricket at clubs is a key one. Houlihan argues that recent governments have been worried about the demise of team-based sport in schools, and have thus involved themselves in various initiatives to improve the situation.[63]

Another argument is that it was the decline of schools cricket that actually presaged the growth of organised junior cricket at local clubs.[64] Between the 1900s and 1930s, a 'junior team' was a second eleven side or a friendly side that perhaps contained a few youngsters; in essence, a lower form of cricket. It is interesting to note that the Ribblesdale Junior League was founded in 1912, 'for the second teams of those members who wished to take part'. Also, 'From the resumption of cricket after the war, the Junior League accepted clubs which were not members of the Senior League'.[65] (In 1977, a third division was added to the Senior League, 'for those who can only play on Sundays and also the opportunity for younger players to gain experience of a good standard of cricket alongside more experienced not to say very mature players!').[66] At Woodlands in Bradford, the first reference to junior cricket was 1912 when Woodlands Juniors entertained Low Moor Wesley Place, but it isn't clear whether this was a team of youngsters or merely second eleven players.[67] During the Great War, the Huddersfield Junior League debated the merits of 'friendly games' and 'point hunting'.[68] We are also told that in the post-1918 period, the club encouraged local schoolboys to play cricket and also set the junior subscription fee at 2s (10p) − half that of the seniors. Some new kit was bought and matches were arranged, but these were friendlies.[69]

The first organised junior cricket − where 'junior' denoted a certain age group − was played in the 1930s. In 1936, a Leeds evening league for under-18s was established; and in 1936–37, an equivalent league was founded in Doncaster. Organisations such as churches and the YMCA also played a part in encouraging junior cricket in this period. The Bradford Central Junior League was established in 1937.[70] The key point to make is that in this early period junior cricket was mainly under-18s cricket. And it was aimed in large part at young apprentices at engineering firms, General Post Office boys and the like.

Malcolm Heywood has written about the history of cricket in Todmorden.

He explains:

> Sam Fielden – the key man in the early history of Todmorden – had an enlightened
> attitude to children. Before the Great War, local children were encouraged to play
> cricket and had equipment bought for them by the club. In the 1930s, schoolboys
> played cricket at Centre Vale – for school teams – but they were not connected with
> Todmorden. After the Second World War, the Lancashire League established a compe-
> tition for 'A' teams, in effect sides of under-18s. They would play 20-over-a-side
> games in the evening and, bizarrely, each side was allowed an over-age captain (who
> wasn't allowed to bowl and would bat no.11! His runs wouldn't count towards the
> team's total, but he could 'baby-sit' the younger lads). But there were no junior sides
> in the 1920s – you couldn't even be a member of the club if you were under 16! The
> club simply didn't want junior members, and would only allow them in exceptional
> circumstances. Things started to change in the 1930s.[71]

Most junior leagues would have been suspended for the duration of the
Second World War.[72] But they resurrected themselves soon after: in 1947,
Haworth Baptist CC entered its first ever side in the 'newly formed West Bradford
Junior Cricket League'.[73] Both the Leeds and Heavy Woollen competitions re-
formed in 1949. By 1952, there were leagues for under-16s and under-14s in the
Wetherby area. The Southport Junior League was established in 1961 as a two-
division competition for under-17s.[74] But the situation differed from area to area.
Mick Bourne grew up in Lincolnshire and then moved to Leeds. He recalls: 'In
Boston in the 1950s and 1960s there was no junior cricket at all. A promising
junior might get a game batting at no.11 for the 2nd XI but that was about it.'[75]
David Thorpe remembers the same period in Huddersfield: 'Under-17s cricket
was played across Huddersfield but that was it. Things were different then. There
were lots of youth clubs – CYCs [community youth clubs] – and we used to play
cricket or football for our school almost every Saturday of the year. So there was
no need for junior teams at local clubs.'[76]

Leagues for under-15s were emerging by the 1970s.[77] Brian Heywood
started playing for Todmorden Under-15s in 1975:

> I initially played for the Under-18s even though I was only 11 or 12. Then in 1975
> I started playing for the new Under-15s side. My main memory is doing a lot of
> batting in the nets. Most of our practice was on the outfield and in the park next
> door. There were two of us who made it from the Under-15s to the 1st XI and we
> both got criticised for playing the ball late and not driving off the front foot. And that
> was because we did most of our practising in the park, where we couldn't trust the
> bounce. Full tosses were OK, but everything else we played really late. The club wasn't
> that amenable to us as young cricketers. We weren't allowed to play on the main
> square; and only on the outfield at teatime during senior matches and in the hour
> after a match.[78]

By the 1980s, under-13s were being catered for at local clubs (they played
eight-a-side cricket and were able to take part in the nationwide NatWest

under-13s competition). But the development of junior cricket was uneven. Evesham's first junior team took to the field in 1980, and a year later, in 1981, the club entered a team in the Worcestershire under-16s league.[79]

In the 1990s, under-11s cricket was popularised, with leagues being formed in Leeds, Sheffield, Wetherby and many other places. And in the last decade, organised cricket for under-9s has taken off. According to Bourne, who became a coach in the Leeds area, 'I'm all in favour of getting very young kids interested in the game. They can be active and enthusiastic but they don't really understand about competition. So I'm against imposing rules and systems on these younger kids – just let them enjoy playing the game. But by the age of 10, 11 and 12 I think kids are ready to be put in teams and play organised sport.'[80] In recent years, clubs have even experimented with under-7s cricket. One example is Thirsk, who equate under-7s cricket to Reception 1 and 2 in terms of school years.[81]

By way of a case study, under-16s had been playing at Great Brickhill in Buckinghamshire since the 1920s. In 1931, the club invested in a 'junior cricket set' to encourage local children to join up, and in 1932 a local dignitary, Sir E.P. Duncombe, offered a monetary prize for the under-17s players who topped the batting, bowling and fielding charts. We are also told that in this period, the club juniors were practising four evenings a week. Junior cricket re-established itself at the club in the 1960s: 'A junior section was mentioned in 1965 and in 1969 extra fixtures were arranged to allow more juniors to play.'[82] In 1992, the club founded a junior section, and in 1993 employed former England fast bowler Greg Thomas as coach to both the juniors and seniors.[83]

Today, in the early twenty-first century, clubs are extremely well organised as regards junior cricket. Brightwell-cum-Sotwell in Oxfordshire have a dedicated junior website and, by way of a mission statement, declare: 'The club will aim to bring the best out of its young players, regardless of their skill or fitness levels.'[84] Beckenham say they have a junior membership of 200 players.[85] Plymouth have sides at under-10s, 11s, 12s, 13s, 14s and 15s.[86] Thirsk are represented in four local Junior Leagues and boast sections for under-7s, 9s, 12s, 13s, 15s and 18s.[87] Bapchild in Kent have a large Colts section and 'run two mini-8s side so children under 9 can play competitive cricket and learn from an early age the joys of team sports'.[88] Didcot have under-11s, 13s, 15s and 17s and a Kwik Cricket section.[89]

In a medium-sized county like Sussex there are now five junior cricket leagues: the Identilam League (operating in the north of Sussex), the North and Mid Sussex League, the East Area Junior Cricket League, the South Area Junior Cricket League and the West Area Junior League. There is a long-running Sussex Junior Cricket Festival and the Sussex Cricket Board oversees the under-10 Cricket Telecom Cup, the under-13 MCC Spirit of Cricket, the under-15 Nationwide Cup and the under-18 Development League.[90]

In the last decades of the twentieth century, junior cricket became a significant part of grassroots cricket. In general terms, clubs with healthy junior set-ups are deemed to be healthy clubs. Moreover, grant-awarding bodies view a good junior section as a key criterion when they are deciding on the allocation of funds. But some observers worry about the future. Where do junior cricketers go? Why is there such a leakage of talent post-junior cricket but pre-senior cricket? Later, in the first decade of the twentieth century, the introduction of tight child welfare legislation would have huge consequences for local clubs.

Finally, clubs now compete to attract junior cricketers. They target parents via mail-outs and the Internet. At Thirsk, the message is: 'We will be looking for parents who wish to help out with coaching, scoring, umpiring and providing transport for the players to and from games. If you are interested in getting involved please come along to your son or daughter's practice night and speak to the coaches involved, I'm sure your support will be greatly appreciated.'[91] They also identify key local schools in their area. For their part, Thurstonland in West Yorkshire recently sent a junior coach into every school in their catchment area.

Junior sport is viewed by the vast majority of people as a 'good thing', and junior cricket is no exception. But a backlash has begun with some commentators arguing that it has been corrupted. One criticism is that some coaches and parents over-emphasise the competitive element. One Internet posting said: 'Having umpired junior football locally and watched junior netball this season, I think some coaches and parents need to be reminded of a few home truths. Junior level is all about development, encouragement and having fun, not all about winning.'[92] And from an academic point of view, Daryl Siedentop has argued that, 'there has been a prevailing mythology that boys will turn into men only if they experience the magic elixer of football competition … This mythology is a vulgarisation of Arnoldism, the mid-19th-century philosophy of fair play that took the name of the headmaster at the Rugby School in England. Arnoldism in its pure form was a philosophy that not only taught how one ought to behave in sport, but used sport as a metaphor for how life should be lived. Needless to say, there is nothing inherently positive about the influence of sport on developing children and youths.'[93]

What can be argued, therefore, is that grassroots cricket reinvented itself in the late twentieth and early twenty-first centuries. The growing contribution of ethnic minority communities and women had a positive effect. Cricket equipment became more rationalised and as schools gave up on cricket to some extent, local clubs developed impressive junior sections and made nurturing young talent a key priority. In the twenty-first century, local cricket has also been assisted by ECB initiatives and the availability of public funding.

Notes

1 Interview: 6 Sep 2009.
2 D. Birley, *A Social History of English Cricket* (London, Aurum Press, 2003), p. 360–1.

3 B. Shaw (ed.), *A History of Evesham Cricket Club* (Evesham, Evesham Cricket Club, 2004), p. 33.

4 www.brickhillcricket.co.uk (last accessed 17 Mar 2012)

5 Over the years the rule has changed and now clubs from South Yorkshire and Lancashire take part in the competition.

6 Anecdote passed on by Brian Heywood.

7 See www.sportsbusinessjournal.com/article/56195 (last accessed 17 Mar 2012).

8 For example, the Huddersfield Central Cricket League. In 1913, Lancashire League side Ramsbottom wrote to the Football Association asking them not to clash with their cricket season! See D. Edmundson, *See the Conquering Hero* (Accrington, Mike McLeod Litho, 1992), p. 32.

9 www.newsshopper.co.uk/.../4453937.BLACKHEATH__Asian_community_group _receives___5_550_to_start_cricket_club (last accessed 17 Jul 2011).

10 www.ckcricketheritage.org.uk/southkirklees/slaithwaite/docs/slaithwaite_the earlyyears.pdf (last accessed 17 Mar 2012).

11 Ashton-under-Lyne CC, *A History of Ashton-under-Lyne CC*, Ashton, p. 27.

12 C. Farnworth and S. Hall, *Bacup Cricket Club: The Authorised History* (Bacup, Bacup Cricket Club, 1999).

13 There followed Indian Nationals CC, Cross Bank Muslims CC, Savile Town Muslims CC and many other predominantly Asian cricket clubs.

14 www.ckcricketheritage.org.uk/northkirklees/mount/clubhome.htm (last accessed 17 Mar 2012).

15 In the company magazine *First Name News* (1:6, December 1955), Darwin is pictured on 19 November 1955 at the cricket section (of the recreation club) dinner leading the gathering in calypso singing. Pros such as Sylvester Oliver and Keith Barker (Todmorden) made their home in England after their careers were over.

16 In Yorkshire, the campaign to rid sport of racism is now embodied in a Yorkshire Cricket Board statement: 'The YCA/YCB are opposed to all forms of racism and are committed towards the elimination of all forms of racism at all levels of sport and to address issues of racial inequality.'

17 According to Solly Adam, Yorkshire have always had an integrationist policy: 'People always say Yorkshire are prejudiced, but there has been a change of policy for some time. Now Yorkshire are helping. They're organising coaching for Asians, all paid for. Yorkshire has gone out of its way to show it's not prejudiced.'

18 It is interesting to recognise the number of Kirklees cricket clubs whose main sponsor is an Indian restaurant. Take, for example, Denby Dale (Palace Tandoori) and Heckmondwike and Liversedge (Spice Kitchen).

19 The same is true of local cricket boards.

20 www.londonnigerianscc.co.uk/archive.html (last accessed 17 Mar 2012).

21 www.londontigers.org/sports/cricket (last accessed 17 Mar 2012).

22 J. Williams, 'Cricket', in T. Mason (ed.), *Sport in Britain* (Cambridge, Cambridge University Press, 1989), pp. 140–3.

23 J. Stanyer, *A Great Survivor: The History of The Exeter Cricket Club in the Nineteenth and Twentieth Centuries* (Exeter, St Leonard's Press, 2000), p. 277.

24 *Woodlands Cricket Club. Centenary Year 1894–1994. The Story of a Cricket Club* (Bradford, Woodlands Cricket Club, 1994), p. 81 – all seemingly recorded.

25 www.ckcricketheritage.org.uk/northkirklees/hangingheaton/clubhome.htm (last accessed 17 Mar 2012).

26 *Ibid.*

27 www.ckcricketheritage.org.uk/docs/081509UHOP1461990.pdf (last accessed 17 Mar 2012).

28 www.ckcricketheritage.org.uk/northkirklees/hangingheaton/clubhome.htm   (last accessed 17 Mar 2012).
29 Williams, 'Cricket', p. 143.
30 The first woman to serve on the Claygate committee – www.claygatecricket. co.uk/page_1229504592788.html (last accessed 17 Jul 2012).
31 (Huddersfield) *Express & Chronicle*, 3 Apr 1998.
32 Williams, 'Cricket', p.141.
33 M. Bishop, *Bats, Balls and Biscuits* (Huddersfield, Cricket Heritage Publications, 2008), p. 109
34 *Brighouse Echo*, 24 Jul 1931.
35 www.towcestrians.co.uk/Ladies/index.html (last accessed 25 Sep 2011).
36 www.orpingtoncc.co.uk/nomads1.asp (last accessed 17 Mar 2012).
37 www.hayescricket.co.uk/pages/ladies.htm (last accessed 17 Mar 2012).
38 The club's website reported: 'On the morning of Sunday 20th May 2007, ten players accompanied by Manager Paul Hancock, assisted by Aaron Hancock and Jo Strick headed to Truro CC to take part in an 8-a-side cricket festival … Cornwall Cricket Board Women's 8-a-side Club Trophy'. See www.redruthcc.com. This Is Bristol also reported on the ambitious Bristol Phoenix Women's CC, raising funds for a South African cricket tournament – see www.thisisbristol.co.uk/localcricket/Bristol-women-s-cricketers-bid-reach-international-tournament/article-1461766-detail/article.html (last accessed 17 Mar 2012). See also http://www.dulwichcc. com/?page_id=384 (last accessed 17 Mar 2012) and *Evening Mail* (Birmingham), 3 May 2001 – the resurrection of the Evesham women's team.
39 Also the work of individuals such as Audrey Collins – www.radlettcc.com/news/default.aspx#news22624 (last accessed 17 Mar 2012).
40 www.chelmsfordweeklynews.co.uk/archive/2000/06/07/Essex+Archive/5510460.Cricket_Southend_maidens_bowled_over (last accessed 17 Mar 2012). See also www.thisisstaffordshire.co.uk/nostalgia/Britton-Crump-traditionalists-stumped/article-936055-detail/article.html (last accessed 17 Mar 2012). On 26 May 2000, the Birmingham Post revealed that there had been a 164 per cent increase in the number of women playing cricket in the previous year. Women's leagues are also attracting sponsors – see www.bscricket.com/index.html (last accessed 17 Mar 2012).
41 www.schoolscricketonline.co.uk/?page_id=133 (last accessed 17 Mar 2012); see also www.thisisgloucestershire.co.uk/gloucestershireheadlines/Cricketer-Jade/article-335286-detail/article.html (last accessed 17 Mar 2012) for a woman who sold her car to finance a trip to Australia to play first grade women's cricket. Catherine Tyler became the first woman to represent her club in a senior league side – see also www.rockhamptoncc.com/history.php, www.webbsoc.demon.co.uk/sussex-home.htm (last accessed 25 Sep 2011), www.thisisbristol.co.uk/localcricket/Female-cricket-rise-thanks-Padgett/article-1251232-detail/article.html (last accessed 17 Mar 2012), and *Grimsby Telegraph*, 2 Feb 2010 – the Ann Boulton Award.
42 www.brickhillcricket.co.uk (last accessed 17 Mar 2012).
43 Interview: 6 Jul 2009.
44 www.caythorpecc.co.uk/new_site (last accessed 17 Mar 2012).
45 Taken from A.A. Thomson, *Hirst and Rhodes*, Epworth, 1959.
46 See www.mongoosecricket.com (last accessed 17 Mar 2012).
47 We also have 'the first bat for women' at www.newbery.co.uk/newbery-senior-cricket-bats/chic-senior-cricket-bat.html (last accessed 17 Mar 2012).
48 Interview: 3 Jan 2011.
49 *Huddersfield League Handbook* 2010.

50 http://stonecc.co.uk/index.php/history-of-stone-cc/ (last accessed 17 Mar 2012).

51 www.brickhillcricket.co.uk (last accessed 17 Mar 2012).

52 www.himbletoncc.org.uk/About%20Pages/History-Peters.html (last accessed 17 Mar 2012).

53 The Huddersfield League are very strong on this.

54 www.fladburycc.co.uk/history.php?history=brief (last accessed 17 Mar 2012).

55 www.brickhillcricket.co.uk (last accessed 17 Mar 2012)..

56 en.wikipedia.org/wiki/Radcliffe-on-Trent_Cricket_Club (last accessed 25 Sep 2011).

57 B. Shaw (ed.), *A History of Evesham Cricket Club* (Evesham, Evesham Cricket Club, 2004), pp. 35–6.

58 www.brickhillcricket.co.uk (last accessed 17 Mar 2012)..

59 syscl.co.uk/cricket/documentation.../league-rules-mainmenu-12.html   (last accessed 25 Sep 2011).

60 www.brickhillcricket.co.uk (last accessed 17 Mar 2012).

61 http://radwaycc.co.uk/Teams.htm (last accessed 17 Mar 2012).

62 www.brickhillcricket.co.uk (last accessed 17 Mar 2012).

63 B. Houlihan, *Sport and Society: A Student Introduction* (London, Sage, 2008), pp. 226, 231.

64 J. Williams ('Cricket', in T. Mason (ed.), *Sport in Britain* (Cambridge, Cambridge University Press, 1989), p. 133) also says that lack of playing fields restricted cricket opportunities at school.

65 A. West, *1892–1992: One Hundred Years of the Ribblesdale Cricket League* (Preston, Cranden Press, 1992), p. 92.

66 *Ibid.*, p. 93.

67 Woodlands Cricket Club, *Centenary Year*, p. 69.

68 *Huddersfield Daily Examiner*, 12 May 1916.

69 Woodlands Cricket Club, *Centenary Year*, p. 69.

70 *Ibid.*

71 Interview: 6 Jul 2009.

72 For example, the Ribblesdale League. See www.ribblesdalecricketleague.co.uk/History%20Second%20World%20War%201940-1951.htm (last accessed 17 Mar 2012). But, at the same time, the Reading Youths Cricket League continued to operate throughout the war.

73 http://www.haworthwestend.com/facts.htm (last accessed 25 Sep 2011).

74 http://www.southportcricket.co.uk/history.html (last accessed 17 Mar 2012).

75 Interview: 26 Aug 2009.

76 Interview: 18 Aug 2009.

77 In South Wales, for example, we have the Bridgend & District Youth Cricket League being founded in 1975 and the South Wales Junior Cricket League being formed in 1972. See www.swjcl.org.uk/index2.htm (last accessed 17 Mar 2012).

78 Interview: 16 Jul 2009.

79 Shaw, *History of Evesham Cricket Club*, p. 33.

80 Interview: 26 Aug 2009.

81 The club states: 'The under 7s is a break off from the under 9s in previous years to allow us to coach in much smaller groups to allow ease the pressure of demand on the young coaches. These sessions will take place on a Monday night from 5:50pm to 7pm. Mark Cook will drop down after a successful one year stint coaching the under 13 to a league and cup double in 2007. He will be assisted by newly qualified ECB Level two coach Mark Nursey. The sessions will start on Monday 7th April and continue throughout the season.'

82 www.brickhillcricket.co.uk (last accessed 17 Mar 2012).

83 Ibid.
84 www.bcsccjuniors.co.uk/aboutus.htm (last accessed 8 Oct 2011).
85 www.beckenhamcc.co.uk/juniors/juniors.html (last accessed 17 Mar 2012).
86 www.plymouthcricketclub.com (last accessed 17 Mar 2012).
87 www.thirskcricket.co.uk (last accessed 17 Mar 2012).
88 www.bapchildcc.co.uk/index.php?option=com_content&task=view&id=20& Itemid=64 (last accessed 8 Oct 2011).
89 www.didcotcricketclub.co.uk/junior_cricket.htm (last accessed 8 Oct 2011).
90 www.sussexcricket.co.uk/the-club/recreationalcricket/clubs-leagues/junior-cricket (last accessed 17 Mar 2012).
91 http://thirsk.nidderdaleleague.co.uk/junior-cricket (last accessed 8 Oct 2011).
92 ECB recommendations, Junior sport is about participation, posted on 22 Sep 2008.
93 http://findarticles.com/p/articles/mi_7673/is_200708/ai_n32255027/ ?tag=content;col1 arnoldism etc jun spt about excellence, fitness, educative (last accessed 8 Oct 2011).

6 Grassroots cricket in the twenty-first century

If Test and county cricket have reached a crossroads in the early years of the twentieth century, so has the grassroots version of the game. The notion of village cricket – conjuring up, as it does, images of genteel competition, church bells and cucumber sandwiches – seems to have passed its sell-by date. Local cricket today is a different animal altogether.

In the first place, grassroots cricket has embraced the idea of competition almost totally. In the past there have been parts of the country that have scorned the idea of playing the game in organised leagues.[1] Here the pure ethos of amateurism held sway, just as it did in rugby union right up until the 1990s. Today, a few friendly sides remain, but on the whole local cricket is highly regimented and has fully embraced the idea of organised competition. The challenge now is to find the right balance of leagues and cups and to work out how best to deal with the Twenty20 revolution.

The world is also getting smaller. In the past, a local club might have had relationships with the local butcher, the landlord at the village pub and the farmer in the adjacent field. It might have pinned its teamsheets up in the local shop window and gone on a September tour of East Anglia or North Wales. In the age of globalisation, this has now changed. A club can secure a professional's services over the Internet (he could come from any country on the globe – from Australia to the Netherlands) and deal with a local sports goods manufacturer who gets his cricket bats from a supplier in India. Weekend line-ups can be posted on the club's website and the September tour could take in various islands in the Caribbean.

Likewise, there has been a commercial revolution. Of course, clubs have always had to make ends meet and search out benefactors. But in recent years, the commercial imperatives in grassroots cricket have grown larger. Outgoings have increased – it is now quite expensive to put on a league match – and this has meant that incomings have had to keep pace. No longer can a club rely on annual subscriptions, match fees and, in a number of northern leagues, gate money. Instead, it has to have a non-stop schedule of fundraising activities. In the early twentieth century, clubs held bazaars and whist drives; a hundred years on, they have scratchcards and fantasy football competitions. They also seek out sponsors for anything and everything connected with the club – from the official website to boundary flags.

In the twenty-first century there are other actors that local clubs and leagues have to interact with. First, the government. There is a Department for Media, Culture and Sport and in its policies and public pronouncements, the government is increasingly shaping the way in which the game is run at grassroots level. Its policy on school playing fields – selling them off or not – and its attitude to PE in schools and issues such as child protection is having a significant impact. The government of the day also holds the purse strings. Through Sport England and the National Lottery, it can dictate how much public money is invested in grassroots sport – whether in coaching schemes, new pavilions or other things. Hill is in doubt that sport and politics have to mix.[2]

Second, the English Cricket Board. The ECB is cricket's governing body and plays a key role in local sport. In recent years it has been proactive in the area of grassroots development. In particular, its Clubmark-Focus Club agenda has put down a clear marker. The bottom line is that only clubs which meet set criteria will be eligible for ECB grants in the future. Critics say that this system will result in the rich clubs getting richer and the poor clubs becoming poorer. The ECB has also launched initiatives in urban areas and state schools to improve participation rates in the sport.

The reality, though, is that in the first years of the twenty-first century, cricket clubs face many problems. It's not just raising funds and keeping afloat that preoccupies club officials, but combating vandalism and other types of anti-social behaviour. Many clubs are managed as a small business would be. Evenley in Northamptonshire, 'is organised by its own management committee, which comprises playing and non-playing members of the club. They meet on a monthly basis to have informal discussions about topical issues, which range from sponsorship, fundraising and social events through to more tactical discussions about selection and organisation of the club in general.'[3]

Leagues, cups and Twenty20

As Chapter 3 made clear, the 'competition' revolution took place in the late nineteenth century. Leagues and cups were a radical idea then and they transformed the nature of the game at a local level. New competitions established themselves across the country and many have survived into the twenty-first century.

However, in some parts of the country, there has been resistance to the idea of 'competitive' cricket. Not until 1961 did Cuckney in Nottinghamshire join the Bassetlaw League.[4] 'Organised competition' arrived in Devon as late as the

1960s.[5] Evesham in Worcestershire played friendly cricket up to 1971 when they joined the Worcestershire League and the 'era of league cricket' dawned.[6] And it was in 1972 that Buckinghamshire side Great Brickhill entered its first knockout cup. In the same period, 'The Club recognised the importance of the introduction of league cricket for the development of the game of cricket and joined the local league'.[7] Even in the twenty-first century, non-competitive cricket still has its adherents. At Evenley, in the South Northamptonshire League, 'There are ... a few friendlies on a Sunday afternoon; this a lesser standard of cricket, played with less emphasis on competition, and more on having fun, and enjoying the sport ... the Sunday team accommodates a wide variation in standards of ability, from the less able to the better players, and from the younger players to the more mature'.[8]

Duncan Stone has examined the situation in Surrey. In the early part of the twentieth century, Surrey embraced league cricket just as other parts of the country did. However, in the inter-war years, with the dominance of the Club Cricket Championship, the authorities basically turned their back on league cricket and opted exclusively for 'friendly' cricket. But, in 1946 a cup competition was established and in 1969 a league format was adopted. What does the Surrey example say about the development of grassroots cricket? Primarily, that cricket's development was different and uneven. Whereas in the north, league cricket was engrained, in the south it was viewed with suspicion, perhaps even contempt. This is a fascinating subplot to the main story, and we should guard against making generalisations and assuming that the development of cricket was even across the country.

Today, there is a new set of issues to be considered. How should leagues be organised? How should grassroots cricket respond to the Twenty20 revolution? In 1997, the ECB published *Raising the Standard*, a document which offered English cricket a blueprint for the future. It was based on the thinking of ex-England coach Mickey Stewart, who had suggested a 'pyramid' structure for league cricket in Surrey.[9] Among other things, *Raising the Standard* said that each county should have its own 'premier league' – the stated aim being to raise standards at the top level of recreational cricket and thus lessen the gap between recreational cricket and county cricket. The ECB wanted a network of premier leagues – they would fund the leagues and also accredit them on an annual basis. The new premier leagues, at the apex of a pyramid structure of feeder leagues, would have links with other leagues and allow aspirational clubs to join. The ECB seemed to have the Australian model in mind: clubs would be allowed only one overseas player and have demonstrated a commitment to junior cricket.

Creating a network of premier leagues was never going to be a trouble-free experience. The ECB and its county boards ran into a number of problems. Some established leagues dug their heels in and, basing their argument on history, tradition and civic pride, said no to the idea – for example, the Bradford League and the Lancashire League (whose membership of fourteen clubs had been unchanged since 1897). In some areas, there was longstanding rivalry between leagues or there were several leagues, each of a similar standard; and, thus, gaining a consensus on how to proceed was almost impossible – for example, in Lancashire. There were also a number of geographical problems and anomalies that had to be overcome. In the north-west, was it really practicable for Stockport to play Settle or Todmorden to play Kendal? Almost certainly not. But in smaller counties, and also in areas where leagues were less well established, the process was easier to manage.

In 2012, there are twenty-five premier leagues in existence. Not all of the country is covered and some leagues – like the Northern Premier League – have not fulfilled the stated criteria (it has no feeder leagues). Critics also argue that if the overall aim is to improve the standard of grassroots cricket, it makes little sense to allow Premier League sides to pay an overseas professional to play for them (the current situation). In general, what the ECB has realised is that it has little power; the leagues control themselves and the one-size-fits-all approach doesn't necessarily work because counties vary greatly in size and demographic distribution.

Less than a decade on from *Raising the Standard*, grassroots cricket had to formulate a response to the Twenty20 revolution sweeping the country. Limited-overs cricket had been played for many decades,[10] but Twenty20 – although not too dissimilar to the format of evening-league cricket – had a distinctive appeal and had been marketed effectively by the ECB. The county game embraced Twenty20 cricket in 2003 and has not looked back. In fact, the number of Twenty20 matches played by a county in a typical summer has almost trebled since the format's inception. The first Twenty20 international took place in 2005 and the inaugural World Cup in 2007 in South Africa. And to add spice to the mix, the Indian Cricket League and Indian Premier League both debuted – controversially – in 2008. These leagues comprise artificial, franchised teams with no history, heritage, tradition, or even a club, supporters having only the name of their city with which to identify. The success of these competitions, despite these handicaps, indicates the power of advertising and the popularity of Twenty20 with the public.

So how would the grassroots game respond? Of course, it was inevitably affected by the tidal wave of enthusiasm for the format that seemed to be sweeping the world, and England in particular. But the evidence suggests that local league cricket has been affected only slightly by the Twenty20 revolution. Why is this?

In the first place, it has to be recognised that local clubs have been playing 20-over cricket for decades. Evening leagues have a long history in England – and most are organised on a 20-over-a-side basis (or equivalent).[11] In addition, when weekend games are, at most, 45-, 50- or 55-over-a-side affairs, the idea of playing only twenty overs is not as novel or innovative as it might appear to a first-class cricketer who regularly plays in matches of three, four or five days' duration. Local cricketers also point out that Twenty20 puts significant demands on their time (unlike professional cricketers, most will be at work during the day) and that in some areas where there is no tradition of evening league cricket, Twenty20 games starting at 6pm are even more of a culture shock.[12] In general, local leagues have embraced Twenty20 cricket, and given it a place in their calendar, but it has yet to usurp the league or the main cup competition as the 'must win' competition.[13]

In terms of structure and playing format, Twenty20 is the latest dilemma that local league cricket has had to face, but there have been others. Should matches be limited overs or based on time or declarations? And if it's overs, how many? Should points be awarded only to the winning team? Or is the concept of a 'losing draw' a useful one?

Globalisation and its effects

In the last chapter we considered immigration and multiculturalism and their effect on local cricket. As a sequel to this, we will now assess the impact of globalisation on grassroots sport. According to Simon Jeffery, globalisation is a complex phenomenon. He writes: '[It] could be a great deal of different things, or perhaps multiple manifestations of one prevailing trend. It has become a buzzword that some will use to describe everything that is happening in the world today. The dictionary definition is as follows. Globalisation (n) is the "process enabling financial and investment markets to operate internationally, largely as a result of deregulation and improved communications" (Collins) or − from the US − to "make worldwide in scope or application" (Webster).'[14]

It could be argued that local league cricket has been affected by globalisation in a number of ways. First, the hiring of overseas professionals. Ever since the early years of the twentieth century, local clubs have signed big-name stars from abroad. Having the foresight, and ability, to sign an overseas pro was a sign of ambition and aspiration. It brought great prestige to a club at a time when there was something quite 'mysterious' and 'of the unknown' about cricketers from foreign lands. In the early days, professionals were generally either English or West Indian or from the Subcontinent. It would be a few decades until it became economic to sign professionals from the Southern Hemisphere.

Today, with clubs able to gather intelligence via www.cricinfo.com, an array of agents and middlemen acting on behalf of players around the world, and cheap air fares, it is relatively easy to sign an overseas player, finance permitting.[15] Likewise, the Internet has made it much easier for overseas cricketers to hawk their CVs around interested (and uninterested) clubs. In 2009, this circular email was forwarded to clubs in the UK by a Chennai-based all-rounder:

hi, there,

may i humbly request you to go thru my mail for a minute or two … I am from chennai in south india and a seasoned allrounder with bags of experience and references in u,k. as i have decided to throw my hat in the ring wrt u.k season of 2009, a tad late b'cos of personal reasons, i am mailing to u to politely and humbly enquire as to whether there r any clubs looking to fill in for an injury vacancy or a last minute SOS call …

> best wishes for a good sunny season.
> pat

Such emails are now par for the course and emphasise how easy it now is for overseas professionals to 'sell themselves' and make contacts via the Web.[16]

Ashby Hastings in Leicestershire have created an online 'hall of fame' for their overseas professionals, 1996–2010,[17] while on their website, Kent club Orpington list their professionals over the last decade:

2008 Brendan Lyon Canberra, Australia
2007 Joshua Scott Sydney, Australia
2006 Wilkin Mota Mhumbai, India
2004–05 Wessels Woolmorans Cape Town, South Africa
2002 Kashif Iqbal (one game) Pakistan
2000 William Stibbs Perth, Australia
1999 David McFarren Perth, Australia
1998 Abi India
1996 Alan Le Pair Brisbane, Australia

Five out of Orpington's nine professionals have been Australian. Cheap airfares have obviously been a factor but also clubs' desire to inject some Aussie 'spunk' and 'attitude' into their team. This has also been evident among county sides in recent years.[18]

Second, the growth of the European Union has impacted on the grassroots game. Clubs and leagues need to be fully aware of EU legislation and how this relates to the local game. One league has stated:

EU Player (No registration restriction)

To qualify to play as an EU player, the person must meet 1 of the following 4 criteria:
1) Hold a Birth Certificate stating that his place of birth is within the EU.
2) Have a Mother or Father born within the EU, and have himself been permanently resident as a citizen of the EU for the preceding year.
3) Be aged 15 years or under and have been permanently resident as a citizen in the EU for the preceding year.
4) Have been permanently resident as a citizen of the EU for at least the last 2 consecutive years, and hold documentary proof from the EU government concerned that he may remain in the EU without any time restriction for a minimum of 3 consecutive years calculated from his entry date into the EU.

Note A: The allowed period of absence from the EU, on holiday for example, in respect of 2), 3), or 4) above, is a maximum of 28 days per calendar year.

Note B: A person holding only an EU/UK 'Subject' passport (including a British Subject, British Dependant, British Overseas Citizen, British National Overseas Citizen, and British Protected Person, or an EU country equivalent passport), as opposed to a full EU/UK 'Citizen' passport, does not qualify him of right as an EU player, under any circumstances, in respect of 1), 2), or 3) above.[19]

In effect, local cricket has had to adapt itself to changed political circumstances. Some leagues have even introduced annual awards such as 'EU Player of the Season'.[20]

Third, the effects of globalisation can be seen in the cricket equipment business. Up to the 1970s and 1980s, companies were almost exclusively 'local' in terms of their suppliers, manufacturers and customers. Now they are part of a global market. Solly Sports, based in Dewsbury, is a good example of a company that has exploited the effects of increased globalisation. Proprietor Solly Adam explains:

> Every autumn I visit business contacts on the Subcontinent and in the Far East. In Karachi, I place orders with clothing companies. In Bangkok, I deal with companies who make cricket shirts and trousers, and also manufacturers of coloured clothing; the quality is good and they can deal in big orders. In Pakistan, I go to Lahore and Sialkot and buy bats, pads, gloves and balls. In India, I visit a variety of sports goods manufacturers in Amritsar. I also have contacts in China who make bags and shoes for me, and in Bangladesh who are specialist manufacturers of cricket caps. Via the Internet, I receive orders from Australia and New Zealand and I am on the verge of opening a store in Florida. Working out of Yorkshire and receiving samples is fine, but I prefer to visit my contacts in person. It is worth my while to do so. The Internet and cheap air fares make it economical. This is a massive change from twenty or thirty years ago.[21]

Finally, English clubs who go on an annual tour are now more inclined to travel abroad. Once upon a time a team might fix up a couple of end-of-season games in East Anglia or Wiltshire or another scenic part of the country.[22] Now, with cheap airfares, it is commonplace for clubs (with the necessary ambition) to arrange tours to the Caribbean (in particular).

The Perkins club in Shropshire have toured Barbados twice:

> At last the 1st of March [1999?] arrived and once again Perkins CC were off on tour to the friendly, sun-kissed island of Barbados. This was our second trip to the island – our first in 1997 was so enjoyable that we decided that we must go back again. We had a party of 38 – which included 15 players. In the two weeks that we were there we were to play 5 games.[23]

The club website reported on the tourists' five games and then announced: 'Our sights are now set on a tour to South Africa in 2 or 3 years time. Wonder if we can win a match there? ... No harm in dreaming is there!'[24]

Commercialisation: sponsorship and fundraising

In his book on the social history of sport, Holt talks about the 'dramatic moves' to 'open sport up to the market' in the modern era. He identifies the need to make profits and notes the way that sport has become 'internationalised', but he also maintains that it is not a business like any other business.[25] As he says, 'Spectator sport may have been partially commercialised but it never became a capitalist leisure enterprise'.[26] So we are dealing here with a sector of society that is 'different' and we need to bear this in mind as we analyse modern clubs' efforts to make money and stay afloat in an ever-competitive world.

In recent years, the grassroots game has undergone a massive commercial revolution. Of course, ever since the early nineteenth century, cricket clubs have been established as mini-businesses, and club treasurers have produced balance sheets, with details of income and expenditure. Jeffrey Stanyer has analysed the workings of Exeter. His research enables us to understand the relative importance of income sources and the seasonal nature of some of them. Given a minor billing are gentlemen's evenings, race nights, advertising boards, play group, one-off hire, summer and winter rents, fruit machine takings, donations, dances and discos, lotteries, gate money and 'big occasions'; emphasised slightly more are subscriptions, catering profits, match fees, bar profits and squash club rent.[27]

So, clubs have always had to make ends meet. Birley says that even the most successful village clubs, like Troon in Cornwall, exist on the breadline.[28] Today, rising costs have forced clubs into professionalising their approach to commercial matters. In the twenty-first century, it is quite expensive to run a local cricket club. In addition to the many background costs a club has to meet – such as ground rent and insurance – there is the issue of matchday expenses, which have escalated in recent years. For a typical league club, expenditure and income on a matchday might be as shown in Table 6.1.

Clubs have been forced to respond. It is not just Premiership football clubs that have an array of sponsors and advertisers (it is actually quite hard to differentiate between sponsors and advertisers at this level). Grassroots cricket clubs are just the same; without these people – who, more often than not, will gain little commercially from their involvement – clubs would find it almost impossible to survive. In some ways, in fact, sponsorship has superseded patronage as the lifeblood of clubs.

The language that clubs use to 'make their pitch' to prospective sponsors is interesting. Milton Keynes emphasise the interlocking nature of the local community and brand awareness: 'Every year we look for opportunities to involve local businesses in our competitive games, and give them the chance to associate themselves with a thriving local club.'[29] Likewise, Norwich make an

Table 6.1   *Matchday expenditure and income for a typical league club*

Expenditure		Income
Fees for two umpires	£60	Gate money
Fee for scorer	£15	Raffle
Cost of matchball	£18	Players' subs
Groundsman	£25	Teas
Cost of producing matchday programme		Bar
Payment to tea ladies (at some clubs)		
Fee for other matchday employee/s (e.g. ball-finder)		
Other fees/costs		
Total £118 minimum		At Golcar in Huddersfield, this income (even without the bar) usually covers the £118 figure

appeal to businesses and individuals and stress the benefits that will accrue from sponsorship: 'For businesses you can advertise your services on custom made boards that surround our two cricket grounds ... A board at one of our grounds costs £250 per season and boards at both grounds cost £450 per season. And of course it is a tax deductible expense for the business concerned.'[30] Meanwhile, Skegness are a fairly traditional club in the way they conceive of sponsorship. They list their sponsors – with little elaboration – on their website.[31] Other clubs not only have a plethora of sponsors and advertisers, but are able to offer a variety of packages. Table 6.2 lists the packages on offer at a selection of clubs.

What does all this demonstrate about grassroots cricket in the early twenty-first century? First, it is clear that sponsorship and advertising are crucial to a local club. With rising costs, local clubs are continually challenged to make ends meet and a major sponsorship deal, or a variety of small ones, can, literally, make the difference between surviving and folding. The official history of Ramsbottom states that the

> philosophy and institution of sponsorship, as part of wider policies being practised by an ever increasing number of business concerns of all kinds, has 'come to the rescue' of Ramsbottom Cricket Club and the [Lancashire] League. From small beginnings around 1980, sponsorship has become a mainstay of Club finances. At Ramsbottom, John Heys has liaised with Sponsors from as far afield as South Wales, Scotland, and Germany. Sponsors are not actively sought. The relationship has been found to flourish best in circumstances where the Sponsor conceives his part as that of a good neighbour or friend contributing to the welfare of the local community while mindful of the needs of his employees.[32]

Second, and this is not to demean local clubs, it is unclear whether sponsors and advertisers gain very much from their investment. Anecdotal evidence suggests

Table 6.2   *Advertising/sponsorship packages offered by clubs*

Hayes CC (Middlesex)	Loyalty Club Sponsor • Match ball sponsorship • Match sponsorship • Fixture card adverts Premium Club Sponsor • Event sponsorship • Corporate sponsorship • Main club sponsors	Special Sponsor Package • Individual teams sponsorship • Boundary board displays • Pavilion advertising boards
Dunnington CC (North Yorkshire)	Ground sponsorship Scoreboard Scoreboard hoarding Boundary hoarding Covers	Matchballs Team sponsorship Website Event sponsorship
Four Elms CC (Kent)	Package 1: Fixtures card advertising Package 2: Website advertising Package 3: Advertising hoarding Package 4: Team sponsorship Package 5: Hire of ground	
Chapel-en-le-Frith (Derbyshire)	Matchball: sponsorship of a match or matchball for a first eleven or second eleven game Team: sponsorship of a senior or junior team Ground: advertising hoardings, boards, banners placed around the ground Club: exclusive sponsorship of the club	
Norwich Coltishall Wanderers (Norfolk)	Major Sponsor • Overseas player and junior sponsor • Shirt and equipment sponsor Smaller Packages • 'Corporate' style hospitality packages • Matchball sponsors • Golf day team sponsor • Six-a-side team sponsor • Club lottery	

that most individuals or companies who put their money into clubs do so for sentimental rather than hard-headed business reasons (often, in fact, sponsors and advertisers have a personal connection with the club – they may have friends there or may be players/members themselves). At Todmorden in the Lancashire

League, local company Videotel recently withdrew their sponsorship because of lack of sales.[33]

Third, cricket clubs have shown themselves to be inventive and innovative as regards sponsorship ideas. Their motto seems to be: if it moves, get a sponsor for it! In addition to the standard items (balls, matches, websites and the rest), certain clubs are now seeking sponsors for boundary flags (Golcar). Other clubs, like Sowerby St Peter's in Calderdale, have erected special marquees for their matchday sponsors.[34] One consequence of this inventiveness is that an individual or business can now pick and choose what kind of sponsorship they want to become involved in and at what price. Finally, it should be pointed out that local cricket is now attracting some big-name sponsors. Supermarket chain Morrisons sponsor Norfolk club Fakenham and Mercedes Benz used to sponsor Almondbury Wesleyans in Huddersfield.[35] These sponsorship deals say a great deal about the appeal of local cricket, the professionalisation of the game at a grassroots level, and the amount of money that is now required to sustain a local club.

Where there is a shortfall in sponsorship, local clubs have to start raising their own money. This has become a reflex, just as it has for other voluntary organisations such as churches and football clubs. In 1947, Ramsbottom, of the Lancashire League, staged a house-to-house collection to help pay for their Riverside Ground.[36]

At local clubs, fundraising takes many and various forms, including 100/200 clubs, 6-a-side/Twenty20 competitions (and variations on the theme), auctions, bonfires, buy-a-brick schemes, car boot sales, club clothing/merchandise, dinners, encouraging individual donations (with special benefits for Community Amateur Sports Clubs),[37] fantasy football/cricket competitions, fun days, golf days, hiring out club premises, lottery/bonus ball draws, members' subscriptions, online shopping (with clubs taking a cut), player fines, prediction competitions, presentation evenings, quiz nights, race nights/snail races, raffles, scratchcards, sponsored walks and runs, sportsman's dinners, supermarket bag-packing, pig roasts, summer balls, teas, and webshops.

In the early twentieth century, clubs used to raise money by staging big social occasions. Ramsbottom held bazaars in 1903 and 1936 (a four-day event) to clear debts of £400 and £1,200 respectively.[38] Great Brickhill in Buckinghamshire had to pay for 'cricket equipment, scorebooks, fixture cards, repairs and painting of sightscreens, work to the pitch, repair of the mower, the umpires' and scorer's tea, transport to away games, carriage of equipment from the railway station and postage. Funds were raised from concerts, dances and whist drives as well as subscriptions and the sale of fixture cards.' And, thus, we are told that in 1933, fundraising took on a new complexion: 'For the first time, a comedian was contracted to entertain at the Club's annual dinner and a hundred tickets were sold.'[39]

The example of Caythorpe in Nottinghamshire is also illuminating. They lost their ground in 1959 but within a few years they had raised £1,400 – including a £400 grant from the National Playing Fields Association – and by the early 1960s they had moved into a new ground. Their main fundraiser was a fête held on Bank Holiday Monday, August 1963. Local man Charles Cappendale remembers:

> The marquee, stalls and games were in place and the helpers arrived … Crowds flooded in all afternoon. By 6pm the helpers were totally exhausted but the Treasurer went home to count the day's takings of £3,000 of which £600 profit was used to purchase the cricket pavilion and which now stands as a symbol of the efforts of a small village with a wonderful heart and to Mr S A Monk, a superb engineer.[40]

The pavilion bar is also crucial. It is difficult to overstate the importance of bar takings to local clubs. In any league, clubs can be divided into those with and without bars – it is a central area of demarcation. Generalising: those with bars have a larger potential turnover and might have the power to recruit a professional; those without powers have a lower turnover and are necessarily limited in their spending plans. Evesham in Worcestershire installed a bar in 1940 and were soon making £30 a year.[41]

What themes and issues are evident in the sphere of fundraising? First, its importance and omnipresence. Take this statement from Malton and Old Malton:

> In 1998 fundraising efforts helped us to demolish the century old pavilion at the Malton Cricket ground and build the new club house and electronic scoreboard, giving much improved facilities for members and visitors alike … 2008 finally saw the construction of our new all weather net facility at the Malton Cricket Ground … Malton & Old Malton Cricket Club has had a good reputation in fundraising and sponsorship for over 10 years, we are now able to provide some of the best cricket facilities in North Yorkshire.[42]

On reading this, club members would be in no doubt as to the reputation of the club and the duties bestowed on themselves.

Second, clubs are continually trying to improve their facilities. Flick through a selection of local newspapers and you will see new clubhouses, pavilions, scoreboxes and net facilities being opened. Sidmouth, by contrast, are trying to raise £40,000 to replace the thatch on their pavilion roof![43] Of course, clubs can take advantage of grants and other funding opportunities, but there will usually be a shortfall or balance that will have to be met through fundraising.[44] Moreover, some clubs will only be able to afford a professional (especially one from overseas, who will need airfare, accommodation and transport covered) if they make an extra effort in the arena of fundraising.

Third, clubs are becoming more professional in their approach to fundraising. Many clubs will have a fundraising officer who will coordinate all fundraising efforts. Occasionally, a club will advertise for a specialist. Saltaire in Bradford were in the market for a part-time appointment:

A fundraiser with experience in either fundraising or a related field is required to help organise existing key fund raising activities and to generate and maximise new income for the cricket club. The post-holder will carry out duties part-time in their own time from their own home. Use of a car would be an advantage.[45]

Fourth, there are ethical problems for some clubs. A club linked to a Methodist church, for example, may not be able to hold raffles or host a bar of any sort.[46] This was the case with the Northowram Methodist Church club in Halifax. In 1952, they fell out with the Methodist authorities over a raffle (at this time the Methodist Church forbade raffles on church premises). As a result, they switched their name to Northowram Hedge Top and severed their link with the Methodist Church.

Fifth, the internet revolution has assisted clubs in their efforts to raise money. A good proportion of clubs now have a website: in the twenty-first century, a modern, well-run website is a symbol of status. It enables the club committee to post news items, minutes of meetings and other information (team selections, for example). It also enables club members to communicate and interact as a virtual community. Anecdotal evidence suggests that junior cricketers particularly enjoy seeing photos of themselves in action on the web. Clubs with websites also have an advantage when it comes to fundraising. They can advertise sponsorship packages, encourage local companies to buy space on their site, publicise club events, sell club merchandise via their own webshop, and benefit from special online money-making facilities, such as easyfundraising,org.uk,[47] Froggybank,[48] www.buy.at,[49] and other schemes.

The involvement of government and other bodies

In his consideration of the state's involvement in sport, Hill identifies two key eras. First, the period from the 1860s to 1945, which he labels the 'golden age' of municipal leisure involvement.[50] And second, the 1970s and 1980s, when there was a significant expansion in what he calls 'local leisure provision' (for example, he refers to the number of leisure centres increasing from zero at the beginning of the 1970s to around 1,200 by the end of the 1980s).[51]

This involvement on the part of municipal authorities is contrasted with the role of central government which, in the view of Hill and other authors, played only a minimal role.[52] (It seemingly had only two concerns: the health of the population and using sport as a vehicle of international diplomacy.)[53] But gradually, in the post-war period, Hill argues, central government 'took on more involvement' in sport, even if this was on an ad hoc basis.[54]

This point is reinforced by Houlihan. He maintains that in recent years there has been a 'growth' in the politics-sport relationship, and in the role of government in sport. He says it was in the 1960s that the government acknowledged that sport was a key responsibility, and that there is now a close relationship between central and local government and sport.[55] He quotes a statistic that makes the point. In 1988–89, the Sports Council had a budget of £45m; in the same year, local authorities spent £738m on sport.[56] He also cites figures on swimming pools and sports halls to emphasise that municipal authorities are now fundamental to the provision of sport at a local level.[57]

Sport is now, today, a major political issue. From the London Olympics to the war on obesity, central government and local councils are having to deal with sport- and fitness-related issues. The stated aim of the Department for Media, Culture and Sport is 'to improve the quality of life for all through cultural and sporting activities, to support the pursuit of excellence and to champion the tourism, creative and leisure industries'.[58] As regards sport, the government states:

> We are committed to providing access to sport and work to encourage the take-up of sport across communities and by children and young people in particular. Sport has an unmatched ability to mobilise and excite people in their millions. Sport matters to most people, but fewer of us play sport or are physically active on a regular basis.[59]

Unquestionably, therefore, the government is now a key player in local sport.

However, in recent years, governments have been sending out mixed messages about grassroots sport. On the one hand, they continue to sell off school playing fields. In 2008, The Observer reported that 187 playing fields had been sold off in the previous decade.[60] In 2000, the BBC stated, 'Despite a series of public commitments from the government to preserve school playing fields, the National Playing Fields Association says that its latest figures – up to March 2000 – show that 96% of sell-off applications are still being approved'.[61] Margaret Morrissey, of campaign group Parents Outloud, said: 'Despite all the Government's wonderful words on this issue, it seems that when we get to the truth playing fields are still being removed. It's something that ministers should be seriously ashamed of. One of the excuses we often hear is that an area of AstroTurf is being built instead. But it just isn't the same thing. Children do not run around in the same way and play on a sterile surface. Ministers are very keen to be seen playing cricket and football and running around gyms with school-children. But when there are playing fields disappearing, they're nowhere to be seen.'[62] Cricket has also been downgraded as a PE sport. In 2005, it was reported: 'Last year a government survey found that cricket was only the sixth most popular sport played in schools, often losing out to football, and not helped by shrinking playing fields and poor resources.'[63]

At the same time, successive governments have said they are committed to local sport. In 2009, Gordon Brown's government said it was taking significant steps to promote cricket. In response to a parliamentary question from Conservative MP Tony Baldry, the then parliamentary under-secretary of state for Culture, Media and Sport, Gerry Sutcliffe, stated: 'Through the PE and school sport strategy, £1.5 billion was invested in the five years to 2008. A further £783 million has been committed for the next three years. That has already helped to ensure that 90 per cent of schools now provide cricket to their pupils.'[64]

In February 2009, schools minister Ed Balls encouraged schools to use cricket in an imaginative way 'to raise standards across the curriculum'. His department announced: 'Cricket has an obvious benefit for children and young people as a competitive sport. It also has the potential to develop their understanding of other subjects in the curriculum.'[65] It was argued that through cricket, children could gain a better understanding of new technologies, maths and statistics, the history of the Commonwealth and historical change. And Balls himself stated: 'From the village green to the Ashes tests to playground scratch games, cricket is part of our national identity. Not only does it have obvious health benefits for young people, it also develops them in other ways – co-ordination, balance, team work, tactics, and remaining calm under pressure. Cricket is one of the most popular school sports and I'm convinced it can have benefits across the curriculum too. Cricket is often called an art and a science – it's time for schools to demonstrate that.'[66]

Sport England – formerly the Sports Council – is the organisation charged by the government with dispensing its money. It states: 'We invest National Lottery and Exchequer funding in organisations and projects that will grow and sustain participation in grassroots sport and create opportunities for people to excel at their chosen sport.'[67] In 2006, Sport England announced that it would be investing £10.7 million in grassroots cricket through a major grant to the ECB. According to Sportbusiness.com: 'Roger Draper, chief executive of Sport England, said that the award recognised the substantial progress made by the ECB in modernising its management and governance structures and its ambitious vision for grassroots development.' In 2009, Sport England and the ECB signed a four-year deal worth £37.8 million. The grant covered investment in all aspects of the grassroots game, with a special emphasis on increasing participation rates, women's cricket and disabled cricket. ECB chief executive David Collier stated: 'This agreement is fantastic news for cricket and will enable us to continue our work to increase opportunities for people to take part in our sport. The ECB has been awarded the largest grant of any national governing body, which demonstrates the confidence that Sport England has in our ability to deliver grassroots programmes.'[68]

In addition to the money they have invested in cricket through the ECB, Sport England have offered 'lottery funding opportunities based on potential priority policy themes such as increasing participation by women and girls, improving school-club links and building sustainable community sports clubs'.[69] As such, the inception of the National Lottery in 1994 can be seen as a landmark in the history of grassroots cricket.[70]

Local clubs now have a new source of potential income. Scores of clubs have already benefited from lottery money. For example, Church and Oswaldthistle of the Lancashire League received an 'Awards For All' grant of £10,000 to help with coaching and their ground.[71] Fladbury in Worcestershire gained £98,280 in 1998 to erect a new brick pavilion.[72] And in 2005, Stokenchurch in the Chilterns secured a grant of £162,272 to help finance a new £250,000 pavilion.[73] Leagues have also benefited. Cheshire Women's Cricket League secured an 'Awards for All' grant of £9,900 to help with coaching, equipment and the introduction of the Cheshire Girls' League in 2010.[74] The overall aim was to increase participation levels.

Sport England have stepped in as potential funders when other bodies have dropped out. A case in point occurred in 2009 when the Coalboard Regeneration Trust told Upper Haugh, South Yorkshire, that they could not find the £250,000 they had promised the club.[75] Local councils have also played a significant role. In 2009-10, for example, West Oxfordshire District Council awarded £5,000 to Bampton-in-the-Bush for the construction of a grass wicket.[76]

A number of charities have played a role in funding local cricket. The National Playing Fields Association (NPFA), which came to be known as Fields in Trust (FIT), was founded in 1925 and 'aims to protect and promote open spaces for sports and recreation in British cities and towns'. Mention should also be made of the Foundation for Sport and the Arts, which was established in 1991 and channels 'money originally donated by The New Football Pools to a wide range of sporting and artistic causes. Since 1991 we have awarded grants worth over £350 million, nearly £500 million at today's values.'[77]

ECB initiatives: Clubmark and focus clubs

The ECB's mission statement states that, 'it provides support for the game far beyond the boundaries of just international and first class cricket'. Its strategic plan for cricket, Building Partnerships, is built on four key pillars: 'Effective leadership and governance; [A] Vibrant domestic game; Enthusing participation and following especially among young people; Successful England teams.'[78] In terms of development, its objectives are:

> Increasing participation, club membership, club affiliation, coaching roles and volunteering roles, together with securing funding, promoting equity, and ensuring strong relationships with all counties – just some of the priorities for ECB's development team.[79]

Today, ECB development work centres on Clubmark and Focus Clubs. All clubs are encouraged to attain the Clubmark accreditation. And only Clubmark clubs can become Focus Clubs (although previously this was not the case). A cricket development officer will recommend Focus Club status for clubs which have attained Clubmark and are well positioned in both geographical and strategic terms. This will be based on a Memorandum of Understanding.

The ECB introduced the Clubmark accreditation in 2002, the official aim being to 'develop a vibrant and healthy club cricket infrastructure'.[80] At the time of writing, there are 950 accredited clubs.[81] The ECB states: 'The ECB Clubmark and community cricket clubs play a central role in all of these programmes and Clubmark will provide the standards that clubs involved in these programmes will aspire to ... The four themes are: Duty of Care and Safeguarding Children, The Cricket Programme, Knowing your club and its Community – One Game, Club Management.'[82] Another perspective on Clubmark comes from Heslerton in North Yorkshire. On receiving their Clubmark award, the club announced: 'Clubmark sets the entry level for cricket clubs to provide good quality cricket programmes for young people. It provides clubs with a structure and direction that will benefit them in several ways: 1) Increasing membership ... 2) Club development ... 3) Developing coaches and volunteers ... 4) Raising the profile.'[83]

The first club in the country to be 'Clubmarked' was Elvaston in Derbyshire in 2003. Club spokesman Dave Bull announced:

> We have since been reaccredited and continue to develop our facilities, links with the local community, sponsorship and membership. Clubmark has been outstanding for us. Since our original accreditation we have grown junior membership from around 50 to over 120 and are now limited by available space ... Partially sighted cricket is also now an integral part of our club, running youth clubs, coaching and matches ...[84]

On their website, another Derbyshire club, Lullington Park, have stressed the link between Clubmark and the club being attractive to parents: 'By taking the time to work towards and achieving ClubMark Lullington Park CC has shown its commitment to its junior players and to its wider local community. The ClubMark logo is recognised by both ECB and Sport England and it tells teachers, parents, community leaders, Local Authorities, funding agencies and all those with a responsibility for the welfare of young children that Lullington Park CC is a safe place for children to enjoy playing cricket.'[85] As such, Clubmark is reflective of its times.[86]

In 2005, the thirty-nine County Cricket Boards across England and Wales started the process of identifying a network of Focus Clubs and their Community Clusters. This process came on the back of the ECB launching its new strategic plan *Building Partnerships*. How is a Focus Club Community Cluster defined? According to the ECB:

> A Focus Club Community Cluster is in essence a geographic area and is a collaboration of:
> – The Focus Club (cricket club)
> – Its partnership of schools / education establishments (including primary, secondary, special education needs schools, high and further education colleges)

- Local community groups (including youth clubs, brownies, guides, cubs, etc ...)
- Local business and sponsors[87]

In short, Focus Clubs are expected to drive cricket development in their locale, support other aspirational clubs and share examples of good practice.

Today, there are more than 1,400 Focus Clubs, including seventy-six in Yorkshire.[88] They are earmarked as being key 'deliverers' of cricket development and, as a reward, are able to access ECB and other resources. According to the ECB, a Focus Club is:

- Affiliated to the ECB via their County Cricket Board.
- Committed to achieving the objectives within 'Building Partnerships'.
- Will work in partnership with ECB, the County Cricket Board, schools and the community to deliver high quality agreed outcomes.
- Has achieved or is committed to achieving and maintaining ECB Clubmark Accreditation evidencing that they are a safe, effective and child friendly club.
- Has a Club Development Plan that has been approved by the County Cricket Board and is reviewed and updated on an annual basis.

The emergence of Clubmark and Focus Clubs symbolises a key stage in the ECB's 'masterplan' for the development of grassroots cricket. They also represent the 'professionalisation' of sport at a local level and the way in which governing bodies (such as the ECB) have embraced the 'quality' agenda that is now omnipresent in business, industry and education. They have unquestionably 'raised the bar' so far as standards are concerned.

However, the ECB's Clubmark and Focus Club agenda has attracted some criticism from within the cricket community. The main charge is that Clubmark (the starting point for any club interested in bettering itself) is too onerous and demanding, and also overly bureaucratic. The argument put forward is that local clubs are voluntary organisations that rely on the goodwill of members; and thus it is unrealistic to expect them to conform to standards and practices that are common in the workplace. Critics see Clubmark as a symptom of a society that has become obsessed by matters of 'quality' and 'quality control'. Nowhere is this better illustrated than in matters of child protection. Here, many ordinary club officials would argue that ECB directives have gone too far.

Another line of thinking is that in 'raising the bar' regards standards, Clubmark is creating a world of 'haves' and 'have-nots', especially as it is only the 'haves' (those who gain the accreditation) who are able to bid for ECB funding. The critics have asked whether it is really the ECB's intention to drive a wedge between upwardly mobile clubs and the rest, as it seems to be doing? The ECB does not view the situation in these terms. Their argument is that as a governing body they would be failing in their primary aim if they did not put a premium on improving the infrastructure of local clubs. (The irony is that many Clubmark clubs would say that they had not suddenly become 'haves' anyway – with few, if any, tangible rewards for having gone through the accreditation process.)

A complicating factor is the attitude of local leagues, for the outlook of a league can condition the attitude of its member clubs. This is difficult to demonstrate but according to one cricket development manager it is a key issue.[89] Some leagues are obstructive; others just unenlightened. Either way, member clubs are not encouraged to go down the road of Clubmark and Focus Clubs. (In the future, some leagues may stipulate that all member clubs must be Clubmark-accredited – this has already started happening in football with the Charter Standard.)

Whatever reservations some might have, it is clear that the Clubmark-Focus Club agenda is now viewed as crucial to the development of grassroots cricket. According to Steve Archer, West Yorkshire Cricket Development Officer, 'Cricket is market leader and setting the trend in England. Other sports have their own accreditation – football has Charter Standard, swimming Swim 21, netball CAPS – but cricket is doing well. I met some development officers from South Africa recently and they were really impressed by Clubmark – they said they had nothing similar.'[89]

There have also been other initiatives. In May 2005, the ECB launched Chance to Shine: the stated aim being, 'to bring competitive cricket – and its educational benefits – back to at least a third of the country's state schools over a ten-year period.'[91] The scheme has been managed by the Cricket Foundation and part-funded by Sport England. Wasim Khan of the Cricket Foundation said that more than 300,000 children a year were benefiting from Chance to Shine.[92] One case study is Hove Park School in Brighton. Humanities teacher Gary Kernan was quoted as saying: 'We now have a four-lane bay with cricket nets that is used for after-school practices and flex-wickets so that cricket can be played on site.'[93]

In 2006, the ECB together with npower – the main sponsors of English cricket – launched Urban Cricket, a grassroots project which was aimed at increasing participation levels among children living in cities. Since 2006, more than 50,000 Urban Cricket kits have been distributed to children.[94] The ECB is also interested in widening participation. Hence the tournaments they put on for girls, women and the over-50s.

Continuity and change

It could be argued that in one sense, local cricket remains rooted in the past. Tim Heald has explored the concept of 'village cricket'.[95] For him, there is something timeless and authentically 'English' about this form of the grassroots game. The fact that, in the twenty-first century, village teams still play each other in front of only a few spectators – with tea ladies happily dispensing food and local pride at stake – could be viewed as an interesting social phenomenon. Moreover, national village knockout competitions are still in existence.[96]

There are other aspects of the modern game that hark back to a distant past. Some clubs devote themselves exclusively to 'friendly' cricket. The Almondbury Casuals, based in Huddersfield, are one such outfit. They have a full fixture list and a burgeoning social scene – including an annual dinner that is usually attended by nearly a hundred people – but they remain loyal to the idea of 'non-competitive' cricket and do not belong to a league. Other clubs put great store on touring, on enjoying the social side of the game. And one or two still play by 'local rules'.[97]

Around the country, there are also men and women who call themselves 'Professional Cricket Watchers'. They enjoy watching cricket at all levels and at all times. With an ageing population, there are an increasing number of retired people who try to watch cricket at all its many different levels throughout the summer months (their motto is 'Every day of the week!'). They are purists and connoisseurs, and feel slightly alienated by the commercialisation of Test cricket and even the county game. So they focus on pre-season fixtures, friendly fixtures, schools and university cricket, fixtures involving academy sides, junior cricket, seniors cricket, midweek matches, fixtures involving touring teams, charity matches, benefit games, fixtures that take place at odd times in the year, one-off games of any type and women's cricket.[98]

In a number of significant court cases, the rights of age-old cricket clubs have gazumped those of local residents.[99] At the same time, local cricket is moving with the times. Many clubs exist as part of multi-sports organisations and others have experimented with indoor cricket.[100] In terms of technology, in 2002, the ECB enabled each and every cricket club in Britain to have its own 'play-cricket.com' website. At the time, the BBC commented: 'Amateur cricket has, thankfully, progressed from the days when 11 villagers would be rounded up in the pub before the night of a game to represent their local side. These days most village sides have embraced the world of e-mail. Rather than spend hours on the phone trying to get 11 players to agree to a fixture, a bulk e-mail gets a much faster response with a lot more ease. But technology moves on apace, and the club website is the latest idea.'[101]

Many areas and leagues now boast a cricket development group. Normally, such a body comprises cricket club representatives, junior team managers, district team managers, cricket coaches, local school teachers, local authority sports development officers and others. The Staffordshire Cricket Board defines a cricket development group as, 'A group of people who come together to volunteer time and energy and take an ACTIVE part in the development of cricket in their local area', the aim being to, 'increase participation and improve the standard of cricket within the local community by producing and co-ordinating a Local Community Development Plan and sharing good practice, resources and ideas'.[102] One specific aim of cricket development groups is to encourage Clubmark applications.

Furthermore, most leagues have embraced the quality-control agenda and now publicise the fact that any club wishing to apply for membership must meet a range of (fairly strict) criteria. Expected standards are also high for member clubs in terms of administration and facilities. Ground inspections are now commonplace. In the Lincolnshire League, clubs are graded on the following issues: 'Levelness of table, Condition of table, Levelness of outfield, Condition of outfield, Evidence of groundsmanship, Covers, Scoring, Sightscreens, Outfield mowers, Table mowers, Heavy roller, Light roller, Changing rooms, Showers/toilet facilities, Catering facilities and Car parking.'[103]

Coloured clothing has also emerged as an issue. In international cricket, the first fixture to feature non-white clothing took place on 17 January 1979. It was a World Series Cricket contest between Australia (in gold) and the West Indies (in pink). Since then, some local leagues have allowed or even encouraged the wearing of coloured clothing (and in these instances, it is usually optional). With new mass production techniques, it is relatively cheap to produce coloured cricketing attire. And for a local league player, a pair of trousers and shirt may only cost between £15 and £20.[104]

Flitwick were the first team in the Bedfordshire County League to wear non-white clothing and it is something the club is very proud of. As their club website states: 'On Sundays, we field two senior teams in the Bedfordshire County League where the club has shown its innovative approach by pioneering the wearing of our own coloured kit.'[105] At Golcar in Huddersfield, coloured clothing is viewed as a bit of fun. Club official David Thorpe says: 'Our kit could be any colour. The key thing is the club badge – that's what provides the identity. Our lads get their names on the back, usually a nickname. And if we're able to get a sponsor, it can work out pretty cheap all round.'[106]

In the north of England, coloured gear has had a strong advocate in former Lancashire and England star Ian Austin.[107] Since 2000, Todmorden and Walsden have played friendly fixtures in coloured clothing, and in 2006 the *Batley News* reported that:

> This season's Priestley Cup and Shield finalists will be allowed to wear coloured clothing for the first time after a postal ballot resulted in an 18–12 vote in favour. The Bradford League's management board announced kits for the teams reaching the finals will be offered free under a new partnership with Surridge, who will provide 16 sets of shirts, trousers and sweaters for each club in the colours of their choice, plus black jackets for the umpires. Surridge have also agreed to provide new shirts for the Bradford League representative side.[108]

In 2008, Illingworth St Mary's took innovation to the limit. They introduced 'double and negative scoring zones as well as coloured clothing, equipment, black sightscreens and white balls'.[109]

Some leagues have experimented with pink balls,[110] and some clubs have established their own system of squad numbers. Blankney in Lincolnshire unveiled theirs in 2009. The accompanying note said that squad numbers had been introduced, 'to assist scorers in player identification, who will be given a list of squad numbers prior to commencing the game'.[111] A club in Bradford have even installed their own floodlights.[112] Some clubs have agreed to the siting of mobile phone masts on their property in an effort to raise extra funds,[113] while others have embraced the green agenda. St Just in Cornwall were the first to install energy-efficient Photo Voltaic (PV) solar panels.[114]

On occasions, the past, present and future coalesce. In September 2009, David Normanton – treasurer of Stones and also president of the Halifax League – spoke at the official opening of the redeveloped club pavilion. He said it was a proud moment for him and referred his audience back to 1884 when the club had been formed. He said: 'In those days, cricket would have been played in any field that looked empty. There would have been no wicket as such and certainly no pavilion. The eleven men who represented Stones in 1884 would be very proud – and also somewhat startled – by the progress the club has made since then.' In effect, Normanton was articulating the view that officials of any club have a responsibility to their forebears and also to future generations.[115]

In recent years, local cricket clubs have encountered their fair share of social problems including vandalism and graffiti. It could be argued that they are particularly vulnerable to anti-social behaviour. Many cricket grounds are set in isolated and exposed locations, and during the winter months there is often little activity at clubs. Take these recent examples:

Vandalism at Whitchurch Cricket Club, 4 December 2008

Vandals have struck twice at Whitchurch Cricket Club, causing an estimated £1,000 worth of damage. Seventeen perimeter fence panels have been kicked in by the culprits…Club chairman Paul Wojda says they suspect a pupil of Sir John Talbot's is responsible – and have furnished the police with a name.[116]

Vandals target Droitwich Cricket Club, 7 August 2009

Hard-working volunteers at Droitwich Spa Cricket Club saw their efforts undone when the ground was targeted by vandals … The most recent vandalism … saw spraypaint daubed across the pavilion and other items …[117]

To add insult to injury, it is the case that the police are often uninterested in such 'petty crime'. What can clubs do to withstand such attacks? The answer is very little. Many clubs go into hibernation during the winter months and, at the same time, do not have the finances to install state-of-the-art security systems.

Three examples from the Huddersfield area are also illuminating. Holmfirth had to contend with a serial graffiti artist in 2002. Meanwhile, Golcar have suffered from bouts of petty vandalism, which has forced them to consider installing shutters on their clubhouse windows. Club officials say that the vandals strike at odd times and that, with minimal assistance from the police, they are powerless to apprehend the perpetrators.

Bradley and Colnebridge joined the Huddersfield Central League in 1975. They were forced to leave their old ground at Colnebridge in the early 1990s and by 1995 had plans in place for a new pavilion at their new abode, Warrenside, Deighton. The pavilion finally arrived in 1997, but a fire ripped through it at Christmas 2006. According to the *Yorkshire Post*: 'A cricket club pavilion built less than a decade ago with £40,000 lottery cash has been destroyed in a suspected arson attack. Bradley and Colnebridge's Cricket Club's pavilion in Warrenside, Deighton, near Huddersfield, will need to be pulled down after it was severely damaged by a fire. A spokesman for West Yorkshire Fire and Rescue service said it was believed the blaze had been started deliberately … Steve Ashwell, the club's sponsorship secretary said: "Inside the pavilion there are changing rooms, a tea room, a scoreboard room and a room for machinery for looking after the pitch but it will all need to be pulled down. We think they have got inside the pavilion through the slated roof."'[118] But an amazing fundraising effort resulted in a replacement building being officially opened in July 2007.

What this chapter has proved is that the world of grassroots cricket has undergone a major transformation in recent years. In many respects it has changed out of all recognition. There are new types of competition, and even the smallest village club is now a player in an increasingly globalised world. With the ECB to the forefront, there is also now a quality agenda in the shape of Clubmark and Focus Clubs. In many ways this has brought cricket into the modern world. And finally, sport is now a major political issue. No longer can government – central or local – stay out of it.

Notes

1 See the research currently being carried out by Duncan Stone at the University of Huddersfield regarding cricket in Surrey.
2 J. Hill, *Sport, Leisure and Culture in Twentieth-Century Britain* (London, Macmillan, 2002), p. 150.
3 www.evenleycc.com/ (last accessed 18 Mar 2012).
4 http://www.cuckneycc.com/history.php (last accessed 18 Mar 2012).
5 J. Stanyer, *A Great Survivor: The History of The Exeter Cricket Club in the Nineteenth and Twentieth Centuries* (Exeter, St Leonard's Press, 2000), p. 257.
6 B. Shaw (ed.), *A History of Evesham Cricket Club* (Evesham, Evesham Cricket Club, 2004), pp. 26, 30.
7 www.brickhillcricket.co.uk (last accessed 18 Mar 2012).
8 www.bosherlay.co.uk/component/k2/item/14-evenley-cricket-club (last accessed 18 Mar 2012).
9 Like non-league soccer.
10 C. Farnworth and S. Hall, *Bacup Cricket Club: The Authorised History* (Bacup, Bacup Cricket Club, 1999), pp. 55, 59.
11 Sometimes they are 15- or 18-over contests, with overs comprising eight rather than six balls.
12 Matthew Jones, first eleven captain at Halifax League club Stones, told us that evening leagues have suffered because of a shift in work patterns. Interview: 5 Jul 2009.

13 In many places entry to Twenty20 competitions is optional, e.g. the Halifax League.

14 www.guardian.co.uk/world/2002/oct/31/globalisation.simonjeffery (last accessed 18 Mar 2012).

15 Some clubs simply advertise – see Worcester Park at www.wparkcc.co.uk/ CricketHome/Overseasplayers.aspx (last accessed 18 Mar 2012).

16 See www.ak-sports.com/Overseas%20PLayers.htm (last accessed 18 Mar 2012).

17 www.ak-sports.com/Overseas%20PLayers.htm (last accessed 18 Mar 2012).

18 On the negative effects of the influx of overseas players, see www.timeshighereduca tion.co.uk/story.asp?storycode=94738 (last accessed 18 Mar 2012).

19 www.drakes-huddersfieldcricketleague.co.uk (last accessed 18 Mar 2012).

20 www.drakes-huddersfieldcricketleague.co.uk/Miscellaneous%20Pages/ Overseas/Overseas.htm (last accessed 18 Mar 2012).

21 Interview: 16 Sep 2009.

22 See, for example, Norfolk club Ingham's tour of Sussex in 1970 – they played against Palmer School Old Boys at Gray's, Morden Rye, Hastings, Eastbourne and Tenterden. See *Norwich Mercury and Norfolk News and Journal*, 24 Jun 1970.

23 www.perkinscc.co.uk/barbados-cricket-tour.php (last accessed 18 Mar 2012).

24 *Ibid.*

25 R. Holt, *Sport and the British: A Modern History* (Oxford, Oxford University Press, 1990), pp. 7, 281.

26 *Ibid.*, p. 282.

27 Stanyer, *A Great Survivor*, p. 273.

28 D. Birley, *A Social History of English Cricket* (London, Aurum Press, 2003), p. 360.

29 www.mkcricket.org.uk/sponsorship.html (last accessed 18 Mar 2012).

30 www.norwichcricketclub.co.uk/index.php?page=sponsorship-opportunities (last accessed 18 Mar 2012).

31 They are: M.H. Electrical Contractors 26 South Parade, Skegness, Lincolnshire, PE25 3HW; Harris Amusements 36 Lumley Road, Skegness, Lincolnshire, PE25 3NG; The Villager Pub Sea Lane, Ingoldmells; George Bateman and Son Salem Bridge Brewery, Wainfleet, Lincolnshire, PE24 4JE; www.bateman.co.uk; Just Cuts 16 Lumley Road, Skegness, Lincolnshire, PE25 3NG; Flippers Restaurant and Takeaway 5–9 High Street, Skegness, Lincs, PE25 3NY; Herick Watson High Street, Skegness, Lincs, PE25 3NW; Duncan and Topliss 27 Lumley Avenue, Skegness, Lincolnshire, PE25 2AT; Jackson Building Centres, www.jacksonbc.co.uk; Roman Bank Social Club Bingo Roman Bank, Skegness, Lincolnshire.

32 J. Rushton (ed.), *Ramsbottom Cricket Club: Sesquicentenary Celebration 1845–1995* (Ramsbottom, Ramsbottom Cricket Club, 1995), p. 96.

33 Point made to us by Brian Heywood.

34 This was a new development for the 2009 season.

35 www.fakenhamcricketclub.co.uk (last accessed 18 Mar 2012).

36 Rushton, *Ramsbottom Cricket Club*, p. 96.

37 www.glasgowaccies.cc/fundraising/other_opportunities (last accessed 18 Mar 2012).

38 Rushton, *Ramsbottom Cricket Club*, p. 96.

39 www.brickhillcricket.co.uk (last accessed 18 Mar 2012).

40 www.caythorpecc.co.uk/history.asp (last accessed 18 Mar 2012).

41 Rushton, *Ramsbottom Cricket Club*, pp. 20, 21.

42 www.maltonandoldmaltoncc.co.uk (last accessed 18 Mar 2012).

43 www.thisisplymouth.co.uk/news/Sidmouth-cricket-club-thatch-appeal/article-1082815-detail/article.html (last accessed 18 Mar 2012).

44 This is the concept of 'match funding'.

45 See www.saltairevillage.info/forum/view_topic.php?id=390&forum_id=16.

46 An old rule – that is now being relaxed.

47 www.mandbcc.co.uk/Easyfundraising.html (last accessed 18 Mar 2012).

48 www.froggybank.co.uk/horsforth-cricket-club (last accessed 18 Mar 2012).

49 http://buy.at/towcestrians (last accessed 18 Mar 2012).

50 Hill, *Sport, Leisure and Culture*, p. 171.

51 *Ibid.*, p. 173.

52 *Ibid.*, pp. 151–3.

53 *Ibid.*, p. 153.

54 *Ibid.*, p. 154.

55 B. Houlihan, *Sport and Society: A Student Introduction* (London, Sage, 2007), pp. 20, 21, 27.

56 *Ibid.*, p. 51.

57 *Ibid.*, pp. 51, 52.

58 www.culture.gov.uk/about_us/default.aspx (last accessed 18 Mar 2012).

59 www.culture.gov.uk/about_us/sport/default.aspx (last accessed 18 Mar 2012).

60 www.guardian.co.uk/education/2008/mar/30/schools.uk (last accessed 18 Mar 2012).

61 http://news.bbc.co.uk/1/hi/education/702537.stm (last accessed 18 Mar 2012).

62 www.dailymail.co.uk/news/article-1202881/200-playing-fields-sold-Labour-How-justified-ahead-Olympics-ask-critics.html#ixzz0Oo8lqiTm (last accessed 18 Mar 2012).

63 http://news.bbc.co.uk/sport1/hi/cricket/england/4252218.stm (last accessed 18 Mar 2012).

64 www.publications.parliament.uk/pa/cm200809/cmhansrd/cm090608/debtext/90608-0002.htm (last accessed 18 Mar 2012).

65 www.dcsf.gov.uk/pns/DisplayPN.cgi?pn_id=2009_0028 (last accessed 18 Mar 2012).

66 *Ibid.*

67 www.sportengland.org/media_centre/press_releases/csr.aspx (last accessed 18 Mar 2012).

68 www.cricket247.org/community/showthread.php?t=8751 (last accessed 18 Mar 2012).

69 *Ibid.*

70 See www.independent.co.uk/sport/a-new-lease-of-life-for-the-far-pavilions-1310673.html (last accessed 18 Mar 2012).

71 www.churchcc.co.uk/latest.asp (last accessed 18 Mar 2012).

72 *Evening Mail* (Birmingham), 16 Jan 1998.

73 www.cricketertalk.com/news/1.asp (last accessed 18 Mar 2012).

74 www.awardsforall.org.uk/england/.../pr_friends_ashfield_valley.doc (last accessed 18 Feb 2012).

75 www.doncasterfreepress.co.uk/news/Cricket-pavilion-is-declared-OUT.5397157.jp (last accessed 18 Mar 2012).

76 www.westoxon.gov.uk/living/sportsgrant.cfm (last accessed 18 Feb 2012).

77 Ending in 2012.

78 www.ecb.co.uk/ecb/publications/building-partnerships (last accessed 18 Mar 2012).

79 www.ecb.co.uk/development/get-into-cricket/cricket-making-a-difference (last accessed 18 Feb 2012).

80 Google this quote and you discover that a host of clubs have used it to go alongside their Clubmark accreditation efforts.
81 www.clubmark.org.uk/news/easton-cricket-club-celebrates-achieving-clubmark (last accessed 18 Mar 2012). One such club is St Albans: www.hertsad.co.uk/content/herts/sport/story.aspx?brand=HADOnline&category=SportCricket&tBrand=HertsCambsOnline&tCategory=SportHAD&itemid=WEED17%20Mar%202010%2016%3A28%3A48%3A060 (last accessed 18 Mar 2012).
82 www.ecb.co.uk/development/clubs-and-leagues/clubmark (last accessed 18 Mar 2012).
83 www.heslerton-sport.co.uk/Cricket-clubmark.htm (last accessed 18 Mar 2012).
84 www.clubmark.org.uk/resources/elvaston-cricket-club-clubmark-delivers-a-culture-change (last access 18 Mar 2012).
85 http://official.sportnetwork.net/main/s215/st103638.htm (last accessed 18 Mar 2012).
86 Changes are being made all the time to Clubmark criteria – see www.ecb.co.uk/development/clubs-and-leagues/clubmark/news/clubmark-criteria-changes.309509,EN.html (last accessed 18 Mar 2012).
87 www.ecb.co.uk/.../clubs-and.../focus-club-community-clusters (last accessed 18 Mar 2012).
88 www.ecb.co.uk/development/focus-clubs,497,BP.html (last accessed 18 Mar 2012).
89 Interview with Steve Archer, West Yorkshire Cricket Development Manager: 5 Jul 2009. He said that 15 out of 35 Calderdale clubs had Clubmark, but only 3 out of 60 Kirklees clubs had.
90 *Ibid.*
91 www.chancetoshine.org (last accessed 18 Mar 2012).
92 www.timesonline.co.uk/tol/comment/columnists/guest_contributors/article6732365.ece (last accessed 18 Mar 2012).
93 http://news.bbc.co.uk/sport1/hi/cricket/england/4252218.stm (last access 18 Mar 2012). See also www.steyningcricketclub.com – Steyning were selected for the scheme and awarded a grant of £6,000 (last accessed 18 Mar 2012).
94 www.ecb.co.uk/development/kids/urban-cricket (last accessed 18 Mar 2012).
95 T. Heald, *Village Cricket* (London, Little Brown, 2004).
96 See the npower Village Cup at http://nvko.play-cricket.com/home/home.asp (last accessed 18 Mar 2012).
97 www.ckcricketheritage.org.uk/docs/091809HOB632009locrules.pdf (last accessed 18 Mar 2012).
98 www.ckcricketheritage.org.uk/professionalcricketwatchers.htm (last accessed 18 Mar 2012).
99 See www.getsurrey.co.uk/.../2056627_draw_declared_in_village_cricket_green_dispute (last accessed 18 Mar 2012).
100 See www.bapchildcc.co.uk/news-and-events-from-bapchild-cricket-club/160-indoor-cricket-league (last accessed 18 Mar 2012).
101 news.bbc.co.uk/sport2/hi/cricket/1952705.stm (last accessed 18 Mar 2012).
102 www.staffordshirecricket.co.uk/devgroups.php (last accessed 18 Mar 2012).
103 www.broughtoncricketclub.co.uk/ground_inspection.htm (last accessed 18 Mar 2012)
104 This information comes courtesy of Golcar in Huddersfield.
105 http://flitwickcc.play-cricket.com/home/home.asp (last accessed 18 Mar 2012)
106 Personal communication.
107 www.cleckheatoncricketclub.com/2003_Season1.html (last accessed 18 Mar 2012).
108 *Batley News*, 29 Jun 2006.

109 www.halifaxcourier.co.uk/Register.aspx?ReturnURL=http%3A%2F%2Fwww.
     halifaxcourier.co.uk%2Flocal%2FCricket-Illingworth-event-has-a.4190626.jp (last
     accessed 18 Mar 2012).
110 On 24 April 2009, the Central Yorkshire League website announced: 'Solly now has
     pink balls available for use in the 20/20 Cup competition. All participating clubs
     should visit the shop to collect theirs.'
111 www.blankneycc.com/page5.htm (last accessed 18 Mar 2012).
112 Bradford and Bingley CC.
113 In the Kirklees-Calderdale area, Kirkheaton and Outlane.
114 www.plugintothesun.co.uk/news/items/st-just-cricket-club-installation   (last
     accessed 18 Mar 2012).
115 Speech at opening of redeveloped Stones pavilion, 5 Sep 2009.
116 See also www.dissexpress.co.uk/news/Vandalism-may-stump-cricket-club.3946
     101.jp (last accessed 18 Mar 2012), www.getsurrey.co.uk/news/s/2061778
     _nursery_and_cricket_club_not_letting_vandals_stop_play (last accessed 18 Mar
     2012), www.bexhillobserver.net/news/Bexhill-Cricket-Club-given-all.6153063.jp
     (last accessed 18 Mar 2012).
117 www.droitwichadvertiser.co.uk/.../4535102.Vandals_target_Droitwich_cricket
     _club (last accessed 18 Mar 2012).
118 www.yorkshirepost.co.uk/news/Arsonists-destroy-cricket-pavilion.1945768.jp (last
     accessed 18 Mar 2012).

Conclusion

There has never been a better time to investigate the social history of cricket. The Indian Premier League and Indian Cricket League have thrust the game onto the back pages and illustrated the fascinating links between the sport, high finance and globalisation. The recent wave of match-fixing has illustrated the corruption that still exists within the game, and reminds us that bookmakers and gamblers – so much a part of the sport in the nineteenth century – are still to the fore. The growth of the Twenty20 phenomenon has indicated the ingenuity of some of the game's administrators and illustrated the popularity of the sport. And the fact that England recently ascended to the number-one spot in the world Test rankings, having won two consecutive Ashes series, illustrates that this is still a country that is passionate about, and successful at, a sport that originated in the Home Counties several centuries ago.

In *Cricket and the Victorians*, Keith Sandiford argues that the Victorians 'glorified' the sport as the 'perfect system of ethics and morals'. His argument is that it is not possible to underplay the significance of the game to them.[1] The game is still important to British society, and it could be argued that even in the twenty-first century there is something quintessentially English about grassroots cricket. What did Sir John Major describe as the essence of Englishness? 'Long shadows on cricket grounds, warm beer, invincible green suburbs, dog lovers and pools fillers and, as George Orwell said, old maids bicycling to Holy Communion through the morning mist'.[2]

We hope that in this book we have traced the evolution of grassroots cricket from the eighteenth to the twenty-first centuries. Our interest has been the social history of the sport, at grassroots level, in England.

Here we have been assisted by the growing literature on the history of sport, and the social history of cricket in particular. Historians such as Dick Holt, Jeff Hill, Jack Williams and Tony Mason have carried out extremely valuable work in tracing the major themes in the history of sport over the past two centuries. This has been the backdrop to the current volume and to our historical research in general.

In a sense, it is a classic case of continuity and change. It is the same game, relatively static in terms of its rules and conventions, and of course there is a timelessness and tradition about the sport which tends to insulate it from radical change. But on the other hand, as we have seen in the six chapters, there have been significant evolutions – the growth of competition, the emergence of clubs and, in the twentieth and twenty-first centuries, a whole raft of changes and modernisations, some inspired by the involvement of outside bodies. All the time, though, in the words of Williams, cricket 'both reflected and strengthened cultural and social harmony in England.'[3]

Our six chapters have hopefully outlined the major events and themes. In Chapter 1, we investigated the nature of early sport and early cricket. We looked at leisure as a theme and explored the economic undercurrents to early sport. Chapter 2 helped us to understand the emergence of local clubs. Paternalists, employers, churches, public houses and social reform groups all played their role. And in Chapter 3, we investigated the nature of organised competition. In the context of nineteenth-century sport, this was a revolution pure and simple.

Moving onto the modern era – the twentieth century – we started by analysing the experience of the two world wars. Chapter 4 assisted us in assessing the relationship between war and sport. But, at the same time, it could be argued that the two sets of post-war effects and consequences were of equal significance. In Chapter 5, we examined the many problems and difficulties that grassroots cricket faced in the last quarter of the century. And in Chapter 6, we brought the story of the game up to date with an investigation into current and contemporary issues.

What we can now locate, from the vantage point of the Conclusion, are a number of major themes in the history and evolution of grassroots cricket.

First, the idea of division. In our early chapters we refer to the tensions that afflicted cricket in its early years. Principally, these related to geography and money. The south was associated with amateurism and amateur players – those who could play the game for 'fun' without the pressure of having to earn an income from it. In the north, by contrast, where there was less wealth, talented cricketers needed to earn a living from the game, or at least get recompensed for their time. (The same was true for talented Rugby League players – hence the 'Great Split' of 1895.) The schism between amateurs and professionals was a significant one, but, with the benefit of hindsight, we would have to conclude that it did not significantly hold back the development of the game.

Second, competition is a major theme. In the early period, we witness the phenomenon of challenge matches and the emergence of 'all star' touring sides. Then, in the late nineteenth century, we see the growth of cups and leagues, which are still with us and accepted as the norm. In the twenty-first century, we have witnessed the sport wrestling with itself again over the best way to format the sport and make it attractive to the viewing public. Hence the birth of Twenty20 cricket, a major revolution for the county game, but it should be emphasised that local leagues up and down the country have been playing 20-over cricket for decades. What does this say about the relationship between the professional and amateur games?

Third, the class basis of the sport is interesting. Of course, amateurism was a bastion of the wealthy and privileged, and the world of professionalism was inhabited by young men who needed money to earn a living, but emphasising this division belies the fact that, at the level of playing the game, the relationship between amateurs and professionals was not as tense as one might suspect. And in no way was cricket like golf, a sport in which a gap started to open up between the privileged, who saw it as their sport, and ordinary people, who were generally excluded.

And what of the future? It is difficult to predict the way that cricket will change and evolve in decades to come. All we can say is that the history of the sport, particularly at the grassroots level, is worthy of further and ongoing investigation.

Notes

1 K.Sandiford, *Cricket and the Victorians* (London, Ashgate, 1994), p. 1.
2 Quoted by the *Daily Mail*, 7 Mar 2009.
3 J. Williams, *Cricket and England* (London, Frank Cass, 1999), p. 191.

Bibliography

Books

Altham, H.S. and E.W. Swanton, *A History of Cricket* (London, George Allen and Unwin, 1947)

Ashton-under-Lyne CC, *A History of Ashton-under-Lyne CC* (Ashton, Ashton-under-Lyne CC, undated)

Bailey, P., *Leisure and Class in Victorian England: Rational Recreation and the Contest for Control* (London, Routledge & Kegan Paul, 1978)

Barker, T., *Cricket's Wartime Sanctuary: The First-Class Flight to Bradford* (Sussex, Association of Cricket Statisticians & Historians, 2009)

Birley, D., *A Social History of English Cricket* (London, Aurum Press, 1999)

Birley, D., *Sport and the Making of Britain* (Manchester, Manchester University Press, 2001)

Bishop, M., *Bats, Balls and Biscuits* (Huddersfield, Cricket Heritage Publications, 2008)

Bowen, R., *Cricket: A History of its Growth and Development throughout the World* (London, Eyre and Spottiswoode, 1970)

Box, C., *The English Game of Cricket* (London, The Field Office, 1877)

Brailsford, D., *Sport, Time and Society: British at Play* (London, Routledge, 1991)

Brookes, C., *English Cricket: The Game and its Players through the Ages* (Newton Abbot, Readers Union, 1978)

Butler, M., *From Batley to Barnsley* (Huddersfield, Cricket Heritage Publications, 2006)

Clarke, P., *British Clubs and Societies 1580–1800: The Origins of an Associational World* (Oxford, Oxford University Press, 2000)

Collins, T., J. Martin and W. Vamplew (eds), *Encyclopedia of Traditional British Rural Sports* (London, Routledge, 2005)

Dowd, J.H., *The Kaiser's Cricket*, undated

Dunning, E., *Sport Matters: Sociological Studies of Sport, Violence and Civilisation* (London, Routledge, 1999)

Edmundson, D., *See the Conquering Hero* (Accrington, Mike McLeod Litho, 1992)

Farnworth C. and S. Hall, *Bacup Cricket Club: The Authorised History* (Bacup, Bacup Cricket Club, 1999)

Ford, F., *Cricket – A Social History 1700–1835* (Newton Abbot, David and Charles, 1972)

From Little Acorns: A Centenary of Cricket at Broad Oak 1880–1980 (Huddersfield, Broad Oak Cricket Club, 1980)

Goodall, D., *Wavertree Cricket Club: 151 Years of Cricket: A Written and Pictorial History* (Wakefield, Charlesworth Group, 2006)

Harris, H.A., *Sport in Britain: Its Origins and Development* (London, Stanley Paul, 1975)

Harvey, A., *The Beginnings of a Commercial Sporting Culture in Britain, 1793–1850* (London, Ashgate, 2004)

Heald, T., *Village Cricket* (London, Little Brown, 2004)

Heywood, M., F. and B., *Cloth Caps and Cricket Crazy: Todmorden and Cricket 1835–1896* (Todmorden, Upper Calder Valley Publications, 2004)

Heywood, M., F. and B., *In a League of Their Own: Cricket and Leisure in 20th Century Todmorden* (Todmorden, Upper Calder Valley Publications, 2011)

Hignell, A., *A Favourit' Game: Cricket in South Wales Before 1914* (Cardiff, University of Wales Press, 1992)

Hill, J., *Sport, Leisure and Culture in Twentieth-Century Britain* (Basingstoke, Palgrave, 2002)

Holmes, Rev. R.S., *The History of Yorkshire County Cricket 1833–1903* (London, Archibald Constable and Co., 1904)

Holt, R., *Sport and the British: A Modern History* (Oxford, Oxford University Press, 1990)

Holt, R. and T. Mason, *Sport in Britain 1945–2000* (Oxford, Blackwell, 2000)

Houlihan, B., *Sport and Society: A Student Introduction* (London, Sage, 2008)

Huddersfield League Handbook, 2010 (Huddersfield, Huddersfield & District Cricket League, 2010)

Kell, J.H., *The History of Menston Cricket Club* (Ilkley, Scolar Press, 1980)

Lawson, J., *Progress in Pudsey* (Sussex, Caliban Books, 1978 (first published 1887)

Light, R., *The Other Face of English Cricket: The Origins of League Cricket in the West Riding of Yorkshire* (Huddersfield, Cricket Heritage Publications, 2008)

Lister, T., *You Couldn't Make It Up! The Complete History of Burnley Cricket Club 1834–2008* (Huddersfield, Cricket Heritage Publications, 2009)

Lodge, A., *Drakes Huddersfield Cricket League Official Souvenir of the Centenary of the League* (Huddersfield, Huddersfield & District Cricket League, 1992)

Lucas, E.V., *The Hambledon Men* (London, Henry Frowde, 1907)

Major, J., *More Than a Game: The Story of Cricket's Early Years* (London, HarperPress, 2007)

Malcolmson, R., *Popular Recreations in English Society, 1700–1850* (Cambridge, Cambridge University Press, 1973)

Mangan, J.A. (ed.), *Pleasure, Profit and Proselytism* (London, Frank Cass, 1988)

Marqusee, M., *War Minus the Shooting* (London, Mandarin, 1997)

Mason, T., *Sport in Britain: A Social History* (Cambridge, Cambridge University Press, 1989)

Mote, A., *Cricket's Glory Days: The Extraordinary Story of Braodhappeny Down* (London, Robson Books, 1997)

Mote, A. (ed.), *John Nyren's The Cricketers of My Time* (London, Robson Books, 1998)

Neal, P. with J. Norbury, *Thank You, Mr Ingham: A History of Mirfield Cricket Club* (Huddersfield, Cricket Heritage Publications, 2006)

Pullin, A.W. ('Old Ebor'), *Talks with Old Yorkshire Cricketers*, Leeds, reprinted from the *Yorkshire Evening Post*, 1898)

Pycroft, Rev. J., *The Cricket Field or The History and the Science of the Game of Cricket* (Longman, Brown, Green and Longmans, Second Edition, 1854)

Razzell, P.E. and R.W. Wainwright, *The Victorian Working Class: Selections from the 'Morning Chronicle'* (London, Frank Cass, 1973)

Rushton, J. (ed.), *Ramsbottom Cricket Club: Sesquicentenary Celebration 1845–1995* (Ramsbottom, Ramsbottom Cricket Club, 1995)

Sandiford, K., *Cricket and the Victorians* (London, Ashgate, 1994)

Shaw, B. (ed.), *A History of Evesham Cricket Club* (Evesham, Evesham Cricket Club, 2004)

Sissons, R., *The Players: A Social History of the Professional Cricketer* (London, Kingswood, 1988)

Stanyer, J., *A Great Survivor: The History of The Exeter Cricket Club in the Nineteenth and Twentieth Centuries* (Exeter, St Leonard's Press, 2000)

Steele, A.G. and R.H. Lyttelton, *Cricket:With Contributions by A. Lang,W.G. Grace, R.A.H. Mitchell and F. Gale* (London, The Badminton Library of Sports and Pastimes, 1988)
Thomson, A.A., *Hirst and Rhodes* (Epworth, 1959)
Underdown, D., *Start of Play: Cricket and Culture in Eighteenth Century England* (London, Penguin, 2000)
Vamplew, W., *Pay Up and Play the Game* (Cambridge, Cambridge University Press, 2004)
Wagg, S. and D. Russell, *Sporting Heroes of the North* (Newcastle, Northumbria Press, 2010)
Walton, T., *One Hundred Partnership: A History of the Huddersfield & District Cricket Association* (Huddersfield, Huddersfield & District Cricket Association, 1986)
West, A., *1892–1992: One Hundred Years of the Ribblesdale Cricket League* (Preston, Cranden Press, 1992)
Wigglesworth, N., *The Evolution of English Sport* (London, Routledge, 2009)
Williams, J., 'Cricket', in T. Mason (ed.), *Sport in Britain* (Cambridge, Cambridge University Press, 1989)
Williams, J., *Cricket and England* (London, Frank Cass, 1999)
Williams, J., *Cricket and England: A Cultural and Social History of the Inter-War Years* (London, Frank Cass, 2000)
Woodlands Cricket Club, *Centenary Year 1894–1994. The Story of a Cricket Club* (Bradford, Woodlands Cricket Club, 1994)
Wynne-Thomas, P., *The History of Cricket: from the Weald to the World* (Norwich, The Stationery Office, 1997)

Newspapers and magazines

Athletic News
Batley News
Bell's Life
Berrow's Worcester Journal
Birmingham Post
Brighouse Echo
The British Journal
Country Journal or the Craftsman
Cricket
Daily Mail
The Era
The Essex Standard and General Advertiser for the Eastern Counties
Evening Mail (Birmingham)
Gazetteer and Daily London Advertiser
General Advertiser
Grimsby Telegraph
Halifax Courier
Halifax Guardian and Huddersfield and Bradford Advertiser
Hampshire Advertiser & Salisbury Guardian Royal Yacht Club Gazette, Southampton Town and County Herald, Isle of Wight Journal,Winchester Chronicle, and General Reporter
Huddersfield Chronicle
Huddersfield Chronicle and West Yorkshire Advertiser
Huddersfield Daily Examiner
(Huddersfield) *Express & Chronicle*
The Independent
Leeds Intelligencer
Leeds Mercury
Leeds Times

The Leicester Chronicle
Morning Post
Norwich Mercury and Norfolk News and Journal
Old Whig or The Constant Protestant
Rotherham Advertiser
St James's Evening Post
Sheffield Independent
The Sowerby Magazine
Weekly Journal or British Gazetteer
Westminster Journal or New Weekly Miscellany
York Courant
Yorkshire Owl
Yorkshire Post

Websites

www.ak-sports.com
http://ashbyhastingscc.hitscricket.com
www.astoncricketclub.co.uk/club-history/4532805863
www.awardsforall.org.uk
www.bapchildcc.co.uk
http://news.bbc.co.uk
www.bcsccjuniors.co.uk
www.beckenhamcc.co.uk
www.benefice.org.uk
www.bexhillobserver.net
www.blankneycc.com
www.bosherlay.co.uk/component/k2/item/14-evenley-cricket-club
www.boxtedcricketclub.co.uk
www.brickhillcricket.co.uk
www.britwellsalomecricketclub.co.uk
www.broughtoncricketclub.co.uk/ground_inspection.htm
www.bscricket.com
http://buy.at/towcestrians
www.caythorpecc.co.uk
www.chancetoshine.org
www.chelmsfordweeklynews.co.uk
www.chippingsodburycc.co.uk
www.churchcc.co.uk/latest.asp
www.ckcricketheritage.org.uk
www.claygatecricket.co.uk/page_1229504592788.html
www.cleckheatoncricketclub.com
www.clubmark.org.uk
www.cricinfo.com
www.cricket247.org
www.cricketertalk.com/news/1.asp
www.cuckneycc.com
www.culture.gov.uk
www.culture24.org.uk
www.cumbriaslevenvalley.co.uk
www.cwgc.org/admin/files/cricket%20leaflet.pdf

www.dailymail.co.uk
www.dcsf.gov.uk
www.didcotcricketclub.co.uk/junior_cricket.htm
www.dissexpress.co.uk
www.doncasterfreepress.co.uk
www.drakes-huddersfieldcricketleague.co.uk
www.dulwichcc.com
www.ecb.co.uk
www.espncricinfo.com
www.fakenhamcricketclub.co.uk
http://findarticles.com
www.fladburycc.co.uk
http://flitwickcc.play-cricket.com
www.freewebs.com/crowhurstcricketclub/history/history.htm
www.froggybank.co.uk
www.getsurrey.co.uk
www.glasgowaccies.cc
www.guardian.co.uk
www.guildfordcc.com
www.halifaxcourier.co.uk
www.harrowcricketclub.co.uk/history/default.aspx
www.haworthwestend.com
www.hayescricket.co.uk
www.henfieldcricketclub.com/articles/history.html
www.hertsad.co.uk
www.heslerton-sport.co.uk
www.himbletoncc.org.uk
http://huttoncc.hitscricket.com
www.independent.co.uk
www.irishexaminer.com
www.londonnigerians.com
www.londontigers.org
www.lydneycricketclub.org.uk
www.maltonandoldmaltoncc.co.uk
www.mandbcc.co.uk
www.midlandhistory.bham.ac.uk
www.mkcricket.org.uk/sponsorship.html.
www.mongoosecricket.com
www.newbery.co.uk
www.newsshopper.co.uk
http://news.bbc.co.uk
www.norwichcricketclub.co.uk
http://nvko.play-cricket.com
www.oakhamcricketclub.co.uk
http://official.sportnetwork.net
www.orpingtoncc.co.uk
www.padihamcc.co.uk
http://palgrave.typepad.com/polley
www.perkinscc.co.uk
www.pitchero.com/clubs/lowdhamcricketclub/a/history-17514.html
www.plugintothesun.co.uk

www.plymouthcricketclub.com
www.potternecc.org.uk
www.publications.parliament.uk
www.radlettcc.com
http://radwaycc.co.uk
www.redcross.org.uk
www.ribblesdalecricketleague.co.uk
www.rodmershamcc.co.uk
www.schoolscricketonline.co.uk
www.smh.com.au
www.southportcricket.co.uk
www.spartacus.schoolnet.co.uk
www.spofforthcc.org.uk
www.sportengland.org
www.sportsbusinessjournal.com
www.staffordshirecricket.co.uk
www.stannescricketclub.org
www.steyningcricketclub.com
www.stockportcc.co.uk
www.stonecc.co.uk
www.sussexcricket.co.uk
www.swjcl.org.uk
www.syscl.co.uk
www.tacc.org.uk/clubhistory.asp
http://thirsk.nidderdaleleague.co.uk/junior-cricket
www.thirskcricket.co.uk
www.thisisgloucestershire.co.ukwww.rockhamptoncc.com/history.php
www.thisisplymouth.co.uk
www.thisisstaffordshire.co.uk
www.timeshighereducation.co.uk
www.timesonline.co.uk
www.towcestrians.co.uk
www.turnhamgreencc.org
www.upton-wirral.co.uk
www.webbsoc.demon.co.uk
www.webwanderers.org
www.westbrettoncc.com
www.westoxon.gov.uk/living/sportsgrant.cfm
http://weybridgecc.co.uk
http://en.wikipedia.org
www.wparkcc.co.uk
www.yorkshirepost.co.uk

Interviews

Steve Archer
Mick Bourne
Brian Heywood
Malcolm Heywood
Matthew Jones
David Thorpe

Index